SETTLING THE WEST

THE AMERICAN STORY

SETTLING THE WEST

by the Editors of Time-Life Books, Alexandria, Virginia

CONTENTS

LOOKING WESTWARD

Spring is slow to come to the northern Rockies, but by mid-May in the year 1862 the alders and willows of Deer Lodge Valley in Washington Territory were hung with tender new leaves and the creeks were brimming with the runoff of melting snow and warming rain. It was a wild and lovely place teeming with elk, deer, moose, bear, mountain sheep, beaver, and fish—and a modest but swelling population of gold seekers. They spent their days looking for "pay streak" in the grit and gravel they scooped from the streams and washed in the frigid snowmelt. On May 20 a young prospector named Granville Stuart didn't find any pay streak himself, but he was encouraged by the success of his miner friends. That evening he wrote in his journal, "Blake and McAdow made ten dollars yesterday and nine dollars today. Higgins worked about three hours . . . and made three dollars and a half." Granville and his brother James "sponged on Blake and McAdow for our grub. We had rice, etc., for dinner; beans, etc., for supper. Blake was the cook, enjoyed our visit very much. They are a jovial set of miners and we had much fun at one another's expense in the way of jokes. I like the appearance of the diggings better than I thought I would. There is plenty of hard work, but I think there is good pay doing it."

Remote though Deer Lodge Valley was, word trickled out about the gold to be had there, and soon more prospectors and miners were traveling north from Colorado, west by steamer up the Missouri River, eastward from the state of California. These men were part of the tide of adventurers and pioneers that was building up on the edges of the Great American Desert—the vast plains that swept from the westernmost contiguous states to the Rockies and from Texas to Canada. Americans had crisscrossed that land, and now they were poised to overspread it and sink their roots into its virgin soil.

On the same day that the Stuart brothers were eating beans, making jokes, and thinking about pay streak in Deer Lodge Valley, back east in Washington, D.C., President Abraham Lincoln put his signature to a congressional bill that would change the West forever. Called the Homestead Act, it provided 160 acres of public land in the western territories to any citizen who could occupy and improve the parcel for five years. Six weeks later, on July 1, Lincoln authorized funding for the Union Pacific and Central Pacific Railroad lines, which would make it possible to cross the continent by train.

Like many Americans, the president was looking beyond a Civil War that would rage on for another three years. In the postwar summer of 1865, former fighting men found their way back to wherever they called home. But for some at war's end, there was no home left, or none that they wanted to return to. Many ex-Confederates, allowed by the terms of surrender to keep their side arms and horses, headed like disinherited knights-errant toward the new western horizon. Their war-weary Yankee counterparts, recruited by the thousands into the Union army, also turned their faces westward, along with blacks fleeing the Old South to explore a newfound freedom. These men, white and black, from North and South, spurred wild-eyed cow ponies after Texas longhorn cattle and wielded picks and shovels digging railbeds and unearthing veins of silver and gold. They drove mule teams over rough mountain roads and guided plows through tough prairie sod. Beside many of them were brides, sisters, and children—apprehensively facing the unknown, yet eager for the promise of a new life.

In each of their lives were stories—many grindingly mundane, a few wildly exciting. Many of those pioneers recorded their stories in diaries or journals, in sketchbooks and on photographic plates. Granville and James Stuart together recorded the life in the mining camps of the northern Rockies, and their exploits became one of the West's enduring legends. So did the entrepreneurial spirit of cattle dealer Joseph McCoy in a tiny Kansas cow town and the fierce determination of transplanted New Englander Theodore Judah to make the transcontinental railroad a reality. And in Wyoming small-time ranchers and homesteaders became heroes by defending their 160-acre pieces of the American dream against wealthy cattlemen bent on keeping the range their fiefdom.

In the pages that follow you will find their stories, as well as those of stalwart pioneer women who walked beside ox-drawn wagons laden with all their earthly possessions; women who baked johnnycake over buffalo-chip fires to feed hungry husbands and children, pausing in the sunset glow to marvel at their strange, barren surroundings; women who nursed newborn infants and tended ailing loved ones—and sometimes buried them along trails they would never travel again.

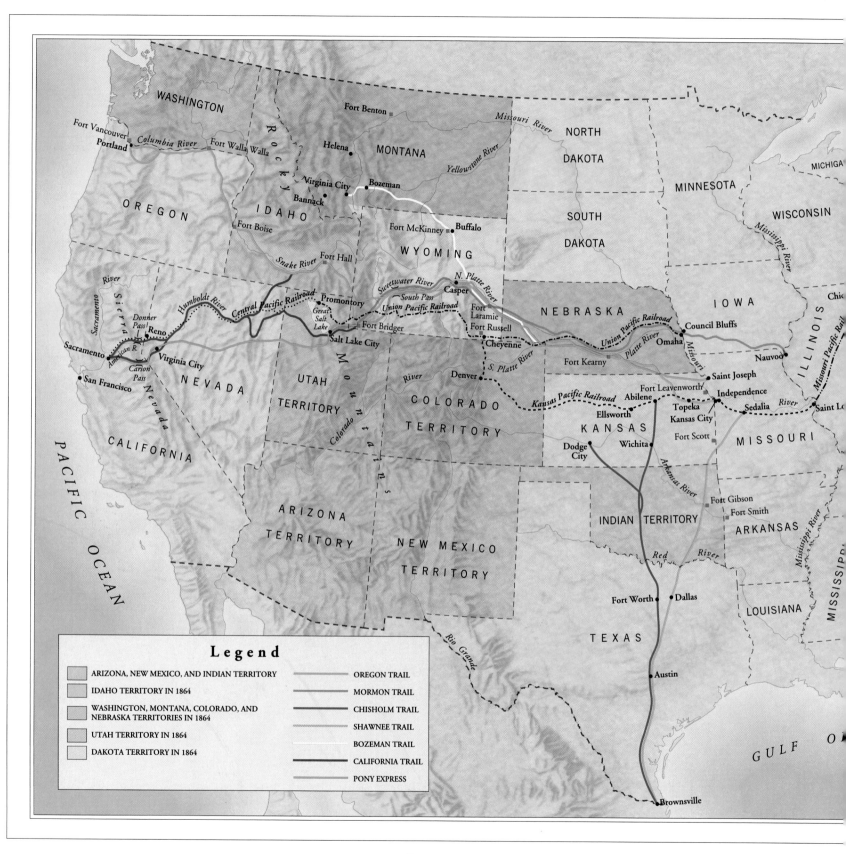

TRAILS WEST

In the 1850s and 1860s westbound pioneers usually set off from Independence, Missouri, on the Oregon Trail or took the Mormon Trail out of Nauvoo, Illinois. Both trails led across Nebraska Territory toward the Rocky Mountains. People lured by the gold fields of Montana Territory might strike north along the Bozeman Trail, while those bound for the Pacific coast made the long climb to the Continental Divide at South Pass and down to Fort Bridger. From there, Oregon-bound travelers headed northwest along the Snake and Columbia Rivers. Those destined for California traversed the Utah and Nevada deserts, paralleling the Humboldt River before crossing the Sierra Nevada.

The trek could take four months or more by wagon, but in 1858 the Butterfield Overland Mail Company stagecoaches could offer passage in three and a half weeks. The riders of the Pony Express made the run from Saint Joseph, Missouri, to Sacramento in 10 days.

In the 1860s, Texas cattle were driven north along the Shawnee and Chisholm Trails to railheads in Missouri and Kansas, to be shipped by way of the Kansas Pacific and Missouri Pacific Railroads to meatpackers in Saint Louis and Chicago. At the end of the decade transcontinental rail travel began, with the meeting of the tracks of the Central Pacific and Union Pacific lines in northern Utah.

In the map at left the western territories as they existed in 1864 are shown in color; dashed lines indicate state and territorial boundaries as they existed in 1890.

THE ROOT OF ALL EVIL

"Many gamblers and desperate characters drifted in, lured by the prospect of acquiring gold dust without digging for it. It became the custom to go armed all the time."

GRANVILLE STUART

W hile she made her way home from school on a chill March afternoon in 1864, Mollie Sheehan paused, transfixed, on a hillside above the little town of Virginia City, Idaho Territory. On every side the Rockies reared their mighty shoulders, still mantled in white. Below her lay a squalid jumble of dirt-roofed log cabins, tents, wagons, false-fronted stores, saloons, and boardinghouses. Once a tranquil, treelined riverbed, the whole of Alder Gulch now lay bare and blackened by gold mining, its earth as roiled as if a giant hog had rooted in the earth along its entire length.

Close to the river was a corral that the town's children called the Elephant's Pen, and it was the scene there that had drawn Mollie's attention. A group of men milled around it, at their center a bareheaded man in fringed buckskins, his arms pinioned, his hands raised as if in prayer. His agonized cry floated up to the girl on the hillside: "For God's sake, let me see my dear, beloved wife!"

Mollie raced home, skirting the crowd. She was only 11, the daughter of a stern and protective father, but she knew what was coming: Virginia City had a vigilance committee, and in the last few months its members had hanged a number of men—sometimes publicly in daylight, sometimes in the dark of night.

Several were people Mollie knew: One had come overland with her wagon train, others had eaten at her parents' boardinghouse. One died on a makeshift gallows so close to her cabin that the girl heard the terrifying creak of the rope as the corpse turned in the wind. This time she recognized the prisoner as Jack Slade, who was known for his courage, his kindness, and his love for his high-spirited wife, Virginia. He had been a vigilante himself, it was said, and certainly had friends among them—at least when he was sober. When Slade drank, he turned into a monster.

By day Slade drove one of the mule teams that supplied the mining camps, but his after-hours drinking and carousing had reached epic proportions—he liked to tear through the town on his horse, Old Copperbottom, shouting abuse and wrecking anything in his path. He rode the horse into stores and saloons, and when he chanced to run out of money, he intimidated bartenders by displaying the leathery ears of a man he had killed back in Colorado. Members of the vigilance committee warned Slade that such excesses would not be tolerated, but his displays only grew worse. During one of his wild forays, Mollie hid in a butcher shop to get out of his way, as the owner muttered ominously that Slade would get what he deserved.

This goldminer needed little else besides his pickax, sledgehammer, chisels, and muscle to work his claim. Excited by news of a major gold strike in 1863, thousands of prospectors descended on Alder Gulch in present-day Montana, giving birth to the town of Virginia City.

The day before Mollie saw him at the corral, Slade tried to pick a fight in a bar with John Xavier Beidler—X, everyone called him—who was possibly the most fearsome of the vigilantes. Later that evening he roared into a theater and shouted obscenities at an actress, driving the audience out and closing the show. He spent the rest of that night roaming the town and singing bawdy songs about the private lives of certain townspeople. Still drunk the next morning, he overturned a milk wagon and then headed up the street on Old Copperbottom to "run it for all it was worth." As merchants closed their stores and the street emptied, Slade's friends tried in vain to stop him. J. M. Fox, the new sheriff, served him with an arrest warrant, which he tore up and stomped on. All along the gulches, miners began to down their tools and move toward the town.

Flaunting a pair of derringers, Slade headed for the store of Paris Pfouts, the euphoniously named president of the vigilance committee. As he backed Pfouts into a corner, vigilante leader James Williams and at least 200 armed miners surrounded the store. "Slade," called Williams, "I want you."

"What do you want with me?" Slade called back. Then, looking outside, he saw the mob, and his bravado turned to fear. "My God," he whispered.

There was no trial. Williams simply told Slade that he had an hour to live and led him into the back room of the store. At that very moment one of Slade's friends was galloping toward Slade's house 12 miles east of town. If anyone could save him from the shame of the gallows, it was Virginia Slade. A black-haired beauty, ardent and proud, she might turn the sympathy of the crowd. Sensing this, the miners hustled Slade to the Elephant's Pen, stood him on a packing box under a scaffold used for slaughtering beef, and put the noose around his neck. He pleaded—eloquently, not cringingly—for his life. People

Perkins
337 HAYES STREET,
San Francisco, Cal.

Mollie Sheehan, pictured here in 1873, moved with her family to booming Virginia City when she was 11 years old. She relished equally the noise of the town and the peace of the countryside, and recalled in later years that "gold dust was the only kind of money I ever saw in Virginia City."

"High above other men and directly beneath the scaffold stood a young man with a rope around his neck.... I slammed the door and rushed into the house."

MOLLIE SHEEHAN

in the crowd knew that Slade had not murdered anyone, nor was he a thief, and those were the hanging offenses in Virginia City. But the mob had its head, and Williams understood. He gave the vigilantes' standard command: "Men, do your duty." The guards kicked away the packing box, and Jack Slade dropped to his death.

Mollie Sheehan, cowering in the cabin just up the road, did not see him hanged. But she heard how the vigilantes, contrary to custom, cut the body down and bore it to the Virginia Hotel so his wife would be spared the sight of her husband dangling from a rope; how Virginia Slade thundered into town on her black horse—too late. When the streets had quieted, the child crept into the hotel to offer comfort. There in a shadowy little room she saw Virginia Slade weeping over a blanket-shrouded form. Words failed Mollie. She stayed a moment, trembling, then slipped away, but the scene remained etched forever in her memory.

So gripping was the story of Jack Slade's death—of a man pleading for his life, of his wife's wild ride and wilder grief—that it became a legend. It was said that the body was preserved (appropriately) in alcohol until it could be sent back east for burial. And for years the Slades' deserted stone house was said to be haunted by a woman's wails and the hoofbeats of a black horse.

Jack Slade, hanged without a trial simply for disturbing the peace, was a murdered man. Yet the men who killed Slade were Virginia City's leading citizens, people who believed in the majesty of law, the primacy of religion, and the orderly pursuit of business. This paradox was one peculiar to an expanding

America: Within the shabby little mining town, set in a splendid wilderness, raged all the conflicting forces that shaped the new land. The West lured legions of men of every sort: prospectors and trappers, traders and farmers, lawyers and merchants, drifters, gamblers, gunmen, and thieves. Most of them were single, though there were a handful of men with wives and children. Some were educated, some ignorant. Some were veterans and deserters from the Union and Confederate armies locked in civil warfare thousands of miles away. Others were freedmen, emancipated from slavery by President Lincoln's recent proclamation. Virginia City had homes and a school, butcher shops and a bakery, saloons, gambling halls, and brothels. It was a place where most men drank heavily and went armed. It was shot through with violence—brawls and gunfights, robberies and murders. It was a town where people did business and shaped political careers—a town that offered literary and historical societies, taffy pulls and sleighing parties, teas and prayer meetings and weddings.

The threads that wove these disparate powers together were spun from gold. Forced up from the earth's molten depths when the Rocky Mountains formed, freed in fragments by millennia of weathering, and washed downhill by ancient streams, deposits of sand, soil, and clay glittered with ribbons of precious flakes and dust that could be mined with minimal equipment and skill. Discoveries of gold had inspired a rush to California in 1849 and to British Columbia's Fraser River in 1855. Now, in the early 1860s, thousands of people were flocking to the gulches on the north slope of Baldy Mountain in what is now southwestern Montana, where claims would yield an estimated 270 tons of gold—worth about $145 million then and more than one billion dollars today.

At first, the adventurers came not from the East but from the played-out California fields. Among them was one who became a legend in the West and a hero to people like Mollie Sheehan—in many ways, a man who embodied the very spirit of the American West. He began as a footloose wanderer,

then a miner and merchant, and eventually became one of the richest cattle barons in Montana. He was a conservative believer in orderly public government, and he did not hesitate to use private violence to achieve it. His name was Granville Stuart.

Granville Stuart typified a distinctively American pattern of men innocent of specific goals but always on the lookout for opportunity. He and his brother James were young and strong, good riders and good shots. They got along fairly well in several Indian languages, knew how to live off the land, and had the skills of farmers, hunters, trappers, carpenters, butchers, and miners—whatever was needed. They were well read for the place and period, curious and observant. They seemed to love the life they led.

They were born in Virginia, but in 1837, when Granville Stuart was three and James was six, their parents immigrated to the Illinois frontier and a year later to the new Iowa Territory. In 1852, the brothers set off with their father to the gold fields of California. The father returned to Iowa in 1853, but the brothers prospected in California for four years. When they decided to return to Iowa for a visit, nine friends joined them. "All our preparations being made on the fourteenth day of June 1857, we started from Yreka, California, on our journey east," Granville Stuart wrote. "Each man had a horse or mule to ride and a pack horse or pack mule for every two. Two of the party had double barreled shotguns. All the others had muzzle loading rifles and all had Colt revolvers. Each man had blankets and a change of underclothing, and food for about fifty or sixty days." They set out with light hearts. Some days they traveled as far as 35 miles, some days only 10; the pace depended on finding good water and grass for the animals, and what struck their fancy. They met and traded with emigrant trains. They saw the smoke of Indian signal fires and kept alert for trouble.

By July 17, 1857, as the party reached the aptly named Malad Creek in the Oregon Territory some 70 miles north of the Great Salt Lake, Granville

Stuart fell ill with what James, who had some medical training, called mountain fever, by which he might have meant one of a number of illnesses—typhoid, malaria, Rocky Mountain spotted fever. Granville could not go on, so he and James dropped out of the party of travelers.

For seven weeks, in a camp of bent willow poles covered with blankets, James Stuart cared for his brother. Granville at last recovered, but in the meantime an obstacle of another kind had been thrown in their path. Brigham Young's Mormon settlement in Utah had revolted against the U.S. government, and the trails leading east toward Iowa and west toward California were being guarded by armed men murderously hostile to non-Mormons. The Stuarts could go neither forward nor back and were hardly safe where they were. They had, however, befriended a trapper and pony trader named Jake Meek, who knew the country well. He planned to take his herd some 200 miles north to the Beaverhead Valley for the winter. The Indians there were friendly and the winters mild. And when the Mormon troubles were over—as they surely would be by spring—the brothers could be on the move again. This suited the Stuarts, and on September 11, 1857, they set off with Meek. A month later, under brilliant autumn skies, they descended into a place of clear streams and rolling hills covered with golden bunch grass that swayed in the wind, Granville Stuart said, "like a field of grain."

The Beaverhead Valley was an earthly paradise—a place of silent, towering mountains forested in spruce, Douglas fir, and tamarack; laced with trout-filled rivers; carpeted in spring with wild violets and iris, moss flowers, rose-petaled bitterroot, snow and timber lilies. On the plains to the east vast herds of buffalo slowly eddied; the mountains sheltered bobcat, coyote, lynx, mink, puma, elk, deer, bighorn sheep, and bear. Flathead, Shoshone, and Kootenai Indians hunted and sometimes warred there, pushed toward the Rockies by other westering tribes displaced by the inexorable advance of white settlers.

Until the 1850s, few whites except for trappers had seen the valleys that lay off the Oregon Trail, a well-worn route stretching from Independence, Missouri, to Oregon and down to California. But now the fur trade was dying, and the U.S. government had already surveyed a rail route from Fort Benton, the highest port on the Missouri River, through the mountains to the Pacific. In 1858 a small army company that was under the command of Lieutenant John Mullan began building a wagon road from Fort Benton to Fort Walla Walla in what is now the state of Washington.

The Stuart brothers wintered comfortably in a camp of elk-skin lodges, hunting, visiting with the few remaining trappers and their families, and trading with Snake, Bannock, and Flathead Indians; for a horse, the Indians wanted two blankets, some clothing, a mirror, a knife, and "a few other trifles"—too much, older trappers complained, compared with what the going price had been before the new wave of adventurers like the Stuarts.

When the weather warmed, the Stuarts rode north to Deer Lodge Valley, about 40 miles from their winter camp. They went there to hunt, but they were also intrigued by the talk they'd heard about a French-Indian half-breed named Benetsee who was said to have found gold at Deer Lodge as early as 1852 but never cared to prospect. A decade earlier, Father Pierre-Jean De Smet, a Jesuit missionary to the Flathead and Nez Perce tribes, had heard that there was gold at Deer Lodge but said nothing, hoping to delay the Indians' inevitable fate as long as possible: "They would tremble indeed," he wrote, "could they learn the history of those numerous and ill-fated tribes that have been swept from their land, to make place for Christians, who have made the poor Indians the victims of their rapacity."

Equipped with only a broken spade and a tin bread pan, the Stuarts found enough gold dust at Benetsee's Creek to convince them the area was worth mining. They ever afterward claimed to be the first white men to mine in Montana. In 1858, though, the Stuarts were more immediately interest-

Threading its way down a steep decline, a Mormon wagon train *(above)* enters the Great Salt Lake Valley. At right, three wagons ford the swollen Platte River in 1866. Enduring cold, heat, and flood, nearly 60,000 Mormon settlers crossed the plains between 1847 and 1867 to find a new home in Utah.

A MORMON'S JOURNEY TO THE PROMISED LAND

Among the thousands of Mormons who immigrated to Utah was Jean Rio Baker, pictured here. She left a moving account of her hardships during this arduous trek.

January 4, 1851: I this day took leave of every Acquaintance I could collect together, in all human probability, never to see them again on Earth. May 4: At first starting one of my teams turned sulky, and would not move in any direction, when all at once they gave a sudden start, and running round broke the tongue of the wagon, I felt heart sick at this beginning. May 31: Our men rose at 4 this morning, in order to make a bridge, when one of the storms we are so used to, came on and in a few minutes they were drenched through; finished the bridge at 8, had breakfast, began to get the wagon over; the creek rising fast, 3 feet in 3 hours; got 4 wagons over, when the bridge washed away . . . , rebuilt the bridge, and got the rest over by 6 o'clock; a right hard days work— mosquitoes plentiful. July 8: Ferried over the Elk-Horn in safety, except one of Chatterley's company, who caught his hand in a chain, bursting one of his fingers. . . . Mrs. Joseph Pierce and I sewed it up between us, and dressed it as well as we could under the circumstances. August 27: Sister Henderson died today at noon, we buried her at 9 P.M., she left seven children.

ed in drying venison to take with them to Fort Bridger, some 300 miles away on the Oregon Trail, where they could get white men's necessities like coffee, flour, sugar, and dried fruit. Nor did the gold of Deer Lodge draw them back directly from Fort Bridger. For several seasons the brothers herded horses in the mountains and traded with emigrant and army supply wagon trains passing through the region. A man could do well buying emigrants' starved and exhausted oxen, horses, and mules; resting and fattening them for a few months on the plentiful, nutritious bunch grass; then reselling them at handsome prices.

Eventually, plagued by Indians who stole white men's horses and killed their cattle, the Stuarts decided to settle, at least for a while, in Deer Lodge Valley. They built a corral for their horses and cows and a cabin for themselves along a creek not far from Benetsee's, at a place they called American Fork. For the winter of 1860 the brothers were well stocked with gunpowder and lead, and they had plenty of their much-treasured coffee, flour, salt, sugar, and bacon. They had traded furs, skins, and dried meat for a plow and seed so they could grow their own grain and vegetables. Antelope, deer, and mountain sheep usually were in good supply.

Even so, no one could call the life easy. While the valley was beautiful, the winters were long, with heavy snow and sub-zero temperatures as early as October. Black frosts that lasted well into June made farming difficult: "No sooner did a vegetable poke its nose out of the ground than it was immediately frozen," Granville recalled. In the dry heat of the short summers, wildfires burned for days along the mountain slopes, while horse flies and mosquitoes tortured man and beast.

In the summer of 1861 James Stuart took a pack-train to Fort Benton to stock up on such staples as sugar and flour. The trip took 38 days and was a failure: The scheduled steamboat *Chippewa* from Saint Louis was still hundreds of miles downstream when a deck hand carried a lighted candle into the hold to sneak a drink of whiskey. The candle ignited the al-

cohol, which in turn touched off 25 kegs of gunpowder that blew up the boat. The outraged James rode home to report that, in a clear failure of retributive justice, the deck hand survived.

Such things mattered. Everyday pleasures like coffee brightened a daily life that was filled with unremitting physical labor. Lumber for cabins and corrals had to be hand sawed in the mountains and brought down by wagon and ox teams. Land had to be plowed and planted. Cattle and horses had to be cared for and retrieved—often from long distances—when they wandered or were stolen by Indians. Theft was so common that during one particularly bad period, Granville kept his best horses tied to the cabin door and, with rifle and revolver at hand, slept next to them night after night.

Prospecting went on when weather and other work permitted. In 1861 James and Granville Stuart started on May 22. They were searching for placers, the loose deposits of gold, sand, and silt washed down from the mountains in streams. When they found one, they panned it, squatting for hours in the icy stream, scooping the sandy water into a shallow tin pan, spinning it to wash away lighter material, leaving a little heavy residue that on lucky days contained a thread of gold specks that could be flicked out with a fingernail or knife blade. A good yield was 10¢ worth of ore per pan, although it was not unheard of for a pan to yield as much as $50 worth. But good days or bad, mining was slow work.

And there was the loneliness. Only a few people lived within 25 miles, among them men whom the Stuarts had known back in the Beaverhead Valley: John Grant, the son of a fur trader, had a place

Although Granville Stuart was one of the first to find gold in Montana, he didn't depend on mining for his livelihood, supporting himself and his family comfortably by butchering beef, trading horses and cattle, and selling groceries. He also helped found the Montana Historical Society in 1865 and was its first secretary.

at the mouth of Little Blackfoot Creek about eight miles from American Fork. Robert Dempsey, who had shared the Stuarts' elk-skin lodges at Beaverhead, built a ranch six miles away, but it was decidedly a mixed blessing. A "ranch" like Dempsey's meant a crude roadside inn where a traveler could corral his horses or oxen, buy a few necessities, and drink a concoction of alcohol that had been enlivened with generous quantities of tobacco and cayenne. Most of Dempsey's patrons appear to have been mindlessly drunk most of the time, and the Stuarts—exceptional in that they did not drink—had little patience with them. Even the genial Granville, who found himself bitterly lonely when James was off on trips, disliked "that gang of drunken loafers." One summer's night he wrote in his journal, "Tolman, Johnny Carr and Co are on a drunk, and as I never drink, of course they had to come and visit me. Oh! For a lodge in some vast wilderness where drunks could never come and where whiskey was unknown."

For the most part, though, the steady trickle of white traders and herders was welcome, as were the Indian hunting groups that often brought trading opportunities. Sometimes warrior bands passed through the valley when tribes were in conflict. In autumn and spring, migrating villages of Nez Perce, Yakima, Coeur d'Alene, and Flathead Indians passed on their way to and from their buffalo-hunting grounds on the plains. Visitors meant company, and perhaps news as well: The Stuarts learned about the Civil War, then several months old, on July 15, 1861, from a fragment of newspaper that someone left at Dempsey's Ranch. Occasionally letters from home, passed from hand to hand along the trails, reached the brothers. And visitors made possible such diversions as card games: James was a keen gambler, although Granville stuck to cribbage. Other amusements were few. Granville, who was a good amateur artist,

James Stuart shared his brother's love of travel and was his business partner. He also led prospecting trips, became a county sheriff, and served in the Montana territorial legislature. The brothers were very close, and when James died at the age of 42, Granville wrote that his death "leaves a gap in my life that will never close."

sketched the scenery, and the brothers took turns keeping a journal.

During the long, dark nights of that first winter, without so much as an almanac to read, the Stuarts were starved for books. Then some Indians mentioned that a man in the Bitterroot Valley had a trunkful: "On receipt of these glad tidings, we saddled our horses and, putting our blankets, and some dried meat for food, on a pack horse, we started for those books, a hundred and fifty miles away, without a house or anybody on the route, and with three big dangerous rivers to cross," Granville recalled. The brothers had $50 between them, and they were ready to part with it. Picking their way over icy fords, they found the tepee of the man who had the books in his care, but he had no authority to sell them. At length, after promising to take the blame and make good in the end, the Stuarts were allowed to choose five books at five dollars apiece—a high price at that time, when a Union private earned $13 a month and a brigadier general's salary was $124. Trembling with excitement, James and Granville chose carefully: illustrated editions of Shakespeare and Byron, a life of Napoleon, a French Bible, and Adam Smith's *Wealth of Nations*. Packing them carefully away in their blankets, they made the long journey home. Granville Stuart kept four of those books to the end of his long life; the Adam Smith eventually fell apart.

Company was so thin in the valley that a social occasion was worth traveling long distances for. All the traders and trappers had Indian wives, as lonely white men had since colonial times. For the tribes, such matches had advantages. At the most basic level, daughters were commodities to be traded, and some families reserved daughters for the purpose. The price was paid in horses, guns, ammunition, blankets, shirts, bed ticking, tobacco, sugar, and flour. Such unions also created social ties between whites

By the light of his small cabin window, a solitary miner relaxes with a book. Books helped relieve the Stuart brothers' cabin fever during the long, cold Montana winters. Granville, who eventually amassed a library of 3,000 volumes, wrote that "many were the happy hours" he and James spent reading.

and the tribal kinship networks, with the women serving as mediators. From the white men's standpoint, the advantages were obvious.

Sometimes Indian wives ran off, but many of them settled into their roles. Robert Dempsey's wife, who was "a lady of uncertain temper," according to Granville, ruled Dempsey's Ranch with an iron hand and "did not hesitate to beat up drunken patrons who tried to order her around." Aubony, the 12-year-old Snake Indian girl Granville Stuart married in May 1862, bore him nine children, and he was faithful to her until she died in 1887.

In any case, everyone was merry at dances. The most memorable was the one John Grant gave on New Year's Day 1862. The men wore their best flannel shirts and fringed buckskin suits but were no match for the women, resplendent in calico, scarlet leggings, beaded moccasins, and ornaments of silver, shell, and feathers. To the music of two fiddles they danced quadrilles all night as a blizzard raged outside. It hadn't let up by morning, so the party simply continued. The soul of hospitality, John Grant produced a good breakfast and spread buffalo skins on the floor, and everyone—men, women, and chil-

dren—slept until early afternoon, then enjoyed another night of feasting and dancing. The guests finally rode away on January 3. Everybody made it home—some as far as 15 miles—without frostbite, Granville reported, on the last New Year before life in the valleys changed completely.

The tribes said the winter of 1862 was the worst in memory. Not until the end of March did the warm, southwesterly chinook wind—the "snow eater"—begin to break up the ice on streams and rivers. Then the world awoke. A steady stream of Indians passed through Deer Lodge Valley on the way back from their winter hunts. At the mouth of the Big Blackfoot River near the future site of Missoula, Captain John Mullan's troops broke winter quarters and resumed work on his road. Jake Meek headed for the Emigrant Trail, to trade with that year's arrivals. Miners drifted in from the west and south, attracted by rumors of gold.

"Our little settlement at American Fork has begun to take on the lively bustling appearance of a new placer camp," James noted in April as he built sluice boxes—the first in the Rockies north of Colorado (*page 28*). He and Granville worked their claims without notable success. In June came news of steamers at Fort Benton loaded with emigrants, provisions, mining tools, and other much-needed supplies; shortly afterward a few travelers stopped at the camp. Among them were families like that of B. B. Burchett: "It looks like home to see little blonde children playing about and to see white women," wrote the newly married Granville. "Every man in camp has shaved and changed his shirt since this family arrived. We are all trying to appear like civilized men."

July brought a 40-wagon train and reports of more on the way. Someone left blacksmith tools with Granville, who found a coal outcrop to fuel a forge and set himself up as a blacksmith. The Stuarts, who could turn their hands to anything, were becoming businessmen. Along with miners and their families came people determined to relieve

DOMESTIC TRANQUILLITY

Aubony, a Snake Indian woman, married Granville Stuart in May 1862, when he was living in the Deer Lodge Valley. They raised nine children of their own and adopted two sons of James Stuart. In 1864, when they were living in Virginia City, their neighbor, young Mollie Sheehan, asked Granville why he had married an Indian woman: "He turned, smiled, put his hand on my shoulder and said sweetly, 'You see Mollie, I'm such an old fellow, if I married a white woman she might be quarreling with me.' "

them of their gold: loafers, hangers-on, and denizens of tent saloons, bawdyhouses, and gambling dens. Trouble was inevitable, but the residents of American Fork had devised a system for maintaining law and order. Although the settlement was technically located in the Washington Territory, the courts and other government offices were hundreds of miles away in the capital, Olympia. To a large extent, American Fork was on its own.

The kind of government found in American Fork and in other remote mining camps was democracy at its simplest. Citizens gathered and agreed what land constituted their district, registering it with the territorial government. They elected a presiding officer, sometimes a marshal to enforce what few laws there were, and—most important—a recorder to register mining claims. In deciding claims rights, every effort was made to give anyone with energy and ambition a fair chance. The first rule, just as with land claims, was priority: The person who found a gold field had first choice of a claim on it. In fact, he alone could have two claims; everyone else got one. The size and shape of claims varied from district to district, but in every case the miner had to mark his claim clearly and file its location and the date of discovery, along with his name, with the recorder. Then he had to work that claim at least one day in three and not dump debris on neighboring claims nor interfere with the water supply at the expense of his neighbors. Claims could be bought and sold in the presence of witnesses, but a claim left unattended for 10 days could simply be taken.

A similarly straightforward approach was taken to crime, which in a mining camp was generally limited to claim-jumping, theft, and murder. To try a charge, the miners gathered and elected a judge, prosecutor, defender, and jury, which sometimes meant the whole group. If the verdict was guilty, the sentence—flogging, banishment, or hanging—was carried out at once, because there was no jail. In any case, swift justice saved time, and time meant money. A miner's work could bring $15 to $100 a day. In

American Fork the system went into action that July, when James Stuart caught a young horse thief. Horse theft was a serious offense for two reasons: Horses were expensive, and depriving a man of transportation in this near wilderness was tantamount to murder. The miners' court convicted the destitute youth, but "in consideration of his age and contrition" decreed banishment, rather than the more usual death sentence. The miners chipped in $15 and gave him provisions to see him on his way, thus tempering justice with mercy.

Three strangers who rode into the camp with six horses were not so lucky. They were followed at a distance by two men who said the horses were stolen from them and asked James's assistance. He was happy to help make the arrests. One of the accused surrendered at once, and another gave up meekly. The third, who was playing cards at the time, went for his gun and was shot dead; he was buried with the cards in one hand and his revolver in the other. At a hastily convened miners' court one of the survivors was acquitted, but the miners convicted the other, whose name was Spillman, and sentenced him to hang forthwith.

Spillman asked only for enough time to write a letter of piteous contrition to his father in the States. Then he went calmly to his death. "It was evident that he was not a hardened criminal, and there was no reckless bravado in his calmness. It was the firmness of a brave man, who saw that death was inevitable and nerved himself to meet it," wrote James, revealing his regret that Spillman's father might never learn what had happened to his son "for, of course, we would not send such a letter to anyone's father."

A gold rush was aptly named. Because claim staking was done on a first come, first served basis, mining communities had highly charged atmospheres, and the rumor of a new strike was enough to start a stampede. At American Fork in the summer of 1862, prospectors reported good placers more than 100 miles away at Grasshopper Creek, a small offshoot of the Beaverhead River. Within days,

"The potatoes, corn, peas, and beets that were planted last are coming up fine. Began to enlarge my prospecting out in the ravine, looks good. This has been a beautiful day, smoky like Indian summer. Read 'Byron' and indulged in many reveries while lying on the bank under the trees by the lovely creek and soothed by its gentle murmur. Woke up by having to return to earth and wash the dishes and roast some coffee. I am becoming very lonesome and long for brother James to return. Was bitten by several mosquitoes and saw the first horse fly of the season."

GRANVILLE STUART'S JOURNAL,
JUNE 12, 1861

people were streaming out of Deer Lodge Valley. By November, Grasshopper Creek had become Bannack, a new mining district whose name was based on that of the Indian tribe pushed out by hundreds of miners and emigrant families.

The Stuarts quickly hired a man to build a 20-foot-square log building in Bannack and another to haul a ton of supplies to it from American Fork. They were now butchers and grocers in addition to being cattle dealers, and they were acquiring the comforts of civilization. In American Fork, for instance, Granville had elected to build a bunk rather than sleep on another split-log floor. The Bannack place was even better: "We have fixed up our cabin quite cozy and home like," Granville wrote in November. "There is a fireplace in one corner and a calico curtain does service for a cupboard, another shelf holds our five books and James's tobacco pouch and pipe. The table and some stools complete the outfit." Besides that, there were more than 30 white women and two fiddlers in the camp, so they could have dances "attended by all the respectable people and enjoyed by young and old alike."

Word of the gold strike at Bannack raced eastward, and warm weather brought the new season's wagon trains to swell its population into thousands. Besides a new crop of miners, there were emigrant entrepreneurs who saw a chance to make their fortunes by supplying the people who were working claims with food, clothing, equipment, and transportation. One man dreaming of a successful business was James Sheehan, Mollie's father. An Irishman from County Cork, he had come to America in flight from the potato famine that starved one million people and sent another desperate million to America between 1846 and 1854. Widowed by the time Mollie was a toddler, he worked as a freighter with horse and mule teams, getting by but not getting ahead. The Sheehans moved from Kentucky to Indiana to Illinois to Iowa, then headed for Saint Joseph, Missouri—where Sheehan remarried—and on to Colorado. In April 1863 he set out from Denver with his mule teams, his new wife and their red-haired infant daughter, and his beloved Mollie for the rich new gold fields at Bannack.

Other, wealthier families were also on the move. New territories offered splendid possibilities for politicians, among them Sidney Edgerton of Ohio: lawyer, former congressman, and now Abraham Lincoln's designated chief justice of the Idaho Territory, which had been carved out of the Washington and Oregon Territories that March. Idaho's capital had not yet been chosen, but Edgerton and his wife nevertheless set off from Omaha on June 16, 1863. The 17-member party included Edgerton's nephew and secretary, Wilbur Fisk Sanders, a tall, thin, pious 29-year-old lawyer who had been invalided out of the Union army after the Battle of Shiloh in 1862; Sanders's adoring wife, Harriet; their two sons; their cousin Lucia Darling; and Amorette Geer, a servant girl.

Two families—one comfortable and well established, the other struggling—could hardly have been more different, but the rutted track west, established for 20 years and more, served as a great leveler. From its starting point in the town of Independence, the Oregon Trail crossed the Missouri River, where the United States ended and the territories began. The long, lumbering wagon trains followed the trail west and then north over the prairies of Kansas and Nebraska and along the winding Platte River to Fort Laramie, then through the high plains of Wyoming into the Rockies. Rolling south along the Sweetwater River, the wagons crossed the Continental Divide at the South Pass through the Rockies and headed down to Fort Bridger. From there a maze of routes led north again. Settlers had a choice of trails besides the Oregon by the 1860s, notably the Northern Overland Trail, which followed the army's planned rail route; Captain Mullan's trail through the mountains to Fort Walla Walla; and the Overland Stage route to Denver, Fort Bridger, and the Idaho valleys.

Granville Stuart made many sketches of the Montana landscape, including this one of Deer Lodge City, near the place where he and his brother first found gold. He also wrote a book, *Montana As It Is,* published in New York in 1865, that included a history of the region, travel itineraries, and a guide to local Indian languages and customs.

A View of the Gold Creek Mountains, from Deer Lodge City. Looking West. August 22nd, 1865. Nº 6

No matter what the route, many overland voyagers depended on guidebooks to teach themselves how to travel. Captain Randolph B. Marcy's *The Prairie Traveler: A Hand-Book for Overland Expeditions*, first published in 1859, offered advice on distances, water, and grass along 28 routes, as well as information on how to organize and what to take. A guide to the gold fields and Bannack did not appear until 1864.

What the guidebooks neglected to include, the pioneers learned along the way. Weather and an abundance of grass for their draft animals were critical: It was best to leave in late April or early May from a place like Independence, where people could buy equipment and join traveling groups. The most practical wagon for a family was small, only about 10 feet long and four feet wide—a simple box made of strong hardwood, with hickory arches on top to sup-

ple ammunition, and a tent were indispensable. So was a stove, preferably cast-iron, which could be bought for $18 to $25 in the States and sold for as much as $200 in the camps. Most travelers chose lighter, cheaper sheet-iron "emigrant stoves," which frequently fell apart. There were, of course, a hundred other necessities—tools, wagon parts, cooking utensils, ponies for riding, perhaps a milk cow. Wise travelers packed food enough to last through the entire trip and the first few months at the camps, where supplies might be scarce. The basics were flour and dried yeast, cured hams and sides of bacon, eggs packed in cornmeal that would later be used for baking, dried apples or peaches, and coffee, the universal drink of the West, which had the virtue of masking the bitter taste of the alkaline water common in the West.

"They would tremble indeed could they learn the history of those numerous and ill-fated tribes that have been swept from their land, to make place for Christians, who have made the poor Indians the victims of their rapacity."

FATHER PIERRE-JEAN DE SMET, JESUIT MISSIONARY

port a canvas cover lined with oilcloth. Although high wheels made the wagon cumbersome and somewhat unstable, they provided enough clearance to ford shallow streams.

To pull the load, most voyagers chose between mules and oxen; horses were expensive and used more often as mounts. Mules were strong, relatively fast, and smart, but they wandered maddeningly if not closely guarded at night and, like horses, were a favorite target for Indian theft. Oxen were stronger, more biddable, and less attractive to thieves. They were, however, very slow compared with mules, and their cloven hoofs splintered on rocky trails. As to cost, oxen were considerably cheaper: Three yoke of oxen—six animals—cost $225, half the price of two span—or four—of mules.

Guides recommended taking nothing but essentials. A few changes of clothing, foul-weather gear, double-soled boots, a dependable firearm with am-

Disregarding the advice of the guides, some people brought nonessentials such as extra linens, sewing machines and hope chests, mirrors, and family bedsteads—much of which ended up lining the trail, thrown out to lighten the load as draft animals weakened. Scavengers from the forts and settlements along the way often lingered at a distance as a train passed, alert for useful castoffs.

Emigrant parties needed organization, with leaders and rules. A wagon train traveling 20 miles a day might be a mile long; it had to find camping places with wood or buffalo chips—dried dung—for fuel, forage for the animals, and potable water. There had to be cooperative, quasi-military routines for getting unwieldy wagons across rivers, up and down mountain passes, and into the corral formation that shielded animals and people at night. The leader had to keep count of wagons and travelers, organize the parties into divisions, appoint lieutenants,

A BRIEF BUT PEACEFUL COEXISTENCE

Among the Indians inhabiting Montana in the late 1850s were the Nez Perce, Shoshone, Snake, Bannock, Flathead, Yakima, Coeur d'Alene, Crow, and, shown above, the Blackfeet. These migratory tribes traversed the mountains and plains following the buffalo herds. They also traded with the whites in the region, and apart from the occasional theft of a horse, there was little trouble between them.

Granville Stuart reported of trading, "We never refused any of these Indians credit for the few things they wanted, such as calico, red cloth for the ladies' leggings, calico shirts, vermilion paint, beads, knives, handkerchiefs, powder, lead, percussion caps, combs, and sometimes blankets. To their honor be it said, they always paid when they passed on their return from the buffalo range. We never lost a dollar through crediting them, for even if the purchaser was dead, or sick, the wife or husband or some relative, as the case might

be, came and paid us in buffalo robes, dried meat, dried tongues, skins or something they had. If a white man came to an Indian's camp he was always welcome to the best he had without money."

When Granville and his brother James had their encampment in the Deer Lodge Valley they had frequent contact with Blackfeet Indians who, he wrote, "were not blood thirsty at this time, for they could have ambushed and killed us almost any day or night."

The years following the Civil War witnessed a tragic change in the relationship: With the ever growing influx of farmers and cattle ranchers and the disappearance of the buffalo herds that followed, the cooperation and trade between Indians and whites gave way to mistrust and open hostilities. During the winter of 1883–1884, some 600 Blackfeet starved. One, named Flint Knife, said shortly before his death: "I wish that white people had never come into my country."

THE
PRAIRIE TRAVELER,
A HAND-BOOK
FOR
OVERLAND EXPEDITIONS.

WITH ILLUSTRATIONS, AND ITINERARIES OF
THE PRINCIPAL ROUTES BETWEEN THE
MISSISSIPPI AND THE PACIFIC,
AND A MAP.

BY RANDOLPH B. MARCY,
CAPTAIN U. S. ARMY.
(NOW GENERAL MARCY, CHIEF OF STAFF, ARMY OF THE POTOMAC.)

EDITED (WITH NOTES) BY
Sir RICHARD F. BURTON, F.R.G.S.,
ETC.

PUBLISHED IN THE UNITED STATES BY AUTHORITY OF THE WAR DEPARTMENT.

LONDON:
TRÜBNER AND CO., 60, PATERNOSTER ROW.
1863.

Emigrants traveling the Overland Trail doff their hats for a photographer in Nebraska. Travelers relied on guidebooks like Captain Randolph B. Marcy's *The Prairie Traveler: A Hand-Book for Overland Expeditions*, which offered detailed information about 28 different trails.

start the trains in the mornings, and stop them in the evenings. He also kept the list of rules that governed the train, the punishments for disobeying them, and the rosters for guard duty.

Even with such safeguards, the way west was long and hard. From his journey from Iowa to California in 1852, Granville Stuart remembered seeing abandoned wagons and a starveling yellow dog lying beside lonely burial mounds. Kate Dunlap, heading for Montana nearly 20 years later, mourned the dead in her journal: "Oh, how many have laid down in death on these plains," she wrote, "and often without the hand of a kind relative or friend to alleviate their sufferings."

Few of the dead were killed by Indians, who almost never attacked large trains. Some emigrants died in accidents, but disease caused the overwhelming majority of deaths. It was rampant in the trains, felling people who were poorly nourished and

had only rudimentary concepts of sanitation. Neither the ill nor the injured could count on a physician to pull them through. The West had few doctors and, considering 19th-century medicine, that may not have been a bad thing. The education and training James Stuart had had, for instance, consisted of a year of high school, a brief apprenticeship with a physician, and a few months of lectures that exposed him to the treatments most country physicians used: bleeding, purging, and sweating patients, bone setting, amputation.

Without the presence of doctors, emigrants turned to self-help books, which reassured readers of their ability to handle medical emergencies themselves: "Any man, unless he is an idiot or an absolute fool, can perform this operation," said one, of amputation. Every wagon carried a few standard medications—calomel as a purgative, quinine for fever, and opium in the form of laudanum to kill pain.

Dysentery was everywhere in the trains. Scurvy, too, was endemic, its sores and swellings brought on by the dearth of fresh fruits and vegetables. So was malaria, which was known as ague, ager, or intermittent fever. The truly unlucky caught cholera, which killed so inevitably and swiftly that, to save time, grieving relatives dug graves as the stricken lay dying. Time was everything on the trains, because the journey had to be completed before supplies ran out or winter came.

Considering the hard work and exhaustion, the dirt and disease and danger, the travelers' buoyancy of spirit and the happiness of their memories is remarkable. A summer's journey to a new life fostered a holiday atmosphere, perhaps because travelers had more free time than they ever had in their lives. Wagon trains averaged about two miles an hour, giving people time to wonder at new sights, to hunt and explore, to read, to knit. Those who were not members of puritanical religious sects sang songs, played cards, and danced in the evenings, when the wagons and animals were secured.

Few can have been more relentlessly cheerful than Wilbur Sanders's wife, Harriet, who traveled in hoop skirts and a silk mask to protect her complexion and took everything in her sunny stride. She recorded it all in her journal—the "grand lightning" on the plains, the singing in tents during thunderstorms, the walks she took, the wildflowers she picked and pressed. She wrote about baking 13 loaves of bread at a time and preparing vast breakfasts—fried venison, fried fish, cream gravy, pancakes, molasses—and about washing and starching sunbonnets. She rhapsodized about the heroism of her revered "Mr. Sanders": When a wagon wheel for which they had no spare broke, he rode alone to find one someone had spotted on the trail several days before—and returned triumphant! When their wagon began to sink while crossing the Snake River, he saved it. She laughed about it all.

Mollie Sheehan remembered her trip with delight, too, and she had special reason to be happy. Because of her mother's death and her father's absences, Mollie's childhood had been peripatetic and often lonely. When James Sheehan remarried

Many miners going west to the Montana gold fields traveled the Oregon Trail to Fort Laramie and turned off there onto the Bozeman Trail. When Granville and James Stuart left Yreka, California, for Iowa in 1857, they left the state by way of the California Trail, going against the westward stream of emigrants. Had they pushed on to Iowa as they originally planned, the Mormon Trail would have been the most direct route for the journey's last leg.

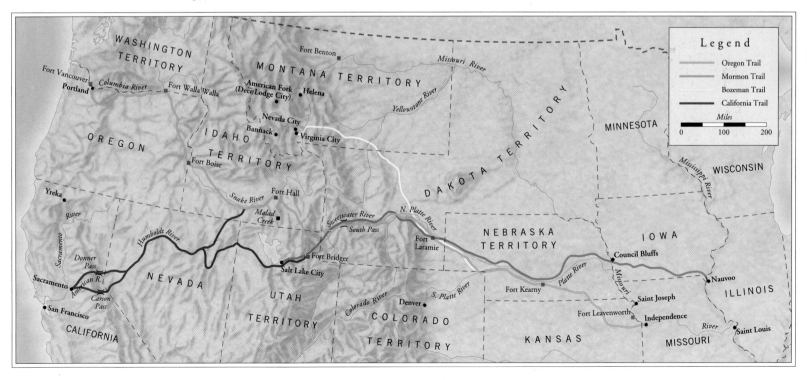

A prairie schooner crammed with possessions left little room for passengers to sit. "What to take and what to leave behind us was the problem," lamented one young westbound wife. "Many of our most cherished treasures had to be left to give place to the more necessary articles."

in Saint Joseph, he left Mollie with relatives and took his bride, Anne Cleary, to Colorado, returning for Mollie a year later. She remembered little of the long trip to Denver, other than the delight of being with her father, who she knew loved her above all else. Mollie grew fond of her young stepmother and her red-haired infant half sister. Her father taught her to ride—sidesaddle for propriety's sake, since even the word "astride" was considered to be too coarse for use in polite society. And as the daughter of a Catholic, she was given religious instruction and made her first communion.

The Sheehan family set out from Denver for Bannack in April 1863, in two wagons pulled by six-mule teams. A hired hand drove one of the wagons, which was loaded with goods to be resold in the camps. James Sheehan drove the family wagon, with their supplies buried among mattresses, blankets, and comforters and with Anne Cleary's rocking chair hanging on the back. The mess box and sheet-iron stove came down only when the family stopped for a couple of days to wash, mend, and bake bread. Otherwise they cooked over a campfire. From time to time other wagons joined them, and at Fort

Bridger they joined an organized train of 25 or 30 wagons, all of them drawn by mules or horses except for that of a man named Nelson Story, who had an ox team. He labored into camp hours after the others, but he always arrived.

Mollie rode beside her father on his high seat and watched the world unfold—"gorgeous sunsets gilding distant mountain peaks and flooding with magic light great valleys," as she later told her children, "the rhythm of going, going, going." When she remembered, she said the five Our Fathers, Hail Marys, and Glorias that her priest had given her to recite each day. Better than that were the songs her father taught her—"Swanee River," "Nellie Gray," and the rollicking "Captain Jenks of the Horse Marines." She had her books, a collection that had been chosen with a Victorian view to the improvement of children: *Bible Stories;* the Little Eva section of Harriet Beecher Stowe's best-selling *Uncle Tom's Cabin*—in which a slave owner's angelic daughter dies in a cloud of sanctity—and *The Life of Mary Magdalene, or the Path to Penitence,* a gift from her father. She liked to read aloud by the campfire, hoping for praise. One of those who gave it was a dark, handsome stranger who listened attentively and spoke in a deep, soft voice. His name was Jack Gallagher, and he joined the train at Fort Bridger. Mollie would have reason to remember him.

The "Land of Gold" that Mollie so romantically expected proved something of a shock. When the Sheehans at last arrived at Bannack in early June, they found the usual collection of outlying ranches and a small town of one-story log cabins with mud and gravel roofs, but few other signs of civilization. As one early arrival put it, there were "no schoolhouses, churches or public buildings of any kind ... there are several stores, hotels, groceries and numerous saloons." Harriet Sanders's four-year-old, James, having heard won-

derful things about Bannack for months, took a look and announced, "I fink Bangup is a humbug," to the great amusement of his elders.

But Bannack would be no more than a stopping place for Mollie. Two days before she arrived, seven prospectors appeared in camp dogged at every step by hundreds of miners frenetically excited by the news that the prospectors' packhorse was loaded with gold. The prospectors, who were led by a Scot named Henry Edgar and Canadian Bill Fairweather, had set out from Bannack in February, heading east with plans to meet a party led by James Stuart to prospect along the Yellowstone River. Instead, each group was captured by bands of Crow Indians. The captives escaped, but several of Stuart's company were killed. Both groups had to take circuitous routes back to Bannack because the Indians had made it clear that they all would be killed if they violated Crow territory again. On May 26, heading for home, Fairweather and Edgar's group camped in the Beaverhead Valley near a branch of the Ruby River, named for the garnets, or "Montana rubies," that were found there. Fairweather and Edgar did a little panning, hoping for tobacco

When Susannah Bristow set out for Oregon to join her husband, Elijah, she packed the leather-covered trunk below with family heirlooms that had already accompanied her on earlier migrations from Tennessee to Kentucky and later to Illinois. Carefully wrapped in blankets, the china that had been part of her dowry survived the bruising journey.

These placer miners working a stream near Lewistown, Montana, diverted the water into the long wooden sluice box to wash gold out of the dirt they shoveled into the box. Gold and other heavy particles sank to the bottom of the box, where they were caught by cleats, or riffles. The water was then cut off and any gold was removed.

money. Before they had finished their first pans, Fairweather shouted, "I have a scad!"—a large gold flake. "If you have one, I have a hundred!" Edgar shouted back. The next day the seven men panned out $150 in gold dust, and the day after that, they staked 100-foot claims; Edgar named the site Alder Gulch, for the green alders that grew along the creek. So they could prospect more thoroughly and get the best claims, the men set off to Bannack for supplies. They agreed to say nothing in camp, but they spent so freely and smiled so broadly that they gave the secret away.

By the time the prospectors left Bannack, they found themselves trailed by a small army of gold diggers who were determined to discover their secret. Granville Stuart ran into some of them about a mile from town: "They were strung out for quarter of a mile, some were on foot carrying a blanket and a few pounds of food on their backs, others were leading pack horses, others on horseback leading pack animals," he observed. "The packs had been hurriedly placed and some had come loose and the frightened animals running about with blankets flying and pots and pans rattling, had frightened others and the hillside was strewn with camp outfits and grub." Recognizing the opportunity at hand, James Sheehan set off after the stampede with a wagonload of supplies to sell at the new gold field.

On the way back to Alder Gulch the prospectors called their anxious followers to a miners' meeting. Henry Edgar explained what they had found but not where they had found it, showed them a sample of the gold, and said, "If we are allowed to have the claims as we have staked them, we will go on, if not, we will go no further." The miners voted their assent but wanted to know where the gold field was. Edgar pointed out that some were on foot and some on horseback, which gave the riders an unfair advantage. He told them, "When we get to the creek you will know and not till then."

The Alder Gulch diggings, extending 12 miles from the foot of Baldy Mountain, were as rich as any placer field ever found in the region destined to become Montana. The bed of the creek and both sides were, according to Granville Stuart, "literally paved with gold." The discovery changed the face of the region. The previous winter its white population was 604 men and 65 women. Within three months of the gold strike, 10,000 people were working in Alder Gulch alone. By June 16 a 320-acre town site had been laid out and registered. At the behest of the large Southern population, it was first called Varina after the wife of Confederate president Jefferson Davis. However, the man elected judge was a Union sympathizer who refused to sign any document bearing Mrs. Davis's name. He could, however, live with the alternative, Virginia City. Virginia, as everyone called it, was just one of several settlements up and down the gulch. Above it were Summit, Highland, and Pine Grove; below were Nevada City and Adobetown. The gateway to the outside world was Bannack, and by August, A. J. Oliver's stage line was plying the route between there and Salt Lake City, charging 75¢ to take a letter and one dollar to bring one back.

The Stuarts left their cattle with Robert Dempsey and joined the throng. The rough road that ran along the gulch soon was jammed with packtrains

and 16- or 20-horse teams pulling chains of wagons. The gulch itself swarmed with long-haired, bearded men digging, wheeling barrow loads of earth, shoveling it into sluice boxes, and rocking the boxes. It was pandemonium punctuated by the steady ring of axes cutting logs for new buildings. Granville Stuart thought it was the first time in the history of mining camps that a bakery got in ahead of the first saloon. James Stuart built a general store with a man named W. B. Dance, and the brothers opened a blacksmith shop. The town soon boasted dance halls, or hurdy-gurdies, and hundreds of houses—almost all of them the standard dirt-roofed log cabin, because the nearest sawmill was at Bannack and 1,000 board feet of transported lumber cost $250 in gold.

James Sheehan's family moved into a cabin on the main street, and Mollie's stepmother soon turned it into a boardinghouse where the "discovery men" Bill Fairweather and Henry Edgar ate. Sometimes soft-voiced Jack Gallagher, who had admired Mollie's reading in the wagon camp, came to dinner. So did tall George Ives, blond, clean-shaven, and handsome; he fascinated the little girl, who knew nothing of the vicious behavior that was making both men notorious.

Everything fascinated this observant child. Along with the few other children in Virginia City, she attended a log-cabin school set up by a frail, Oxford-educated Briton named Thomas J. Dimsdale, who had come west in the hope that the mountain air would cure his tuberculosis. She thought he knew everything. When school was out, the children roamed the hills above the town, and Mollie learned to recognize the remarkable high-country wildlife—badgers and gophers, rabbits and rockchucks, deer and elk. To the end of her life she could name its pines and cedars, its wild berries and carpets of early flowers, its array of bright birds—mountain bluebirds, yellow-breasted meadowlarks, huge blue Steller's jays, and goldfinches, which she

Prospectors used a short-handled pick *(above, left)* to loosen the dirt of a promising stream bank, then swirled a shovelful in a shallow pan of water *(above, right),* washing the lighter-weight sand and silt over the rim. When only the heavy residue, or "drag," remained, the prospector would pick out the gold specks with a knife or fingernail and transfer the precious particles to a can or bottle.

called canaries because of their color and sparkling song. Back in the noisy town Mollie freely visited such solid neighbors as Granville Stuart, fascinated by his Indian wife and the hammock in which she rocked their baby. She deeply admired the home of Wilbur and Harriet Sanders. It was a whitewashed frame house with green shutters and a board floor—much nicer than a log cabin. Harriet Sanders brought furniture and carpet from the States, although she had sold most of the carpet in strips to the saloon keepers who "besieged her for it." The rest of the town—the gaudy prostitutes, the drunks, the doorstep loungers, the men fighting in the streets—the child viewed with detachment. They were simply part of the scenery.

As were the miners. She was safe around them, in any case. Miners were so lonely, it was said, so indulgent of and protective toward the young that in large camps they might wait hours just to see a white child playing. They might have shot a stranger who touched one of their sluice boxes, but it amused them to see bonneted little girls carefully brushing up traces of gold dust left in the cracks after the boxes were emptied. On a good day Mollie sometimes gleaned as much as one dollar's worth of dust, which she kept in a little inkwell and used for buying candy. However, James Sheehan disapproved of his daughter's being out and about where strange men could speak to her. After a time he forbade her expeditions and, disturbed by the rumors about the characters who gathered at his table, he closed the boardinghouse and moved the family to a little cabin on a quieter side street.

Other people in Virginia City and in Bannack as well were growing unhappy with the state of affairs—conservative, respectable citizens who had built businesses, who held property, and who believed in law and order. James and Granville Stuart had won offices in the first elections held in Deer Lodge Valley, and Granville had joined others to discuss the

Virginia City shopkeepers kept scales with a set of graduated weights for the gold dust customers used to pay for their purchases. Gold was reckoned at $18 an ounce, and, Granville Stuart wrote, the "dust flowed in a yellow stream from the buckskin bags of the miners into the coffers of the saloons, dance halls and gambling dens."

prospect of Montana's becoming a territory in its own right. Merchant Paris Pfouts, who had come from Denver at the same time as the Sheehans, was also concerned, as were schoolmaster Thomas Dimsdale; Sidney Edgerton, still waiting to assume office as the Idaho Territory's chief justice; and Wilbur Sanders, who was setting up his law practice. Most of these people were Union sympathizers—Edgerton had been a fervent abolitionist in Congress—and churchgoers, when there were services. Many were members of such organizations as the Freemasons, which formed a lodge in Virginia City. They disapproved of the miners' disorderly ways and were disturbed by the growing number of men who went about their daily business armed. Recalling the fatal brawls and frequent robberies of 1862, Granville later observed, "Those were dark days."

The situation worsened in 1863, and the root of the evil was gold. It was the only currency in those parts, worth $18 an ounce. The miners carried the precious dust in buckskin pouches; every commercial establishment had a balance scale on the counter sensitive to as little as half a grain—less than five cents' worth. When a visiting priest held the first mass in the town, the miners' offering was a pouch full of the dust worth several hundred dollars.

Paid exclusively in gold by their customers, local businessmen also paid their suppliers in Fort Benton in gold, since Virginia City had neither a bank nor a telegraph to send a money order. As a consequence, tens of thousands of dollars' worth of dust was transported in the mule trains led by people like James Sheehan. The seemingly inexhaustible stream of treasure flowing out of Virginia City attracted criminals from all over the West. So frequent were murder and robbery by the autumn of 1863, so dangerous the Bannack road, that respectable citizens concluded that the outlaws were organized as a gang, with spies in the towns who watched for departing gold shipments and alerted highwaymen, or "road agents," who carried out the robberies. Behind it all, people began to suspect, was Henry Plummer, sheriff of Bannack and Virginia City.

Plummer was something of an enigma. He came from a family of New England sea captains and sailed as a teenager to California in 1852, where he staked a rich claim in the gold fields and was elected a marshal. But he had also served time in San Quentin Prison for second-degree murder before being pardoned by the governor. He made a reputation as a gambler in Lewiston, in what was soon to become Idaho Territory, and it was rumored around town that he led a secret life masterminding a gang

of robbers. But no one knew about Plummer's shady past when he arrived in Bannack. Granville Stuart, who met him quite by accident on the road, liked the man so much that he invited Plummer home and suggested he stay in the area. Thanks to their forge, he and James even fixed Plummer's shotgun for him.

Everybody liked Plummer, who drank very little, who was well spoken and extremely courteous, and who was darkly handsome and dashing in his red-lined overcoat. He was also a fine shot and a bold rider, skills people respected in the West. He had been in Bannack only a short time when he shot a man dead in a saloon. The victim, Jack Cleveland, had been a pal of Plummer's back in Lewiston, but

By 1864, Wallace Street, the major thoroughfare in Virginia City, boasted a bank and a two-story legislative hall a few doors down. Mollie Sheehan's family ran a boardinghouse on Wallace Street where, she recalled, "My stepmother's dried apple pies and dried peach pies were rare delicacies, much in demand."

the two had fallen out; a woman was said to be the cause of the trouble. Bannack's sheriff, Hank Crawford, insisted that a miners' court try Plummer for murder. He was acquitted, the general feeling being that it was a private quarrel, and in any case, Cleveland was suspected of being a road agent and was better out of the way. Plummer promptly set out to avenge himself on Crawford, but Crawford sent a bullet into Plummer's right arm, shattering his wrist and elbow. Plummer taught himself to shoot left-handed, and Crawford prudently left for Wisconsin, to be heard from no more.

No one ever properly explained why the citizens of Bannack elected Henry Plummer sheriff in the spring of 1863. It may have been because he was backed by the town's leading Democrat, or it may simply have been that Plummer himself was a good politician. True, he had been tried for murder, but it was a murder of revenge, and in this culture, personal vengeance was a right, if not actually a duty. The deputies Plummer appointed, however, were another matter: Although nothing was known against D. H. Dillingham, many believed Jack Gallagher, Buck Stinson, and Ned Ray to be road agents. And after being deputized only a few weeks, Stinson, Hayes Lyons, and Charlie Forbes, with the covert assistance of Gallagher, murdered Dillingham in cold blood and in full view of the citizenry because he had been interfering with their plans for a robbery. A miners' court sentenced the three men to hang for the killing, but with the help of a touching last letter from Lyons to his mother, deputy Gallagher and George Ives, the Sheehans' former boarder, roused the crowd to a fever of sympathy and forced a second vote. The men were set free.

Respectable citizens were outraged. The miners' court had been openly manipulated by the kind of men who robbed and threatened and shot one another in the street. Some men quietly began to count the deaths and disappearances around the area; the tally came to 102.

Among several robbery victims that autumn was young Henry Tilden, a protégé of Wilbur Sanders. A

few miles out of town he was held up by three hooded men, one of whom he recognized by the red lining of his overcoat to be Henry Plummer. Just after Tilden was robbed, Sam Hauser and N. P. Langford, heavily armed, set out with $14,000 in gold for James Stuart's suppliers back in Saint Louis. One night, Langford spotted four masked men lurking around his camp. They rode off when he challenged them, but he recognized them as Plummer, the two deputies Stinson and Ray, and George Ives.

Everyone knew the handsome, flamboyant Ives as the leader of a gang of toughs and a friend of Plummer and Jack Gallagher. Oddly enough, amid the threats and the violence, it was a callous remark by one of Ives's unsavory friends that goaded the citizens of Bannack and Virginia City to bring him to justice. According to one version of the story, Ives's downfall began with Nicholas Thiebalt, a likable German youth who worked for a freighter named Clark. In early December Thiebalt, who was sometimes called the Dutchman, went to retrieve a span of mules Clark had been boarding at Ives's 160-acre ranch on the Bannack road. When Thiebalt failed to return, Clark went in search of him at Ives's. He found neither boy nor mules, but he did find blood on the snow. After some ugly words with Ives and a number of his friends, he left convinced that Ives had killed the boy.

About 10 days later, saloon keeper William Palmer, out bird hunting not far from the huddle of corrals and shacks that made up the Ives ranch, dropped a grouse into the brush, and when he went to get the bird he discovered it had landed near a frozen body. It was Nicholas Thiebalt's, and it had been gnawed by animals. Looking for someone to help load the body onto a wagon, Palmer tried one

With local fauna adorning its walls, the Bale of Hay saloon in Virginia City hosted many an impromptu boxing match. Despite their rowdiness, frontier saloons also served as important meeting places: The *Montana Post* reported in 1865 that a miners' meeting to settle a civil dispute was held in J. H. Hughes's saloon in Bagdad City, Montana.

of Ives's shacks, where he found Long John Franck and George Hildebrand. They shrugged at his request and refused to go out into the cold. "Dead bodies are common enough in this country," Hildebrand said. "They kill people every day in Virginia City. Why should we trouble ourselves about this man when he's dead?"

Enraged at their heartlessness, Palmer loaded Thiebalt's body by himself and took it up Alder Gulch, where he made sure that everyone heard the story of the men in the shack and had a good look at the ways in which the luckless youth had been tormented. His neck bore the marks of a rope, and his hands clutched bits of sagebrush that he had grabbed while being dragged across the ground; over the left eye was a bullet wound. This was too much. When night fell, 25 riders set out after Thiebalt's killer. Leading the posse was James Williams, a large, stolid, taciturn man who, along with his brothers, ran a livery stable. One of Williams's riders was X Beidler, formidable gunman and survivor of a number of quarrels, including disagreements with George Ives and Jack Gallagher.

In the morning the posse surrounded the shack at Ives's place and arrested Hildebrand, Franck, and George Ives himself at gunpoint. They escorted the men back to Alder Gulch and kept them under guard all night. The trial was held in Nevada City, just down the gulch from Virginia, because that was the district located closest to Ives's place. At least 1,500 people gathered for the miners' court, among them an intimidating group of Ives supporters, who had secured advocates to defend him. Thanks to their threats, no one stepped forward immediately to act as prosecutor.

Then Wilbur Sanders, who was passing through town on his way from Bannack to Virginia City, volunteered his services. People had remarked Sanders's clumsy riding, his poor shooting, and his Bible thumping—but no one questioned his courage. When Ives's supporters threatened him, he said he would be in town after the trial and they could find him when they wished. When the crowd argued

John X. Beidler *(below)* and James Williams *(bottom)* led many vigilante raids out of Virginia City. When asked, "What's up, X?" Beidler usually replied, "After tracks." An acquaintance stated: "From X no criminal ever got away."

HELENA, *Keller,* MONTANA.

about whether Ives would be judged by the entire community, as the miners preferred, or by a jury, as Ives and his friends demanded, Sanders explained Ives's rights. In the end, a jury of 24 was selected, its verdict to be ratified by all assembled. Sanders and a miner named Charles Baggs, who unlike the lawyer was well known in Nevada City, prosecuted. Ives's friends James Thurmond, John Ritchie, and Harry Smith defended. Dr. Don Byam of Nevada City, assisted by a miner, served as judge.

The trial was held in the street around two wagons, one of which was for the officials and one for the witnesses. The jurors sat around the wagons on chairs borrowed from a hurdy-gurdy hall; an open fire gave them some warmth. Around the principals James Williams placed a cordon of armed guards; gunmen stood on the roofs of cabins, and pickets watched the road to Bannack. Rumors spread that Ives's friends had threatened to kill anyone who testified against him and that Sheriff Plummer was on his way from Bannack to free the prisoners. The air crackled with tension.

But like Williams, lawyer Sanders and Judge Byam worked with dispatch. The evidence against Ives was frightful: Infuriating the defense, Long John Franck turned state's evidence against Ives not only for the murder of Thiebalt but also for six other murders and several stage robberies. The witnesses took two days to testify, and the lawyers needed another to finish their arguments, with the assembly asking questions and voting on disputed points of evidence. Each time a vote was called there was a rush from the saloons, where many retreated for warmth. In the end, the jury was out only a half-hour. Long John Franck was released. Hildebrand, who was weak-minded and elderly, was banished. As for George Ives, he was found guilty.

As Ives's supporters roared in astonished protest, Sanders leaped to his feet and shouted the motion required by a miners' court: "I move that George Ives be forthwith hanged by the neck until he is dead!" Judge Byam put the motion, and most of the miners agreed. Williams's guard drew tight around the prisoners. Ives asked Sanders for a night's grace to write his family and make a will. Sanders hesitated. Then from the cabin roof where he stood guard, X Beidler shouted, "Sanders, ask him how long he gave the Dutchman."

That reminder of the merciless death dealt out to Nicholas Thiebalt sealed Ives's fate. In an atmosphere of near riot, some miners wedged a pine log through the roof of an unfinished cabin, while Williams's circle of guards, shotguns at the ready, kept Ives's friends at bay. He claimed innocence throughout, and just before the noose tightened around his neck he blamed the murder on his friend Alex Carter. The execution proceeded.

So seriously did the miners take the death threats made against Wilbur Sanders that they protected him with an armed guard day and night. Charged by a sense of duty, he stayed in Virginia City for a week on new business—the formation of a committee of vigilance. Vigilantes—groups of men who organized in secret to pursue and punish people they had judged guilty of crimes—had existed in America as early as 1767 but were most common during the settlement of western territories, where the only legal systems most people could avail themselves of were the settlers' and miners' courts. Vigilantes were typically decent citizens who felt called on to defend their communities against outlaws; when they had reason to believe that elected or appointed officials were part of the problem, they took the law into their own hands. They were exercising, they believed, the sovereign power of the people.

George Ives's trial convinced the men of Virginia City, Nevada City, and Bannack that the time had come to take charge of dispensing justice. The testimony they heard confirmed their suspicions of an organized band of road agents; Long John Franck had admitted as much. The outcome of the trial showed them that there were like-minded people with enough power to battle the band. And it provided them with the most chilling of reasons to resort to vigilanteism: The legal system was too slow and expensive. The trial had cost several dozen wit-

nesses and officials four valuable days, not to mention the time of hundreds of spectators who would otherwise have been working. There was no doubt about it: It was faster and cheaper to dispense with the legal system and form a vigilance committee.

The secret nature of the committee meant that most facts about its membership and activities were later subjects of debate. It is generally accepted that the original committee met in late December 1863 in a house on Wallace Street, the main street of Virginia City. Paris Pfouts was made president; a Nevada City merchant, John Lott, was treasurer, in charge of collecting citizens' money to meet expenses. Wilbur Sanders was chief prosecutor. James

Meeting in a house on Wallace Street, the original members of the Virginia City vigilance committee signed a secret oath *(below)* in December 1863. "In a few short weeks," wrote schoolteacher Thomas Dimsdale, "it was known that the voice of justice had spoken, in tones that might not be disregarded."

Williams was made executive officer and put in charge of conducting manhunts. Like other vigilance committees, they developed a set of legalistic bylaws—one of which read, "The only punishment that shall be inflicted by this committee is death." In total darkness, 24 men then swore an oath, the original version of which read, "We the undersigned uniting ourselves in a party for the Laudible purpos of arresting thievs & murderers & recovering stollen propperty do pledge ourselves upon our sacred honore each to all others & solemnly swear that we will reveal no secrets, violate no laws of right & never desert each other or our standerd of justic, so help us God as witnes our hand & seal this 23 of December A.D. 1863."

Early in the new year a mounted party of two dozen men led by James Williams rode out of town in double file, down the Ruby River and the Big Hole River and across Deer Lodge Valley to a hamlet called Cottonwood. A bitter wind was blowing, and the mountains were deep in snow, but that did not deter the vigilantes from their mission. They were after Ives's friend Alex Carter and D. H. Dillingham's murderers, freed by the miners' court months before. But when the vigilantes got to Cottonwood, the outlaws had fled, thanks to a warning from George Brown, a bartender at Dempsey's Ranch. Brown's message had been delivered by Erastus "Red" Yeager, a bartender at the Rattlesnake Ranch, whom the vigilantes had seen on the ride out. They nabbed both men and questioned them separately: Brown admitted to writing the warning and Yeager to carrying it. When he learned that he was to be hanged for his troubles, Yeager told the vigilantes everything they wanted to know—the names of the men in the outlaw gang, their roles, even their password: "I am innocent."

If Yeager thought confessing would save his life, he was mistaken. Williams hanged both men just before midnight, January 4, from a cottonwood tree at a place called Laurin's Ranch about 10 miles from Virginia City. Notes pinned to the dead men's coats announced, "Red! Road agent and messenger" and

THE HANGING OF JAMES DANIELS

On November 19, 1865, James Daniels and A. J. Gartley quarreled over a game of cards, and the enraged Daniels stabbed Gartley, killing him instantly. Vigilantes arrested Daniels and turned him over to the civil authorities. Three weeks later he was brought before the newly organized territorial district court in Helena, sentenced to three years for manslaughter, and then summarily released by acting governor Thomas Francis Meagher. Not content with his reprieve, Daniels began threatening witnesses who had testified against him in court. On March 1, 1866, a vigilante group that was dissatisfied with the course justice had taken seized Daniels and hanged him from a tree.

"Brown! Corresponding secretary." In Yeager's pocket was a letter from his sister, and when the hangmen showed it to Granville Stuart, he realized that Red Yeager had been one of his schoolmates back in Iowa. It made Stuart sad.

Using Yeager's information, the vigilance committee recruited hundreds of men to their cause. Night after night they rode up and down the countryside in search of men they believed to be outlaws. Accounts of the names on the vigilantes' list vary, but the names of the dead men and the dates of their deaths do not. On January 10, in Bannack, they hanged Sheriff Henry Plummer alongside deputies Ned Ray and Buck Stinson on a scaffold Plummer himself had built for executions. The next day in Bannack they hanged Dutch John Wagner and killed a

spells of pale sunshine. James Williams stationed 400 heavily armed pickets 50 yards apart on snowy foot trails in the hills around the town. In the gritty streets below, smaller squads were on a manhunt. The first man they seized was Frank Parrish, who ran the Rattlesnake Ranch, the roadhouse where Red Yeager had worked and reputed to be a road agents' haunt. Next was "Clubfoot" George Lane, a cobbler who kept his bench and bed at James Stuart's store; he was said to be a mule thief, but worse, he had ridden to Bannack to warn Henry Plummer of George Ives's trial. The vigilantes found Jack Gallagher asleep in his bedroll in a gaming room. They surprised Boone Helm, self-confessed desperado and cannibal, outside the Virginia Hotel. Hayes Lyons, condemned for murdering D. H. Dillingham and then reprieved thanks to Gallagher and Ives, was in-

"Is it lawful for citizens to slay robbers or murderers, when they catch them; or ought they to wait for policemen, where there are none, or put them in penitentiaries not yet erected?"

THOMAS J. DIMSDALE IN *THE VIGILANTES OF MONTANA*

Mexican called Joe Pizanthia. When they surrounded Pizanthia's cabin he shot two of the vigilantes, one of them fatally. Infuriated, the attackers blew the cabin open with a howitzer, strung Pizanthia up, shot him, and set fire to his cabin.

On January 16 they captured Steve Marshland hiding out in a freezing shack near the Big Hole River. He had been wounded trying to rob a wagon and was nearly dead of the gangrene that had attacked his frostbitten flesh. The stench had attracted wolves, and before he died Marshland begged, "Bury me deep, boys, so the dogs don't get me." On January 19 they hanged Bill Bunton; on January 24 George Shears; on January 25 Cyrus Skinner, Alex Carter, and John Cooper; on January 26 Bob Zachary and Whisky Bill Graves; and on February 3 Bill Hunter.

But of all the executions, perhaps the hangings on January 14, 1864, in Virginia City were the most gruesome. The day was bleak and cold, with brief

terrupted while eating griddlecakes in a cabin.

None of the men hanged in those weeks was tried. What they got instead was an interrogation by executives of the vigilance committee. The five were held until completion of the gallows—a beam in a roofless, partially built house, with five packing boxes set underneath. Williams formed his guards into a hollow square around them and marched the condemned men to the place of execution as a crowd gathered in the streets to watch.

The hanging was an amateurish operation. An experienced hangman would have adjusted each rope to give the sharp drop that broke a man's neck cleanly. With nobody attending to such details, the condemned men died especially horrible deaths. Lane wept, prayed, then leaped from his box, but his rope was so long that he could push himself up from the floor with his boot tips, twisting and bouncing as he strangled to death. Cursing, Gallagher jumped

too, and thrashed at the end of his rope until he died. Helm, a Southerner, cried, "Hurrah for Jeff Davis; every man for his principles," and kicked away his box. He was a big man and, considering everything, lucky: The drop broke his neck. Parrish and Lyons, the last to die, died hard.

The crowd slowly broke up and drifted away. Mollie Sheehan, coming down a hill in the cold, charged air, looked into the cabin. She saw the dangling bodies, the blackened faces and protruding tongues, the long blue Union overcoat that identified Jack Gallagher, the little form of George Lane, whom she had seen almost every day at his cobbler's bench. She trembled so much, she told her daughter years later, that she could hardly run for home.

The worst of the killing was over, but the vigilantes' reign of terror had equaled that of the outlaw gang's and generated its own mythology, including the cryptic sign 3-7-77 left on each victim's body or house. Some surmised that it stood for the dimensions of a grave, three feet wide, seven feet long, and 77 inches deep. Only the vigilantes knew for sure what it meant, and none ever revealed the secret.

Tales about the aftermath of the killings circulated for years. It was claimed that people pawed through Joe Pizanthia's ashes looking for the trove of gold dust they thought he had; that Dr. John Glick of Bannack, curious about Henry Plummer's old wound, dug the corpse up one night, amputated the right arm, and put it in a snowbank while he went to a dance, and that a dog dragged it into the dance hall. George Lane's deformed foot ended up displayed in a saloon; someone bragged about boiling the flesh from Jack Gallagher's head and putting the skull on show.

After the hanging of Jack Slade on March 10, 1864, open criticism of the vigilantes' activities became more frequent. Following the scent of blood, national newspapers denounced the executions as "cruel, barbarous, and criminal." Such avid executioners as X Beidler found themselves receiving death threats. In some towns notices were posted decrying vigilante activity; one such notice warned

that the citizens would hang five vigilantes for every person that they executed.

Realizing that popular dislike was growing, Mollie Sheehan's teacher, Thomas Dimsdale, wrote a series of articles for the *Montana Post*—Mollie Sheehan saw him writing while the children did their lessons—that were published in 1866 as *The Vigilantes of Montana*. Dimsdale portrayed the events of 1864 as a struggle between good and evil: The vigilantes were decent men fighting a criminal army in a territory where the only legal recourse was the easily dominated and expensive courts of the "uneducated and unprincipled" miners. The vigilance committee, he wrote, changed the face of society. "It was a dreadful and disgusting duty that devolved upon them," Dimsdale wrote, "but it was their duty, and they did it." In fact, frontier society remained disorderly for decades, and vigilance committees—themselves part of the disorder—disappeared only after effective law, first territorial and then state, came to the region.

Sidney Edgerton helped bring about those changes. He traveled to Washington in the spring of 1864, his overcoat stuffed with gold dust to demonstrate to the federal government, then burdened with the costly Civil War and hungry for gold to pay its growing debts, why the region should become a territory; by May it was. In 1889, Montana became a state, and he was its first governor. In 1890, Wilbur Fisk Sanders was elected one of its two senators.

As to the Stuarts, James died in 1873, to the great sorrow of Granville, who made a fortune in the cattle business and became something of a grandee. When he died at 84 he was mourned as Mr. Montana, the personification of the state. Mollie Sheehan's memoirs of her life as a pioneer woman earned her lasting fame, and a lovely Montana lake now bears her name. Gold seekers abandoned Virginia City long ago. The vigilantes are mere ghosts, but Montanans cherish the legends, and many still see those men who took the law into their own hands as heroes. They are honored with plaques in the State House in Helena, and the badges of the Montana State Police bear the secret number 3-7-77. ◆

Sixteen years after arriving in Virginia City as a lively 11-year-old, Mollie Sheehan Ronan posed with her husband, Indian agent Peter Ronan, and six of their eight surviving children in front of their house on the Flathead Indian Reservation in western Montana. "I was delighted with the beauty of the place," Mollie recalled. "There I spent twenty years, the most interesting and difficult of my life. Something stirring, exciting, dangerous was always pending, threatening, happening."

BOOM AND BUST IN A NEVADA MINING TOWN

July 1, 1863—soon we were in the far famed "Virginia City"—of course it is no use for my pencil to try & describe this place—big bustling, noisy city—all in process of creation—streets full of wagons, horses . . . crowd—evening took turn round city & saw the sights . . . like San Francisco in '49—lots of money flying around in this city & no mistake.

One year after recording these impressions of Virginia City, Nevada, Alfred Doten, a 35-year-old former goldminer, took a job with the *Virginia Daily Union* and began an eventful career as a local newspaperman. Doten also kept a private journal chronicling life in the raucous boom town he called home.

Virginia City and neighboring Gold Hill were spawned by the largest silver strike in history—the Comstock Lode. Situated near the route used by forty-niners bound for the California gold fields, the area had for years attracted a few passing prospectors. By the mid-1850s about 100 miners were sifting three or four dollars' worth of gold a day from loose deposits known as placers. Mixed in was a bluish rock that the miners simply threw aside. In June 1859 an alert prospector had this "blue stuff" assayed. It proved to be high-grade mixed ore with a value per ton of $3,000 in silver and $876 in gold. The rush was on. Virginia City and Gold Hill sprang up practically overnight.

The rich veins of the Comstock Lode, named for a placer miner, extended far into the earth. Deep shafts had to be sunk through unstable rock and clay to extract the ore. The original claimants, lacking sufficient capital, sold their interests to speculators, about 20 of whom became millionaires.

Other Virginia City residents profited by catering to the labor force of up to 2,000 miners. Those

Alfred Doten, pictured in his volunteer fireman's uniform on July 4, 1867, began keeping a journal in March 1849 when he sailed from Massachusetts for California in search of gold. He continued to jot down entries like the one above until he died on November 11, 1903, filling 79 leather-bound volumes with pithy accounts of life in the mining towns.

workers, including immigrants from Mexico and Ireland, ran the risk of fires and cave-ins on the job and bloody altercations after hours. But their efforts did not go unrewarded. In 1866 they formed a union that won them an eight-hour workday and a minimum of four dollars a day—a generous wage for the time.

By the mid-1870s the town was heady with prosperity. "Men walked the streets of Virginia City as if pacing the roof of a fathomless treasure house," wrote an observer. Fortune smiled on Doten, who had invested in mining stock. He owned the *Gold Hill News* and was the town's most influential newspaperman.

The Comstock Lode eventually yielded nearly $400 million in precious ore. Once the large pockets of ore were depleted, however, investors like Doten took a beating. "Stock down again," he noted more than once in his journal. By late 1881 he had lost his home and his newspaper. To support his family he accepted a job as editor of a small newspaper in Austin, Nevada. "Quite a large crowd saw us off," he wrote with a full heart on January 26, 1882. "Good bye Gold Hill—*Good Bye Gold Hill*."

Perched on Mount Davidson, the mining district that included Virginia City and Gold Hill grew from a population of 3,400 in 1860 to 20,000 at the height of the boom in the 1870s.

October 15, 1864

Busy as usual at my vocation as Local Editor of the Virginia Daily Union–About 10 oclock I went with Ossian E Dodge up to the Mexican mine–Went down in it–& all through it.

September 16, 1865

Clear & pleasant–localized as usual–Evening Ex Gov & US Senator Nye spoke at Court house–I attended & reported–splendid speech–Couldn't been better–Hall crowded–speech on political topics & questions of the day–Mexican murdered this evening–down on North C Street, in little whore house–He was called Pinto or Pete–woman's name Manuela–she probably killed him with hatchet, as big gash was found in left temple–no other wound–I attended Mexican ball at Armory Hall awhile–bed at 3.

Alfred Doten, far right, sits with other reporters from Virginia City and Gold Hill for this portrait, taken in December 1865.

Newspapermen work in the composing room of the *Daily Territorial Enterprise*, the leading paper among the three local dailies. In 1862 the editor of the *Enterprise* hired as a reporter a part-time prospector called Samuel Clemens, who took the pen name Mark Twain.

VIRGINIA CITY ADVERTISEMENTS.

THE DAILY TERRITORIAL ENTERPRISE

Is published every morning, Sundays excepted,

—BY—

GOODMAN & McCARTHY,

J. T. GOODMAN, ... D E. McCARTHY.

PUBLICATION OFFICE,

A STREET, . . VIRGINIA CITY

TERMS OF SUBSCRIPTION :

ONE YEAR, in advance $16 00
SIX MONTHS 10 00
THREE MONTHS 6 00

☞ Subscribers in VIRGINIA CITY, SILVER CITY, GOLD HILL, DAYTON, and CARSON CITY, will be

Served by the Carriers at Fifty Cents per Week.

ADVERTISING

DONE AT REASONABLE RATES.

Enterprise Job Printing Office

As we have the finest assortment in the Territory, of

PLAIN AND FANCY TYPE, BORDERS,

etc. etc., and employ none but good workmen, we are prepared to execute, in the best style and at reasonable prices,

EVERY DESCRIPTION OF JOB WORK

— SUCH AS —

Visiting Cards,	Ball Tickets,	Certificates of Stock,
Wedding Cards,	Bill-Heads,	Real Estate Deeds,
Business Cards,	Circulars,	Mining Deeds,
Justices' Blanks,	Programmes,	Posters, etc.

GOODMAN & McCARTHY.

Clutching their lanterns, three miners prepare to descend into the Consolidated Virginia mine. In the deep, hot galleries men worked 30 minutes each hour and cooled off between shifts in rooms stocked with ice.

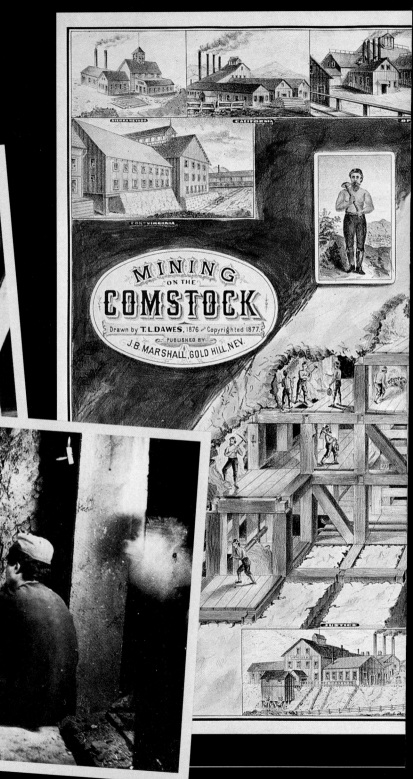

A miner toils by the light of a candle attached to a sturdy column. To guard against cave-ins, the mineshafts were reinforced with wooden columns arranged in boxlike frames called square sets.

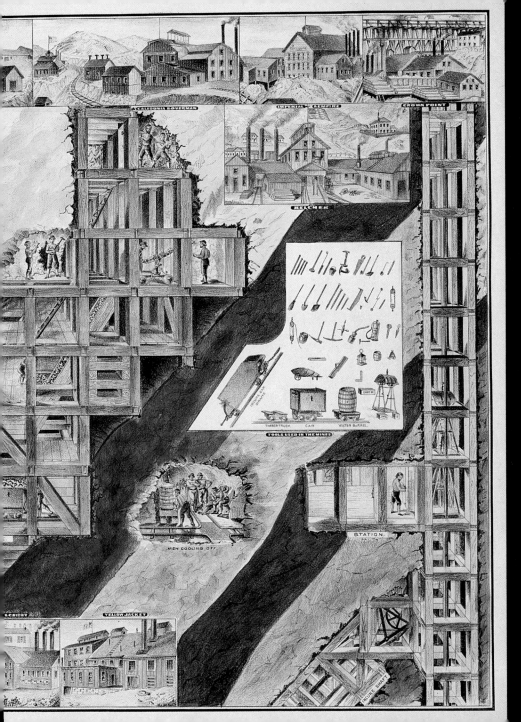

April 7, 1869

Alarm of fire at 7 o'clock in morning of whistles blowing at the Hill–Hurried down without waiting to get breakfast–fire in Yellow Jacket 800 level near the Kentuck mine–timbering on fire– Saw no less than six corpses brought up out of the mines–great excitement.

April 1, 1870

At 10 AM I went into Yellow Jacket mine–down south shaft to 900 foot level & through it to 300 ft north of shaft & took look at new body of ore just discovered–Very hot–all the miners worked stark naked, with only a breech clout on–I sweat furiously–Then I went down to 1020 ft level & took look at body of ore discovered & being worked there–Cooler and better place to work– Jim O'Donnel was there (foreman of mine) and he gave me all the points he could–Out at 11.

This 1876 lithograph illustrates the support system of square sets that allowed the excavation of deep shafts through the unstable deposits of the Comstock Lode. The ore was brought to the surface via the verti-cal shaft at far right.

Oct 23, 1865

Evening I attended Madam Anna Bishop's concert awhile at Maguire's—Mr Henry Lascelles is with her & played the piano—He also has a splendid voice—they sang beautifully together—House crammed with the beauty & fashion of the City—plays again tomorrow evening—I got through at 11.

April 1, 1872

1st appearance of Miss Aline Le Favre and Johnny Manning at the Theater—She is queen of the Can-Can and "shape"—Showed all she could conveniently in the last piece—"Paris by Gaslight"— Manning 1st rate in trapeze act—one of best I ever saw.

ADAH MENKEN IN HER GREAT CHARACTER OF MAZEPPA.

As a reporter, Alfred Doten covered the Virginia City social scene, including Piper's Opera House, whose curtain displayed advertisements *(left)*. Piper's offered an eclectic mix of entertainment, ranging from fights between bears and dogs to feats by actress Adah Menken *(above)*, who performed one of her more memorable parts in flesh-colored tights while tied to the back of a stallion.

Townspeople stand amid an array of poultry and other provisions offered for sale by Hatch Bros., billed as Headquarters for Thanksgiving Delicacies. By the 1870s grocery stores in Virginia City attracted customers with fresh produce shipped in by rail from California. The workers could afford such items, having demanded and received the highest rate of pay for miners anywhere in the world.

Jan 1, 1875

Egg nog seemed to be plenty–No paper today, it being New Years Day–Evening at home–Fixed up copy for tomorrow–Bed at 2–Happiest "New Year" of my life–Have cleared my property & insured it, have a wife and baby, and am worth $20,000 or more–Am much better fixed than I ever was before in my life.

FROM THE *VIRGINIA CITY DAILY REPORT*, DECEMBER 19, 1881:

"The leasing of the Gold Hill *News* involves the retirement as its editor of Alf. Doten, one of the oldest journalists of Nevada, who has been connected with the *News* almost since its founding, some eighteen years ago, and who owned the paper during the most prosperous time of the Comstock. The *News* was a bonanza at one time, but like other Comstock bonanzas, it pinched out."

In July 1873 Doten visited Lake Tahoe with Mary Stoddard *(below)* and reported: "We had an *interesting* talk–I proposed and was accepted." They were married the next week.

Doten plowed his earnings into the Enterprise Gold & Silver Mining Co. and other local outfits. When their stock prices began to sag in late 1877, his fortunes fell with them.

Horsemen of the Emmet Guard, a volunteer militia unit made up of Irish immigrant miners, parade through the flag-draped streets of Virginia City on a holiday in 1880. Mining continued in the area on a reduced scale for decades after the boom, as small, overlooked pockets of high-grade ore were discovered in the old shafts of the venerable Comstock Lode.

CHAPTER 2

NORTH TO ABILENE

"McCoy was a man of advanced vision. He had what all men need but many lack–imagination. Joe did not see cattle only; he saw a future."

CHARLES GROSS, FRIEND AND ASSISTANT TO JOSEPH McCOY

English-born E. C. "Teddy Blue" Abbott, sporting the broad-brimmed hat and bandanna that were trademarks of the Texas cowboy in the 1870s, typified the adventurous young man attracted to life on the range. He reflected in his memoirs that cowboys "used to brag that they could go any place a cow could and stand anything a horse could. It was their life."

Young Jim Daugherty tugged the sweat-soaked bandanna over his nose and mouth and scrunched his greasy sombrero tighter on his head, but they offered scant protection from the biting black buffalo gnats that peppered his skin. Putting spurs to his cow pony, he galloped up a grassy hummock, where a hot breeze from the west momentarily scattered the vicious insects. Turning in the saddle and wiping away the dust that sweat had caked on his face, he saw spread out below and behind him on the rolling Texas landscape a ragged line of cattle—his cattle. Their bony flanks shivered under the biting swarms, and they kicked up clouds of dust as they funneled their way into a shallow creek bed, splashed through the muddy water, and clambered up the opposite bank.

Jim Daugherty was a mere 16 years old, but he was destined to be recognized as one of Texas's legendary cattlemen. Born James M. Daugherty in Missouri and transplanted to Texas as a baby, he had learned the cattle business down in Denton County near a little settlement named Dallas. He had just made his first business deal, buying 500 longhorn steers from his boss, James Adams, and with five hired cowhands he meant to drive that herd north to the new railroad that had recently penetrated into

Missouri and Kansas. The grueling journey might take the better part of two months, across nearly 500 miles of prairie marked by raging rivers, tornadoes, snakes, and—as things turned out—marauding humans. But the longhorns might also bring the saddle-toughened 16-year-old five times the three dollars to four dollars a head that steers were worth in Texas—a handsome payoff.

Young Daugherty wasn't alone. Scores of Texas cattlemen had the same idea in the spring of 1866. Most were older, many of them veterans of the terrible Civil War that had ended a year earlier. Though fighting had scarcely touched Texas, the farms and ranches they had vacated were as tattered as their gray Confederate uniforms. But one resource that could put hard cash in a poor man's pocket was virtually theirs for the taking: millions of longhorn cattle that roamed the unfenced grasslands.

Over the next 20 years, Jim Daugherty and hundreds of other drovers herded more than five million cattle up the trails from Texas to Kansas, where they were sold to cattle buyers and shipped off to the commercial markets of Chicago, New York, and other cities east of the Mississippi River. Supported by deep-pocketed entrepreneurs who established the markets, such cattle drives gave birth to boom towns

51

in Kansas and boom times in Texas. The legendary cattle drives of the 1860s and 1870s helped to fuel the westward thrust of the railroads, create a burgeoning meat-packing industry, and put affordable beef on the tables of hungry American consumers. The drives also inspired an enduring body of fact, fable, and folklore about the American cowboy—from mournful ballads that soothed his cattle to the roar of the six-shooter that sometimes settled his quarrels.

The animals that Texans rounded up and trailed to market were longhorns, a distinctive breed descended from stock brought to the New World by Spanish settlers and toughened by three centuries of drought, flood, and blizzard on the open ranges of northern Mexico and the regions that were to become the American Southwest. Unlike domestic breeds, the Texas longhorn could fend off swarming insects, wolves, and rattlesnakes. Its long-legged, straight-backed, lanky body was built for speed. Its tapered head and narrow face gave it a mean, sullen look. Its graceful, pointed horns swept five feet or more from tip to tip, and they could gore a cow pony or skewer its rider in the blink of an eye. A four-year-old longhorn steer stood nearly five feet high at the shoulders and averaged 900 pounds in weight—nearly half a ton of tough, belligerent muscle. Cattlemen said a longhorn could walk 15 miles to water and then make one drink last two days. The older it grew the meaner it got, and most cowboys would rather face a wounded bear or a charging buffalo than a provoked longhorn bull.

By the mid-1800s, a motley mix of longhorns dotted the Texas grassland, and many were wild creatures that had never felt the touch of a rope or a branding iron. Wild longhorns naturally resisted being herded together; cows and their calves typically grazed in small groups, and mature bulls were almost always found alone. Some of these free-ranging animals bore an owner's distinctive symbol, which had been burned into their hides when they were calves, but they grazed the open grassland just as if they were wild. To the cowboy a single mature animal was a beef, and a herd of them were beeves. Newborn calves or strays whose owners had neglected to brand them were known as mavericks, after Samuel A. Maverick, a San Antonio lawyer and cattle owner whose negligent ranch hands gave rise to a new word for unfettered obstinacy.

Rounding up Texas beeves called for rough-and-ready men who knew how to use a rope and a branding iron. Some were native Texans, but the diverse lot of cowboys included vaqueros from Mexico, adventuresome immigrants from the British Isles and Europe, and former slaves from the American South; some authorities estimate that one in every four cowhands was black. In the cow hunts that were the forerunners of full-scale cattle roundups, a handful of cowboys might drive together several hundred wild beeves and the motherless calves they called dogies. They learned to keep the cattle moving for the first two or three days just to tire them out, since burning a brand into a longhorn's flank for identification was dangerous work. On the open range, before the days of specially built cattle pens, the usual practice was to rope the beast, but the grandstanding cowboy preferred a more daring maneuver. He would grab hold of the tail and either twist it around the horn of his saddle or "bulldog" the longhorn, wrestling it to the ground by its horns. The cowboy then tied the animal to a nearby tree or hogtied it, binding its feet together. His partners built a fire and heated a branding iron hot enough to burn through the animal's matted hair and permanently sear its hide. In some cases a slash of the cowboy's knife gave the beast a distinctive earmark, and if a young bull was destined for the feedlot rather than fatherhood, a castrating cut quickly altered him into a steer.

Lean and tough, the longhorns were admirably suited to enduring the rigors of the open range. Their meat was just as lean and tough on the table as it was on the hoof—fit for stewing, not for juicy steaks. Before the mid-1800s in the eastern United States, the meat in most people's diet came mainly from poultry and pigs, and cows were raised primarily to supply milk, cheese, and butter. Until 1845,

> *"I believe I could walk along the streets of any town or city and pick out the real cowboy, not by his clothes especially, but because one can nearly always notice that he has a very open countenance and almost innocent eyes and mouth. He is not innocent of course; but living in the open, next to nature, the cleaner life is stamped on his face. His vices leave no scars, or few, because old mother nature has him with her most of the time."*
>
> BULAH RUST KIRKLAND, DAUGHTER OF A TEXAS TRAIL DRIVER

THE ORIGINAL AMERICAN COWBOY

Long before Texas cowboys began rounding up longhorn cattle, Franciscan missionaries had brought European cattle breeds to the ranges of Mexico, which included the region stretching from present-day Texas to California. Ignoring laws that prohibited Indians from using horses, Spanish ranchers taught native Indians and mixed-race workers to tend their herds. These vaqueros (from the Spanish *vaca,* or "cow") became skilled horsemen and expert cattlemen, developing such techniques as cutting individual animals out of a swirling herd, subduing the animals with ropes, and branding them for identification.

In California the local vaqueros, or *californios,* developed a distinctive style of decorating their clothing with silver ornaments called conchas and favoring the broad-brimmed sombrero, or shader. This style, portrayed in the 1830s-era painting above, eventually became widespread.

Because eastern cattle-herding techniques weren't suitable in the West, American cowboys adopted and adapted many of the vaqueros' ways. Their saddle, a modified Spanish war saddle, underwent more changes. The horn and the stirrups were strengthened so they would withstand the strain of heavy-duty roping, and the tapaderos, leather covers over the stirrups that protected the rider's feet, were shortened. To protect their legs, cowboys wore the leather coverings that vaqueros called chaparajos but knew them simply as chaps. A vaquero might use a 60-foot braided rawhide rope he called *la reata,* but most cowboys used store-bought "lariats" made of twisted grass or manila fiber, tougher than leather and less expensive. The wide-brimmed hat the Americans wore evolved from the sombrero, and they even Anglicized *vaquero,* calling themselves buckaroos.

But in one area the vaquero and cowboy differed significantly. Many of the young Texas cattle drovers had served in the Civil War and were used to carrying side arms. The typical vaquero thought using a firearm was unmanly and preferred to defend himself with his wits and his rope.

when Texas was admitted to the Union, longhorns were valued primarily for their hides and for tallow, which went into making soap, candles, and lubricants. Yet the lure of readily available beef had begun to create lucrative cattle markets in the increasingly populous northeastern states: In 1854 Texas longhorns carried by train to the stockyard at Fourth Avenue and 44th Street in Manhattan brought as much as $80 a head.

In the years before the Civil War, Texas cattlemen had shipped beeves to the port of New Orleans, Louisiana, and had trailed cattle as far as Chicago, Illinois, and even to California in the wake of the 1849 gold rush. The practice of trailing cattle to far-flung markets had slowed to a trickle during the Civil War, however, and by the end of the fighting Texas had more longhorns than ever, while beef stocks in the North were practically exhausted from feeding the Federal army.

Jim Daugherty originally planned to drive his herd up to west central Missouri, where the Pacific Railroad of Missouri had built a new stockyard siding at Sedalia, something of a boom town, with more than 3,000 residents. If all went well, a buyer there would purchase his 500 beeves and load them aboard freight cars bound for Saint Louis. Daugherty felt his men could make 10 or 12 miles a day over the old Shawnee Trail, a route that began in south Texas and ran north through Austin and Dallas, where he joined it, and on to the Red River. Near the town of Preston, Texas, a natural chute in the rock bluffs along the riverbank and a slight slope on the opposite side made crossing the Red easy. The trail then veered northeast across the Indian Territory—present-day Oklahoma—to Fort Gibson near the Arkansas River, one of the oldest frontier army outposts. From there the trail cut across the southeastern corner of Kansas and on into Missouri.

With the confidence born of growing up quickly while older men were away at war, Jim Daugherty felt assured that his drovers could handle the hazards of the journey: long, hot, dusty days in the

saddle; nights spent guarding the herd after a day's trek; swimming frightened cattle across rain-swollen rivers; or the rare Comanche party swooping down to steal horses or beeves. In truth, the greatest threat from Indians was financial. The Cherokees, Creeks, and others of the so-called Five Civilized Tribes had been forcibly transplanted from the southeastern United States to the Indian Territory three decades earlier. These tribes adapted readily to the white man's ways, to the point that their legislature had imposed a tax on Texas cattlemen whose herds grazed on Indian land.

Of all the hazards a cattle drover was likely to encounter, the worst was a stampede, so to calm a nervous herd, cowboys kept the cattle moving at a slow but steady pace during the day and developed the habit of singing to them when the drive stopped for the night. A cowboy on one side of the herd might sing one verse of a hymn, a dance hall tune, or a song brought back from the war, then the man on the other side would take up the next verse. Besides soothing range cattle unaccustomed to being in a large herd, singing also distracted the longhorns from sights and sounds that might frighten them. If a sudden flash of lightning or a coyote's howl spooked one longhorn, its reaction could easily panic the rest, sending the herd into a wild rush that might go on for miles and destroy everything in its path and the animals themselves. At the first sign of a runaway, one cowboy would dash to the head of the herd, using his pony to turn the leaders and bring the swirling animals into a more compact mass. As the longhorns got worn out, the cowboys gradually brought the herd together until they quieted down—ever watchful of letting them pack together too tightly, lest a fallen cow be trampled under the sharp hoofs of the others. After a big

Getting a herd to cross even shallow streams like the one at left was a challenge. One drover described crossing cattle over the fast-running Washita River in 1877: "Some of them would turn and try to come back, but the swift current had carried them down to where the steep banks . . . kept them from coming out, and they had to go across."

stampede, rounding up scattered strays could take hours—even days.

While the trail had its hazards, drovers like Daugherty worried most about the reception they could expect when they reached their goal in Kansas or Missouri. Farmers raising dairy cows wanted no part of longhorns—for good reason: Longhorns were typically infested with ticks that carried the lethal disease known as Spanish or Texas fever. Although the range-hardened longhorn was virtually immune, domestic Holsteins, Jerseys, and other cattle bitten by ticks carrying Texas fever were as good as doomed. The symptoms were unmistakable: The afflicted beasts stared with glassy eyes, staggered from weakness in their hind legs, trembled violently, stopped eating, and almost always died. Severe

had killed a Texas drover, stolen his herd, and run off the cowboys. The bandits were Jayhawkers—anti-slavery guerrillas who had marauded along the borders before and during the Civil War. After the war, they began bedeviling the Texas drovers, demanding payment for safe passage or simply stealing their cattle. On hearing the news, Daugherty galloped back across into the Indian Territory, halted his herd south of the Kansas border, and told his men to stay put. While the cattle rested and grazed, he headed back to Kansas. At Fort Scott he met a dealer named Ben Keys and quickly made a deal to sell Keys his entire herd. Daugherty knew he might run into Jayhawkers in trailing the cattle up to Fort Scott, but it was a risk he had to take. Back in the Indian Territory, he and his cowboys got the herd on the move

"Upon approach of the Jayhawkers John attempted to draw his gun and the Jayhawkers shot him dead in his saddle. This caused the cattle to stampede and at the same time they covered me with their guns and I was forced to surrender.... After I was freed and had joined the herd, two of my cowboys and I slipped back and buried John Dobbins where he fell." JIM DAUGHERTY

epidemics before the Civil War had killed thousands of domestic cattle in Missouri and Kansas, so the outraged legislatures in these states enacted quarantine laws preventing the entry of diseased or disease-bearing cattle during summer months. However, a combination of lax enforcement and determined trail drivers made the statutes ineffective, forcing farmers to take matters into their own hands. They formed vigilance committees to turn back at gunpoint any Texans trying to trail herds through their homesteads. When longhorns started back up the Shawnee Trail after the war, these vigilantes returned to action.

Once Jim Daugherty's herd passed Fort Gibson in the Indian Territory, he packed several days' provisions in his saddlebags and rode on ahead alone. He didn't encounter any vigilantes, but at Baxter Springs, in the southeastern corner of Kansas, he heard alarming reports about an outlaw band that

again, keeping a constant lookout for trouble.

That trouble came soon enough. Some 20 miles south of Fort Scott, a band of armed riders suddenly appeared over a rise, outfitted in hunting shirts, coarse homespun pantaloons, crude homemade cowhide shoes, and coonskin caps. The strangers rode in close with guns drawn and ordered the Texans to halt immediately. Daugherty's lead cowboy, John Dobbins, started to resist but toppled from his saddle, dead from an assailant's bullet. The gunfire panicked the herd, and another Jayhawker started flourishing a striped blanket and yelling in order to start a full-scale stampede. "The rest of the cowboys stayed with the herd, losing part of them in the stampede," recalled Daugherty. "The Jayhawkers took me to Cow Creek which was near by, and there tried me for driving cattle into their country, which they claimed were infested with ticks which would kill their cattle. I was found guilty without any evidence, they not even having one of my cattle for evidence." They tied him to a tree and, arguing over what to do with him, began beating him with hickory branches. One shouted, "Hang him!" Others favored whipping him to death. One of the Kansans, taken aback by Daugherty's youth, finally persuaded the others to let him go.

Daugherty dragged his lacerated body back into the saddle and set out in search of the scattered herd. Hours later he spotted his cowboys' campfire. They had managed to escape from the marauders and head off a full-scale stampede, but they lost some 150 longhorns in the process. Daugherty and two of his men sneaked back to where John Dobbins had fallen and buried him, cutting down a small tree to make a marker for his grave. Daugherty then rode to Fort Scott and told Ben Keys what had happened.

In a contemporary sketch showing him much older than his 16 years at the time of the incident, Jim Daugherty is beaten by three Jayhawkers as other members of the renegade band overpower one of Daugherty's men and stampede his herd. Describing the hazards drovers faced, Joseph McCoy wrote that "for but a single misstep or wrong move . . . he may lose his entire herd, representing and constituting all his earthly possessions. None understood this fact better than the mobs of outlaws that annually infested the cattle trail."

Determined to get his beef, Keys sent a scout back with Daugherty to show him a safe route to Fort Scott. For five nights they drove the herd through thinly settled areas, hiding in secluded valleys and bottom land during daylight. Finally, as dawn broke on the fifth night, the herd arrived at Fort Scott. Daugherty and his men were in no mood to whoop it up at the end of the trail. They slept all day and headed back to Texas that night under cover of darkness, happy to get out of Kansas with their lives and a tidy profit besides.

Another, older drover bound for Missouri faced a different threat from the other side of the law during that tumultuous spring of 1866. R. D. Hunter, a Scottish-born stockman based in Missouri, had purchased a herd of 400 longhorns from a Texas

Cowboys enjoy a relaxing break from the hard work of the trail. After reading other cowboys' memoirs, Teddy Blue Abbott observed that they "told all about stampedes and swimming rivers and what a terrible time we had, but they never put in any of the fun, and fun was at least half of it."

cattleman in the Indian Territory and, like young Daugherty, intended to trail them to Sedalia. About 20 miles into Missouri, Hunter and several other drovers using the same trail encountered the Barton County sheriff, who promptly arrested them and seized their longhorns, about 10,000 in all. Hunter persuaded the sheriff to ride with him to the county seat, Lamar, where he claimed friends would put up his bail. As soon as they rode out of sight, the other cattlemen hurried the herds back into the Indian Territory. Once in Lamar, Hunter took the lawman to a saloon and started plying him with whiskey. Soon enough, the canny Scotsman simply walked out of the saloon unmolested and rejoined his herd.

Even so, in order to market the cattle they had saved from the sheriff's clutches, he and the other drovers had to take a most roundabout route. They headed westward 150 miles, skirting the southern border of Kansas, then turned northward through sparsely settled parts of the state and cut eastward to a rail connection of the Chicago, Rock Island & Pacific Railroad in northwestern Missouri.

Drovers by the score were forced into taking such circuitous routes past both lawful and vigilante blockades and renegade raiders at the Missouri-Kansas border. Some avoided a showdown by edging eastward along Missouri's southern border with Arkansas and trailing their longhorns on to Saint Louis or ferrying them across the Mississippi to Illinois, where the footsore and emaciated cattle brought poor prices. Others simply stopped their herds in the Indian Territory and waited until November 1. Kansas law permitted entry of longhorns after that date, because freezing weather was known to kill the disease-bearing ticks. By the long, hot days of July 1866, nearly 100,000 Texas longhorns found themselves grazing in the northern section of the Indian Territory—the so-called Cherokee Strip

of present-day Oklahoma. However, there wasn't enough grass to keep all of them well fed because of destructive prairie fires that had swept the territory.

A year that had begun with such high hopes ended in bitter disappointment for much of the infant Texas cattle industry. Although some 260,000 cattle had been driven out of Texas that summer, many of them had been held back until the arrival of cold weather by their cautious drovers, and untold thousands—as well as a few of their owners—had been lost to vigilantes and outlaws. It was clear that in order to prosper and grow, the cattle industry had to be able to get beeves to market over routes that were direct, efficient, and, above all, safe from the difficulties that had made 1866 such a financial disaster.

During the following winter, a solution to the cattlemen's problem began taking shape in the imagination of a man far removed from the Texas range. Joseph Geating McCoy was a 30-year-old businessman who operated out of Springfield, Illinois, the heart of midwestern livestock feeder country. The youngest of 11 children in a family of prosperous farmers, the ambitious Joseph had left Knox College in Galesburg, Illinois, to start raising mules. In 1861 he showed his commercial acumen by shipping a carload of prime mules by way of five separate railroads to Paris, Kentucky, where he sold them at a handsome profit. But despite the Union army's demand for mules to transport war matériel, the fattening and sale of cattle became McCoy's main interest. In the 1860s more cattle were raised in Illinois than in any other state except Texas, and McCoy's older brothers, William and James, specialized in the beef trade. At the beginning of 1867 Joseph joined their thriving partnership, William K. McCoy & Brothers. The firm was shipping as many as 1,000 cattle a week, and their annual business with one bank alone amounted to $2.5 million.

Joseph McCoy was intrigued by tales of the Texas herders, and he mulled over the problem with his friend Charles Gross, who knew the McCoys through his brother, their family lawyer. The son of a

Baptist minister, Gross had gone to school in Springfield, Illinois, with Abraham Lincoln's son Robert and had joined the Union army as a teenager. He became a telegraph operator and at the end of the war was sent into Texas in search of the best route for a new telegraph line between Brownsville and Shreveport, Louisiana. Back in Springfield that winter he regaled Joe McCoy with stories of "the immense amount of Cattle & Horses running wild" on the Texas range "only awaiting for some one to gather & drive to the northern Market." What would have been just stories for many listeners was much more than that for McCoy; he seized the stories and ran with them. Gross was impressed with how "progressive and far ahead of most men" McCoy was. "Joe did not see cattle only; he saw a future," Gross commented. "I started to fire that imagination of his, which ran far ahead of me. Before I knew anything of his plans, they were half completed."

From another source who had sold him some Texas cattle, McCoy learned how hard it was to get those free-ranging animals to market. W. W. Sugg, an Illinois native who had driven a herd of longhorns from Texas in 1866, described the violent blockades and showed McCoy the scars he wore from hickory branches wielded by vengeful border ruffians.

For the farsighted Joseph McCoy, the goal was clear: "to establish a market whereat the Southern drover and Northern buyer would meet upon an equal footing, and both be undisturbed by mobs or swindling thieves." Poring over a map of the western states, he first considered transporting longhorns northward by water, driving the cattle overland to a depot near Fort Smith on the bank of the Arkansas River, just east of the Indian Territory. Dealers could then ship the beeves down the Arkansas to the Mississippi, up the Mississippi to Cairo, at the southern tip of his home state of Illinois. From there they could go by rail northward into the pastures and feedlots of Illinois or even be forwarded eastward on the Ohio River.

But on a business trip to the booming frontier town of Kansas City, Missouri, he learned that

COME AND GET IT

On a cattle drive or roundup, the chuck wagon was the nearest thing to home. Hungry cowboys gathered around it three times a day and bedded down near it at night. The ideal vehicle was a converted army wagon with iron axles tough enough to withstand miles of rough trails. The wagon carried bedding, bulk foods such as salt pork and dried beans, long guns and ammunition, and an extra wheel. On one side hung a water barrel, on the other a toolbox that held branding irons, horseshoes and nails, a Dutch oven, and other equipment. A canvas cover stretched over bentwood bows kept out rain and the midday sun.

Second in rank only to the trail boss, the cook had to outpace the drovers and have their meals ready on time. His cupboard was the chuck box, and its hinged door dropped down to serve as a worktable. Compartments held such staples as coffee beans, flour, sugar, dried fruit, potatoes, onions, and beans. Stuffed into corners were assorted items such as plugs of tobacco, bandages, needles and thread, a razor and strop, and perhaps a bottle of whiskey reserved for medicinal purposes.

The cook usually dished up corn bread and bacon for breakfast. Beans or stew, coffee, and perhaps a pudding or pie sufficed for the other two meals. The men scraped leftovers into the fire and dropped their dishes into the "wreckpan" for a wipe clean.

A painted-on brand identifies the Littlefield Ranch chuck wagon. On rainy days the cook worked under a canvas canopy held up by the poles stored on the side of the wagon.

tracks of the Union Pacific, Eastern Division, soon to be renamed the Kansas Pacific, now extended as far as Salina in central Kansas. McCoy saw at once how to link the growing east-west network of railways with the north-south trails traversed by the Texas cattle drives. He discussed the scheme with a railroad agent who realized that Mc-Coy's plan could be a moneymaker for the railroads: Eastbound freight cars, which were frequently empty on their return trips from western destinations, could be filled with cattle. McCoy's next step was to investigate the shortest routes from the Texas ranges north to stations on the railroad. On a voyage westward to the end of the rail line, his train stopped briefly at a tiny prairie village 15 miles east of Salina while a bridge was being repaired. McCoy took advantage of the hour's delay to talk with some of the local folks, who struck him as friendly and receptive to his ideas. The place was called Abilene.

McCoy gained additional advice and support in Junction City, Kansas—buffalo hunters called it Junk Town—which was already a thriving railroad center. At the town's hotel he sought out Colonel John J. Myers, a distinguished-looking gray-haired man who had crossed the western territories in the company of explorer John Charles Frémont nearly three decades before. Myers himself had brought herds to west Kansas from his ranch in Lockhart, Texas, and he now had them pastured waiting for a buyer. The two men strolled down the dusty street to a vacant building lot and sat down to talk on a pile of lumber. Myers struck McCoy as "a sincere, honest man, who spoke with a firmly fixed determination to give only correct information." When McCoy explained his idea, the rancher said his colleagues would welcome and eagerly patronize a location on the railroad where they could dispose of their herds to willing buyers. The two-hour conversation so stimulated Joseph McCoy that he quickly tried to purchase some property for his stockyards

Despite a dour appearance in front of a camera, Joseph McCoy tended to "look most upon the bright side of the picture and never feel inclined to look at the dangers or hazards of a venture." McCoy's farsightedness turned Abilene into a boom town, but his impulsiveness led to bad investments and financial ruin. As another Kansas businessman observed, "Had he stuck to his original plan of running his yards he certainly would have added largely to his fortune, but . . . he could not forbear entering into . . . his pet scheme, let it cost what it would."

six miles from Junction City, but he found that the price was too high.

Now more determined than ever to make his scheme work, McCoy pursued the other half of the equation—picking out the individual railroads that could be linked into a route to the east. Dressed in his rough frontier garb—soiled shirt, seedy coat, and unpolished boots—he made the rounds of elegant offices presided over by well-heeled railroad executives. One of the men he met with was John T. Perry, the president of the line McCoy had taken west through Kansas. Perry had his doubts about McCoy's scheme and commented, "It looks too visionary, too chimerical, too speculative." But he went on, "If you think you can get cattle freighted over our road and are willing to risk your money in a stock yard and other necessary appendages, we will put in a switch and, if you succeed, I will pledge that you shall have full and fair recompense." The railroad executive reckoned that the amount might be five dollars for each carload of cattle shipped that year from McCoy's proposed, but still nonexistent, stock depot.

The deal with Perry was sealed, and McCoy now had one part of his route in place. Continuing his rounds, he paid a call on the president of the Pacific Railroad of Missouri—soon to be renamed the Missouri Pacific—whose eastern terminus was Saint Louis. After hearing McCoy explain his project, the president was less than impressed: "It occurs to me that you haven't any cattle to ship and never did have any; and I, sir, have no evidence that you ever will have any." He imperiously ordered McCoy out of his office. Less than 12 hours later, however, the undaunted McCoy had made a deal with the Hannibal and Saint Joseph Railroad, which linked nicely with Perry's railroad. The Hannibal and Saint Joseph line traversed Missouri well to the north of Saint Louis, and the cattle it carried would be delivered straight to Chicago. A few minutes of shortsighted arrogance on the part of the Missouri Pacific's president cost the city of Saint Louis a key role in the market for Texas cattle and assured Chicago the title "the nation's stockyard."

With his railroad connections established, McCoy hurried back to central Kansas. He pitched his idea to leading citizens in Salina and in nearby Solomon City, but they had no interest in attracting the cattle trade. McCoy thought they regarded him as a "monster threatening calamity and pestilence." Then he went back to the tiny prairie village of Abilene.

Abilene, to be sure, did not amount to much. Only six years old, it lacked even a rudimentary rail station. Instead, a wooden post with the mail pouch slung from a hook marked the stopping place for trains. McCoy described the village as "a very small,

dead place, consisting of about one dozen log huts, low, small, rude, affairs, four-fifths of which were covered with dirt for roofing." On the east bank of Mud Creek huddled the six-room Bratton Hotel, Thomas McLean's blacksmith shop, William Moon's combination store and post office, and the saloon operated by Josiah Jones, characterized by McCoy as "a corpulent, jolly, good-souled congenial old man" who supplemented his income by selling prairie dogs to railroad tourists at five dollars a head. On the other side of the creek stood a stagecoach station, the second floor of which was favored by the widely scattered settlers for an occasional dance. Eliza Hersey, the station owner's wife, charged her customers a steep one dollar for a meal described by one dismayed traveler as "strong black coffee, strips of pork fat fried to a sandy crispness and half-baked

Seen from the railroad trestle over Mud Creek on the west side of Abilene, Joseph McCoy's newly built Drover's Cottage dominates the town's skyline in this 1867 photograph.

soggy, indigestible biscuits." But in spite of Abilene's sparse population and rough-hewn character, the place appealed to McCoy. Lying some 400 miles north of the Red River and about 1,000 miles from south Texas, it was surrounded by the grass and water that was needed to put valuable weight back on the cattle after their grueling journey, and it had lots of cheap land to build on. Just as important, there were not many farmers and other settlers to complain about Texas cattle and cowboys. Barely a month after his search began, McCoy had discovered the right place.

Acting in the name of McCoy & Brothers, he bought from Abilene's founder, Charles Thompson, 250 acres adjoining the railroad northeast of town. Two weeks later he began constructing his shipping depot with lumber brought in by rail from points east. McCoy commissioned a large barn, a one-story office building, and enough pens for 1,000 cattle, complete with specially designed chutes to guide the beeves directly into the rail cars at the rate of 20 carloads an hour. He hauled in a pair of 10-ton scales, each capable of weighing a carload of about 20 beeves. After much arm-twisting, he persuaded the railroad to lay enough siding track for up to 100 cars. To house cowboys weary from the trail, he contracted for construction of the Drover's Cottage, an elegant three-story hotel with a livery stable to care for the cowboys' mounts. He also built a bank to care for their money.

To make certain that the cattle and cowboys would come, McCoy launched an ingenious promotion campaign. He had handbills printed up and sent to post offices all over Texas and the southwestern territories announcing Abilene as a convenient and safe shipping town. He also dispatched into the Indian Territory his new cattleman friend W. W. Sugg, whose experiences as a drover had helped inspire McCoy's vision. Sugg's assignment was to intercept cattlemen on the trail and "proclaim the good tidings of Abilene to the wandering and mob-fearing drovers." McCoy thought that the sales pitch of this "man upon whose counte-

nance truth and honesty sat enthroned supreme" would be persuasive to drovers in desperate need of a safe market.

What McCoy did not trumpet was the fact that trailing cattle to Abilene was technically illegal. Outbreaks of Texas fever the previous year had inspired new quarantine laws in a half-dozen states. In February 1867 the Kansas legislature banned Texas cattle outright, for all but three winter months—with an exception being made for the sparsely settled southwestern quarter, where drovers like Colonel Myers had the foresight to take their herds. That exception, interestingly, was largely the result of lobbying by a group of influential entrepreneurs from the state capital of Topeka, who had independently arrived at the same idea as McCoy. They evidently had planned to establish a shipping depot just inside the free zone when the railroad tracks extended that far west, but then failed to follow through on the scheme.

Abilene was a good 60 miles inside the quarantined part of Kansas, and McCoy almost certainly would have discussed this fact with Charles Thompson, Abilene's leading citizen and a member of the state legislature. In any event, McCoy visited Governor Samuel J. Crawford in Topeka in the hope of persuading him that the trails leading up to Abilene crossed far enough west of the settled area not to pose a serious threat to local farmers. The governor, quickly sensing the economic potential of McCoy's scheme, decided that he would make a quiet exception to the new quarantine law. As the governor himself put it, he "approved the undertaking in a semi-official manner."

Predictably, however, as the first herds recruited by W. W. Sugg approached Abilene in early August 1867, some farmers east of town became concerned about Texas fever—so concerned, in fact, that a group of them banded together and threatened to stampede every incoming herd. Catching wind of the threat, McCoy met with the hostile farmers at the cabin of their leader, bringing with him several drovers who had arrived ahead of their cattle to check out the new facilities. It was a masterly performance. While McCoy preached the economic benefits of the cattle trade, the drovers circulated among the farmers contracting to buy their butter, eggs, vegetables, and feed grain at up to twice the prevailing price. Most of the farmers quickly came to the conclusion that the potential profits they could reap from provisioning hungry Texans overrode any fears of the damage that their cattle might bring.

The herds began arriving in mid-August, unmolested, and so did the trains. On September 5, 1867, the first shipment of longhorns left McCoy's Great Western Stockyards aboard 20 rail cars destined for Chicago. Confident that this marked the beginning of a new era, McCoy had invited meat packers, cattle dealers, and old friends and as-

ABILENE'S RISE AND FALL

Tim and Eliza Hersey *(below)*, among Abilene's earliest settlers, moved into the two-room log house Tim had built in 1858 and became influential. Called Mud Creek or Dog Town earlier, the town was renamed by Eliza. A devout Methodist, she got the idea that Abilene, the name of a biblical city, meant "grassy plain" and applied it to her town.

Abilene's heyday as a cow town was short-lived. Photographed in 1875, the main street *(bottom)* was quiet and nearly deserted, unlike the bustling marketplace it had been a few years before.

sociates from Illinois to help him celebrate. The Drover's Cottage was still in the throes of construction, so several large tents were set up, and Eliza Hersey, who evidently managed to rise to the occasion, prepared a banquet. "A substantial repast was devoured with a relish peculiar to camp life," wrote McCoy with a flourish, "after which wine, toasts, and speechifying were the order until a late hour at night. Before the sun had mounted high in the heavens on the following day, the iron horse was darting down the Kaw valley with the first trainload of cattle that ever passed over the Kansas Pacific Railroad, the precursor to many thousands destined to follow."

Actually, there was little else to celebrate that first year. Due largely to a late start, only about 35,000 longhorns reached Abilene in 1867, far fewer than expected. The McCoy yards shipped about 20,000 in nearly

1,000 carloads, but the remaining 15,000 wintered on the prairie or were trailed as breeding stock to ranges located farther north or west. Even worse, McCoy had to contend with cattle that were less than prime. Heavy rain during the previous spring had turned the prairie grass coarse and made it nutrient poor, which did little to improve the stringy flesh of the wild longhorns.

Because not enough buyers came to Abilene in that first year, some drovers risked shipping beeves to Chicago on their own account, hoping to find willing buyers there. McCoy himself bought more cattle than he had bargained for. One of his shipments of nearly 900 head failed to find a buyer in Chicago and ended up in Albany, New York, selling for $300 less than the freight bill. "Texan cattle beef then was not considered eatable," he wrote later, "and was as unsalable in the Eastern markets as would have been a shipment of prairie wolves." Brokers and consumers had yet to be convinced that well-fatted Texan beef could be as good as any other kind, and cheaper to boot.

McCoy's venture had begun on such a dismal note that the railroad men in Saint Louis were, he learned to his chagrin, "regarding it as the big joke of the season. The enterprise was considered a failure, and everyone, save the parties directly interested, freely expressed themselves that no cattle would be driven there the next year." But McCoy was an irrepressible optimist, and even before the first season ended he had taken steps to ensure success in the next. He realized that providing a direct link from the western railheads to markets in the East was not enough. In order to corner the pass-through market for Texas cattle, he also needed to formalize a single, direct route for trailing the longhorns north from Texas. Most of

Mexican cowboys were skilled in handling cattle and proud of their vaquero heritage. "The Mexicans would not accept paper money or gold," an American cowhand noted. "Silver was the money of their country and silver they would have."

the herds in 1867 had come north up the old Shawnee Trail and westward along the Kansas border. A few, however, had chosen a newer route some 150 miles to the west—a route that in time would come to be known in story and song as the Chisholm Trail.

Jesse Chisholm was the mixed-blood son of a Cherokee mother and a father of Scottish descent. For years he had operated a trading post near a Wichita Indian camp in south central Kansas along the Arkansas River; the town that eventually developed on the site took the tribe's name and became one of the West's wildest boom towns. In addition to being a trader, Chisholm was much in demand as an interpreter and guide for the government and commercial agents because he could speak 14 Indian languages. Beginning in the autumn of 1864, he made frequent use of an old trail that ran south from his trading post to the North Canadian River in the Indian Territory. Although Chisholm didn't blaze the trail—it had been trodden previously by migrating Indians, vast herds of buffalo, and even a few units of the U.S. Army—he plied it with cattle and other trade goods so often before his death in 1868 that it had come to be known by his name.

McCoy envisioned a convenient route that would begin near the Rio Grande, tie in with the Shawnee and other feeder trails in Texas, then shoot due north through the Indian Territory and into lower Kansas. The trail along which Jesse Chisholm drove cattle was ideally located for elaborating into the route he had in mind, since it could easily be extended south across the Red River into Texas and north from Wichita to Abilene (map, pages 8-9).

To make the new northern segment easy for the drovers to find and follow, McCoy recruited an informal engineer corps captained by his new friend Tim Hersey, a good-natured, multitalented native of Maine and one of the earliest settlers around Abilene. In addition to operating the local stagecoach station, the energetic Hersey had helped survey the original town site, run a gristmill, acted as county clerk, and eventually served two terms in the state legislature. Hersey's hastily assembled work crew blazed trees where they could find them and elsewhere made mounds of soil and sod to serve as trail markers.

In comparing the Chisholm with other trails, its chief promoter was characteristically positive and unequivocally blunt: "It is more direct. It has more prairie, less timber, more small streams and fewer large ones, altogether better grass and fewer flies— no civilized Indian tax or wild Indian disturbances—than any other route yet driven over. It is also much shorter because direct from the Red River to Kansas." It was said that a drover did not even require a compass: All he had to do was point the tongue of the chuck wagon toward the North Star in the constellation of the Little Dipper when he stopped the herd at night and start in that direction the following morning.

To publicize this new trail to Abilene, McCoy allotted the considerable sum of $5,000. With part of his advertising budget he sent a pair of emissaries— "two gentlemen of tact and address"—into Texas to blanket the state with circulars and other advertising. "All Texas," he crowed, "was reading and talking of the new star of hope that had arisen in the north to light and buoy up the hitherto dark and desponding heart of the ranch man." He could even boast that the governor of Kansas, Samuel Crawford, had endorsed the trail. McCoy had finagled the governor to send a commission south as far as the Red River to persuade Indians not to interfere with the herds. McCoy could then announce to buyers and sellers alike that the trail was "established and sanctioned in a semi-official manner."

Sellers taking the trail north from Texas would, of course, need buyers when they got to Abilene, so some of McCoy's advertising money was aimed at reaching potential purchasers of the cattle through newspapers in the North.

Once slavery was abolished, many blacks went west to start new lives. Recalling his partners on the trail, one cowboy reckoned that "about one-third were negroes and Mexicans." In typical cowboy fashion, James Arthur Walker (above) carried a pistol wherever he went and bragged he could hit a string at 100 yards. Ned Huddleston, alias Isom Dart (below), rustled Mexican cattle and sold them to Texas ranchers.

McCoy's flair for promotion paid off: In late March 1868, as the herds moved up the new Chisholm Trail—the vanguard of a massive flow of longhorns that would make up the greatest migration of domestic animals in history—buyers flocked to Abilene. They lodged at his Drover's Cottage, newly completed and furnished at a cost of $15,000. The hotel, which could accommodate 80 guests and had the facilities to feed three times that many, was one of the finest in the West, featuring such amenities as plaster walls and green venetian blinds within, and a coat of tan paint on the exterior. And as Abilene's main center of entertainment, it possessed a billiard room and saloon; it also had a veranda from which guests could watch in shade and comfort as trains were loaded with longhorns and then departed for the East. The Drover's Cottage also had the benefit of experienced managers, Jim Gore and his wife, Lou, imported from Saint Louis. Lou Gore in particular was an asset, having grown up in a hotel in Niagara Falls, New York, where her father was the manager of the operation. In Abilene she manifested a maternal concern for cowboys that became legendary. "In their sickness a true guardian and nurse," wrote McCoy, Lou Gore was "one whose kind motherly heart was ever ready to provide for their proper want."

McCoy's ambitious promotion of Texas cattle attracted four categories of buyers: ranchers from Colorado, Wyoming, and other territories in need of fresh beef stock to expand their herds; government contractors who bought cattle to feed Indians on federal reservations; middlemen in Illinois who fattened longhorns for market; and eastern packing house agents who sought beef intended for slaughter. A determined McCoy primed the pump by giving away $5,000 worth of hotel and livery stable services for his guests, and he hired 10 men at an extravagant $50 a month each to meet herds on the trail and make sure they headed for Abilene and not farther north or west.

In return the buyers paid good prices. Beeves worth three dollars or four dollars a head on the

Texas range brought $15 to $18 at the railhead, and when fattened for several months on good Kansas grass, might earn the drover as much as $25 a head. One Texas drover, M. A. Withers, made a net profit of $9,000 on a single herd of 600 steers. By mid-June Abilene already had surpassed the previous year's shipments, and by the end of June the railroad could not supply enough cattle cars to keep up with demand, and they were forced to build improvised frames on flatcars.

Meanwhile, settlers around Abilene had been relatively content to share in the new prosperity. They took advantage of drover contracts for their farm products and liked the occasional gift of a newly dropped calf. Some homesteaders actually let drovers bed cattle on their lands so they could collect the dried dung, or chips, which they valued for fuel in a land virtually without timber. To be sure, a few settlers pressured the governor to enforce the quarantine against Texas cattle, accusing McCoy of bribing local officials to look the other way—a charge that probably had some truth to it.

But with the new herds came a new outbreak of Texas fever that struck local livestock. "Hell was to pay," said Charles Gross, McCoy's general assistant. "It was almost open gun war." McCoy restored at least partial peace with the Kansans by making good a promise to compensate local stockmen for their losses. He personally paid $3,300 and raised another $1,200 from drovers by levying a five-cents-a-head tax on cattle arriving in Abilene. But in late July an even worse epidemic of Texas fever erupted in Illinois. Local livestock were so severely affected that vigilance committees were formed to stop importation of Texas cattle.

Suddenly the booming market in Abilene went flat, and 25,000 unsold steers were grazing in the immediate area. Never one to flinch in the face of crisis, McCoy organized his most spectacular promotion, brazenly designed to distract cautious buyers. He put together what may have been the first Wild West show, complete with wild buffalo and ponies, an elk, and a collection of Mexican vaqueros and Texas cowboys in full regalia, and shipped the traveling extravaganza east in a specially rigged circus car. Although McCoy wound up another $6,000 in debt, the show helped bring buyers back to Abilene. The breathtaking stunts of riding and roping delighted audiences in Saint Louis and Chicago, and before winter set in, every animal offered at McCoy's stockyards was sold.

The year 1868 had been twice as good as 1867—75,000 cattle were herded into Abilene and about 50,000 were shipped out by rail. "Abilene as a cattle market was at last established beyond cavil or doubt," McCoy wrote. He was confident of doubling his business the following year, and perhaps the one after that, and he was right. Flowing north over the Chisholm Trail, the rapturous McCoy gushed, was a great stream of cattle "that inspired the drover with enthusiasm akin to that enkindled in the breast of the military hero by the sight of marching columns of men."

Abilene looked, smelled, and sounded like a boom town. Thanks to Joe McCoy and the entrepreneurs he attracted, stores and saloons soon sprang up, then churches and a schoolhouse, a railroad station, a hardware store that sold everything from shotguns to sewing machines, and a combination furniture store and funeral parlor. The pungent stockyard aroma soon mingled with the redolence of freshly sawed pine, brought in by rail to construct houses. Beneath the prairie sun, optimistic new residents planted quick-growing cottonwoods and box elders for shade. Above the jingle and rattle of horses and buggies rose the whoops and curses of sweating men as they shoved recalcitrant beeves into the rail cars, then prodded them with poles in order to keep them on their feet—a technique that gave rise to the term "cowpuncher."

Even so, the town's growing reputation exceeded its actual size—the 1870 census counted a mere 849 residents—but Joe McCoy bragged that it was the best-known small town in America. He liked to tell the story of the Texas drover who supposedly rode into the village one morning, looked around its dusty and deserted streets, and asked someone how far it was to Abilene. When the resident assured the stranger that he had arrived, the Texan replied, "You don't mean this here little scattering trick is Abilene? Well, I'll swar I never seed such a little town have such a mighty big name."

At the center of Abilene's new renown and prosperity stood the cowboy, and Abilene helped introduce him to the national consciousness in all his gaudy but functional trappings. His sombrero with its low crown and wide brim shielded him from the sun, his boots with two-inch heels kept his feet from slipping through the stirrups, the bandanna around his neck kept trail dust out of his mouth, his old Confederate army coat served as both slicker and blanket, his calfskin chaps warded off the thick brush, the knife in his waistband served as an essential tool, and the revolver at his hip provided the last line of defense against snakes, steers, and, occasionally, other cowboys.

McCoy, who admired the breed, thought cowboys were as hardy and sometimes as ornery as the longhorns that shared their lives: "He lives hard, works hard, has but few comforts and fewer necessities. He has but little, if any, taste for reading; loves danger but abhors labor of the common kind; very quick to detect an injury or insult, and not slow to avenge it nor quick to forget it; would rather fight with pistols than pray; loves tobacco, liquor and women better than any other trinity."

As soon as the cowboy hit town, he collected his pay. The accepted wage for cattle drovers was "a dollar a day and found," meaning as much as $90 for three months on the trail, plus beef, beans, coffee, and whatever other grub

A COWBOY'S SADDLE

Riding tall in the saddle he had bought in San Antonio *(below)*, A. J. "Gus" Bellport drove 4,000 cattle and 60 horses up the Chisholm Trail to Ellsworth, Kansas, in 1870. The western-style saddle's high cantle at the rear and the pommel at the front helped him keep his seat. The horn angling up from the pommel secured his lariat, and the leather ties were handy for a bedroll, saddlebag, and other necessities. The broad leather fenders hanging down on each side protected rider and mount from chafing and protected against horse sweat.

the trail cook managed to rustle up. First the dust-encrusted drover visited the barber for a shave, haircut, and bath. Then he headed over to Jacob Karatofsky's Great Western Store at the corner of Texas and Cedar Streets for a new shirt, suit, or other fancy garb. Then perhaps he would stop in at Thomas C. McInerney's emporium, where up to 20 bootmakers cut and stitched leather footwear—a high-heeled model spangled with lone star and crescent moon set in red morocco front and back sold for up to $20 a pair.

Thus outfitted he embarked upon two or three evenings of revelry to compensate for a similar number of months of arduous labor on the trail. Like a sailor in port he cut loose. Raising a little hell was one reason every boy on a Texas ranch dreamed of going up the trail, and Abilene was ready to fulfill all his fantasies. By 1871, Texas Street—the main thoroughfare south of the railroad tracks—sported no fewer than seven saloons, not counting bars in the four hotels. The most celebrated watering hole was the Alamo—through its triple set of glass doors glittered a rococo world of ornate mirrors and shameless paintings of female nudity. A "brightly lit array of felt-topped gambling tables" tempted cowboys to try their luck at dice, poker, monte, and faro. At the polished brass bar, reported a visitor, the "bartender, with a countenance like a youthful divinity student, fabricates wonderful music, while the music of a piano and a violin from a raised recess, enlivens the scene."

From there, a visitor might repair to the Novelty Theater—certainly a novelty to cowboys unfamiliar with the performing arts. This establishment, which catered to "a better class of people," according to one contemporary, seated 400 and featured thespian companies from as far afield as Kansas City. The less refined cowboy, if able to walk at all, proceeded to one of the town's dance halls to consort with a species conspicuously lack-

Cow town dance halls were frequented by prostitutes, who plied their trade in the back rooms. More tolerant of the cowboy's diversions than many Abilene citizens, Joe McCoy wrote, ". . . the more he dances and drinks, the less common sense he will have, and the more completely his animal passions will control him. Such is the manner in which the cowboy spends his hard-earned dollars."

ing on the Chisholm Trail: women. For the price of a drink for himself and one for the lady, he could, in Joe McCoy's words, "fandango to lascivious music in company with maidens to whom virtue is an unknown and unrespected grace and to whom modesty is a lost sensibility." The cowboy, McCoy said, plunged into "this vortex of dissipation" without bothering to lay aside hat, spurs, or pistols. "With the front of his sombrero lifted at an angle of fully forty-five degrees; his huge spurs jangling at every step or motion; his revolvers flapping up and down like a retreating sheep's tail; his eyes lit up with excitement, liquor and lust; he plunges in and 'hoes it down' at a terrible rate; often swinging 'his partner' clear off of the floor for an entire circle; then 'balance all' with an occasional demoniacal yell, near akin to the war whoop of the savage Indian."

Practically all of the women at the dance hall were prostitutes. After the evening of dancing was finished, they were likely to invite prospective clients back to a nearby brothel. In the first cattle driving season of 1867, a few prostitutes had arrived by rail from Memphis, Saint Louis, and other cities. "Then they came in Swarms," said McCoy's assistant, Charles Gross, "& as the weather was warm 4 or 5 girls Could Huddle together in a tent very Comfortably." These soiled doves, as one shopkeeper delicately termed them, were not to be trifled with: Many concealed a dagger or small pistol in their handbag for self-defense and to ensure payment for services rendered.

Everybody made money in Abilene, though the typical cowboy was relieved of every dollar he had after two or three days of revelry. Joe McCoy labored day and night "to make the Abilene enterprise a complete success." He often made do on only two hours of sleep, and his booming voice seemed to resound everywhere. A Texas drover once remarked,

"You could hear him all over town." He even spent considerable time—and $2,000 of his own money—successfully lobbying back in Springfield to stifle legislation that would have kept Texas cattle out of the state of Illinois.

But McCoy was too ambitious and headstrong to be content just with running stockyards and other enterprises. "He was a man of hasty temper with strong likes and dislikes," observed Charles Gross. "He never ask any Ones opinion of any act of his or any proget he started or had in view, his will & wishes were law." He was "Mr. Know it all & then some. I am the whole cheese & you are skim milk." Without consulting Gross or anyone else, in the autumn of 1869 he scraped together enough cash to buy a herd of 900 longhorns, intending "to winter them on hay, fatten them on grass the following summer" along the Smoky Hill River, and then make a killing of perhaps $15,000 or more. To cover feed bills and other expenses in the spring of 1870, he was counting on the money due McCoy & Brothers from the Kansas Pacific Railroad. Under a new agreement, he had been promised $2.50 for every carload of cattle shipped out of Abilene. When he went to Saint Louis to collect the $5,042.50 payment for 1869, railroad officials insisted they had no knowledge of such an agreement. McCoy promptly filed suit in U.S. District Court, but while the case awaited trial McCoy's creditors clamored for their money.

He had already sold the Drover's Cottage and had bought out his brothers' shares in the stockyard, promising that he would pay them as soon as the railroad fees were paid. But without those fees in hand, he faced the specter of financial ruin. "Then, with only

AN ORDINANCE
To Prohibit Drunkeness and Disorderly Conduct.

Be it ordained by the Trustees of the town of Abilene,

That any person found in a state of intoxication within the corporate limits of the town of Abilene, or any person guilty of noisy, riotous conduct, or threatening violence against any person or persons, or against the town of Abilene, or running horses on the public streets or alleys, or of lassoing any animal, or leading any wild animal with lasso, or lassoing any person or persons, or of discharging fire-arms within the town limits, shall on conviction thereof before the Court, be fined in any sum not less than five dollars nor more than twenty-five dollars for the first offense, and for the second offense not less than ten dollars nor more than fifty dollars, with costs of prosecution added in both first and second offense, and may be committed to the town jail for any length of time not exceeding five days, provided at the end of that time all costs and fines are paid.

This ordinance shall be in full effect and force from and after the 20th of May, 1870.
T. C. HENRY, Chairman.
Attest: G. L. BRINKMAN, Clerk.

AN ORDINANCE
Relating to the Carrying of Fire Arms and other Deadly Weapons.

Be it ordained by the Trustees of th[e] Abilene,

SEC. 1. That any person who shall c[arry within] the limits of the town of Abilene, or [a] pistol, revolver, gun, musket, dirk, b[owie knife] or other dangerous weapon upon his [per]son or persons, either openly or concea[led] to bring the same and forthwith deposi[t] at their house, boarding house, store ro[om]...

AN ORDINANCE
Relating to Houses of Ill-Fame.

Be it ordained by the Trustees of the town of Abilene,

SEC. 1. That any and every person or perso[n] who shall keep or maintain, in this town, a ho[use] of ill-fame or prostitution, or a house in [which] disorderly, licentious, obscene, lewd, p[...] indecent conduct or language is perm[itted or] tored, shall be fined not less than [two hundred] dollars nor more than two hundred [dollars and] the fact that such language occurring [...] shall be prima facie evidence that the [...] mitted or allowed by the person who ma[...] keeps such house.

SEC. 2. That any and every person who [is] an inmate or resident of a house of i[ll-fame or] prostitution in this town, or who sha[ll] frequent any such house, for lewd, lice[ntious,] scene or indecent purposes, shall, on [conviction] be fined not less than ten dollars nor [more than] one hundred dollars, and the fact of [...] being found in any such house in the [night time] between the hours of eight o'clock, P. [m. and five] o'clock, a. m., shall be prima facie evi[dence of] or her frequenting the same for such p[urpose.]

SEC. 3. That any and every person who shall [at]tend, visit or frequent any place in the last p[art of pre]ceeding section mentioned, and engage or [...] part in any of the acts, conduct or language there[in] specified, shall be fined not less than ten dolla[rs] nor more than one hundred dollars for each a[nd] every offense.

SEC. 4. That any person or persons who sh[all] hereafter knowingly let, lease or rent any hou[se,] hall, tenement or other place in this town to [any] person or persons, for the purpose of keeping [or] maintaining therein any place as described in [the] preceeding sections of this ordinance, shall, [on] conviction, be punished by a fine not exceed[ing] one hundred dollars, and not less than ten dol[lars] for each day that he, she or they allow the sam[e] to be tenanted for such purpose or purposes, or [shall] shall suffer the same to be used after any of [the] Constables of this town have given notice that [the] same has been declared a house of ill-fame.

SEC. 5. Be it ordained, that any person con[victed] for keeping a house of ill-fame, or k[...]ons, mate thereof, as provided in the fo[...]stables shall be removed by any of the t[...] without the corporate limits of this town, upon the [or]der of the Court.

a single ten-dollar note," McCoy wrote, he retired from business, "compelled by adversity and sickness, induced by overwork and anxiety, causing complete nervous exhaustion." In May 1870 McCoy was forced to sell the Great Western Stockyards business and mortgage his own little cottage. Fair-weather friends, he noted bitterly, passed him on the street without bothering to speak, or merely "deigned to nod their head in cold recognition."

While McCoy retreated into his shell of despair, trouble flared up between settlers and cowboys. One controversy occurred in the late summer of 1869 over a painting that adorned the front of the Bull's Head Saloon on Texas Street depicting a large red bull with lifelike genitalia. Although mature bulls paraded daily in the streets, some of Abilene's more respectable citizens found the painting too realistic, too suggestive, an insult to women, and a bad influence on children. The issue raged for weeks until, just in time to avert a threatened gun battle between factions, the saloon owner decided to have the picture painted over.

Harder to gloss over were settlers' prejudices against cowboys. Texans were rough-hewn southerners, many of whom fought on the wrong side in the Civil War. To more reserved settlers, they dressed and talked differently, and they often crowded local folks off the dusty streets: One resident supposedly counted 4,000 persons on Texas Street during one summer day. Even worse, they wallowed in drink, gambling, and prostitution, which in turn lured scoundrels of various stripes—pickpockets, crooked

Although Abilene and other Kansas cow towns passed ordinances against vice and disorder, enforcement was often lax. Prostitutes like Dodge City's Squirrel-Tooth Alice *(near left)* were tolerated because they kept the hard-earned dollars of their cowboy clients in local circulation.

The midnight shootout in this painting by Charles Russell typifies cow town life at its most violent. Drawing on his father's first-hand observation of the cattle season of 1870, Abilene chronicler Almon C. Nixen wrote that a week seldom passed without a man or two being killed in a fight.

gamblers, whores, and confidence men. Most annoying to the locals was the Texans' abandon with firearms. At any hour of day or night, the crack of pistol shots punctuated the summer heat. J. B. Edwards, who delivered blocks of ice to the saloons at six cents a pound, witnessed such unsettling gunplay. "When a man from Texas got too much tanglefoot aboard," he said, referring to cheap whiskey, "he was liable under the least provocation to use his navies"—referring to the .36 caliber navy revolvers highly favored by Civil War veterans. "If his fancy told him to shoot, he did so—into the air or at anything he saw. A plug hat would bring a volley from him at any time, drunk or sober."

Citizens grew so outraged at the promiscuous behavior that in September 1869 they took steps to restore law and order. They successfully petitioned the county probate court to incorporate Abilene as a

town, which meant they could hire a police force instead of relying on ineffectual county officials to deal with lawless elements. The court appointed five leading citizens, including Joe McCoy, to serve as town trustees. Before the start of the volatile 1870 cattle season, the trustees had created the office of town marshal and approved a number of restrictive ordinances, including one that forbade carrying firearms in public. Neither action seemed to help. A succession of local men hired as marshal proved to be failures, and posters advertising the firearms ordinance were riddled with bullets as soon as they could be put up. The first patron of the town's new jail was quickly sprung by fellow Texans, who shot up the office of the chairman of the trustees on their mad stampede out of town. In desperation, the trustees hired two professional officers from Saint Louis to help get the town under control. The pair spent a day being hazed mercilessly by cowboys and took the next train home.

Despite his personal financial setback, McCoy's concern for the town had not diminished. Recognizing the need of an experienced hand with impressive credentials, he and his fellow trustees settled on Thomas James Smith, a handsome, husky, Irish ex-policeman from New York who had served successfully as a marshal in Wyoming and Colorado. Remarkably, Smith did not drink, gamble, or use profane language. Pledging to enforce the law against firearms, the new marshal said a man might just as well "contend with a frenzied maniac as an armed and drunken cowboy." Soon after pinning on his badge, Smith encountered a rowdy cowboy known as Big Hank. The cowboy, a pistol at his belt, swaggered up to Smith and delivered an unmistakable challenge. "What are you goin' to do about that gun ordinance?" Big Hank demanded. "I'm going to see it's obeyed," replied Marshal Smith, "and I'll trouble you to hand me your pistol now." Big Hank swore and twice refused the marshal's quiet request. Suddenly Smith's fist flashed out and felled the Texan with a single blow to the jaw. He then took Big Hank's pistol and ordered him out of town. The next morning, the ritual was reenacted with another desperado called Wyoming Frank. After Smith disarmed this bully, others in the saloon began offering up their own weapons. Smith told them to check their guns with the bartender and strolled out.

Smith's quiet courage and unusual style impressed the trustees, who raised his salary from $150 to $225 a month after just two months on the job. Potential lawbreakers respected his fists as much as the pair of Colt revolvers he carried but rarely brandished. Smith patrolled Texas Street mounted on his horse Silverheels and prided himself on never having to kill a rowdy cowboy. But on November 2, 1870—five months after taking over—he faced a test from an unexpected direction. A homesteader named Andrew McConnell killed a neighbor in

During five months as Abilene's marshal in the rough-and-tumble cattle season of 1870, Tom Smith restored civic order by moving brothels to the outskirts of town and enforcing the town's ordinance against carrying guns in public. He won universal respect by using his fists rather than his pistols to subdue wild cowboys. Smith was killed in the course of making an arrest in the county outside Abilene. Under ordinary circumstances the sheriff would have made the arrest, but he was too ill to venture out that day and Smith filled in for him.

a dispute over the neighbor's cattle grazing on his land. Though McConnell claimed self-defense, neighbors swore out a murder warrant, so Smith and deputy James H. McDonald rode out to arrest McConnell at his dugout home. McConnell was waiting with a friend, Moses Miles, and a Winchester rifle. Before the marshal could disarm him, McConnell shot Smith in the chest, and as the two men grappled, Miles struck the wounded marshal over the head with a gun. Then he picked up an ax and virtually beheaded the marshal. Deputy McDonald, who had evidently stood rooted to the spot in fright, turned and fled.

McDonald galloped into Abilene and told his version of what happened over a whiskey at the Drover's Cottage. "He blubbered out his yarn," said a skeptical Charles Gross. "There being no one to dispute him, his story had to go. But I still recall the looks that passed between men who had been raised from birth to eat six-shooters. It was so rank that no one could say a word." McDonald kept his job but was thereafter widely regarded as a coward.

Abilene's residents turned out in force to honor the slain marshal. The funeral procession moved from the little frame Baptist church through Texas Street and up a knoll into the town's tiny cemetery. Behind the flower-strewn hearse walked Silverheels, the pommel of his empty saddle draped with the pair of pearl-handled revolvers recently presented to Smith by the grateful community. McConnell and Miles were sentenced to prison for the killing, though everyone in Abilene agreed they deserved nothing less than hanging.

Finding a new marshal became a priority in the spring of 1871 before the arrival of more cowboys. A district court ruled in Joe McCoy's favor in the suit against the Kansas Pacific, so he came out of his forced retirement and was promptly elected mayor. Knowing that "Joe wanted A Marshall with nerve & who would act," Charles Gross told him about a tough fellow he had known back in Illinois and had recently become reacquainted with—a man named James Butler Hickok, now known as Wild Bill. On April 15 McCoy hired Wild Bill Hickok at $150 a month, plus 25 percent of all fines he collected and 50¢ for every stray dog he killed.

A striking six-footer in his early thirties, Hickok had a style that differed markedly from Tom Smith's. Instead of his fists, he asserted his authority with a pair of Colt revolvers and a bowie knife thrust into the sash he wore around his waist; in reserve he had a sawed-off double-barreled shotgun that could be slung from his shoulder on a strap. Unlike Smith, Hickok walked down the middle of Texas Street twice a day to keep an eye on things but usually could be found at the Alamo Saloon, where he drank sparingly, gambled frequently, stayed abreast of town gossip, and kept his back to the wall—"looking at every-

high license fee in order to retain an under-the-table kickback on profits from gambling and prostitution. The licensing issue so antagonized the council that three of the more righteous members resigned. Needing a quorum of members to fill the vacancies, McCoy instructed Marshal Hickok to bring in one of the derelict councilmen, which Wild Bill did—over his shoulder like a sack of corn. That pragmatic gesture was only one of the reasons McCoy considered Wild Bill "the squarest man I ever saw."

Few cowboys dared to challenge Wild Bill, whose reputation as a gunman was already well established. One of the exceptions was John Wesley Hardin, a teenage Texas killer who came up the Chisholm Trail in 1871 with a price on his head. Though Hardin flouted the ban on carrying firearms, the marshal obligingly bought the young

> "As ter killing men, I never thought much about it. The most of the men I have killed it was one or t'other of us, and at sich times you don't stop to think;and what's the use after it's all over?...I am a fighting man, you know."

JAMES BUTLER "WILD BILL" HICKOK, QUOTED IN *HARPER'S NEW MONTHLY MAGAZINE,* FEBRUARY 1867

thing and everybody from under his eyebrows," said a cowboy, "just like a mad old bull."

Marshal Smith had chased the soiled doves out of town, but they returned in greater numbers than ever in the spring of 1871. Though their behavior was not as outrageous as that of the whores in Wichita, who enjoyed running in nude footraces in public, their presence so offended the ladies of Abilene that more than 100 of them petitioned the city for "active measures for the suppression of brothels." McCoy's solution was to authorize the "Devil's Addition"—a red-light district on a 40-acre tract southeast of town. Abilene's lumberyard owner, Theophilus Little, figured it was "rightly named, for Hell reigned there—Supreme."

While helping to isolate one form of vice, McCoy embroiled Wild Bill in another—city politics, where the hottest issue concerned saloon licenses. McCoy argued against raising the relatively

desperado a drink and gave him some fatherly advice about behaving himself in Abilene. One night in August, however, annoyed by the loud snoring of a neighboring hotel guest, Hardin fired through the wall and killed the offender. Hardin left through the hotel window just as Wild Bill arrived to investigate, hid in a haystack, and headed back to Texas on a stolen horse.

Another troublemaker was Phil Coe, a 32-year-old adventurer from Texas whose dislike of Wild Bill was common knowledge. Coe had deserted the Confederate army after one day of service and fled to Mexico before taking up residence in Abilene. He stood well over six feet, with black hair styled in a pompadour and gray eyes that some men swore were the coldest they had ever seen. Coe was agreeable enough when sober—he even played the violin in his spare time—but he was trouble when drinking. In August 1871 he sold his share of the Bull's Head

Saloon but stayed on as a house gambler. Rumors circulated that Coe and Hickok were rivals for the affections of the same woman, and Bill supposedly had accused Coe of running a crooked poker game. Whatever the reason, Coe reportedly threatened to kill Hickok "before the frost."

On the night of October 5, 1871, Coe was living it up with a bunch of cowboys. As the rowdy mob wandered up Texas Street, Wild Bill was at the bar of the Novelty Theater with his friend Mike Williams, a private policeman hired to protect the chorus line from amorous advances by the Texans. Hearing a pistol shot, the marshal hurried to where Coe and the others were gathered in front of the Alamo Saloon. Wild Bill asked who had fired, and Coe replied that he had shot at a stray dog. Wild Bill ordered everyone to disarm and leave town. Coe demurred and then, only a few paces apart, both men drew and fired. One of Coe's pistol balls made a hole in Wild Bill's coat; another passed harmlessly between his legs, but Wild Bill's shot found its mark. Another man came rushing up in the darkness, pistol in hand. Wild Bill dropped him with an instinctive burst of gunfire, then whirled to confront the mob: "If any of you want the rest of these pills, come and get 'em!" The cowboys scattered. Only then did Wild Bill realize that the man he had gunned down in darkness was his friend Mike Williams, who had been attempting to come to his aid.

Hickok got a preacher out of bed to pray for the mortally wounded Coe, who survived in agonizing pain for three days. Williams had died instantly, and the marshal in his sorrow saw to the funeral and burial expenses. Then, grief-stricken at having killed an innocent friend, Wild Bill swept like an avenging angel through the saloons of Abilene. Anyone tempted to resist had only to look at the determination in his eyes.

Things quieted down in Abilene with the approach of winter, but Wild Bill began receiving death threats

A Gift of Thanks

Presenting a law-enforcement officer with an ornate firearm became a tradition among grateful frontier citizens. In 1884, the citizens of Dodge City, Kansas, honored lawman Patrick Sughrue with this engraved, nickel-plated, ivory-handled Colt single-action revolver (below)—a model popularly known as the Peacemaker. The Irish-born Sughrue served as a constable under Sheriff Bat Masterson, and later, as sheriff himself, he was credited with restoring order to the trouble-plagued town. During one arrest he deflected an outlaw's gun upward as it discharged, calmly telling the offender, "I ought to kill you, but you may consider yourself under arrest."

from Texas, including a report that Phil Coe's mother had put a $10,000 bounty on the lawman's head. Hickok started carrying his shotgun and soon found need of it on a train trip to Topeka. Five Texas desperadoes joined Wild Bill on the train, and only his threat to give them both barrels prevented mayhem.

In December the Abilene city council discharged Wild Bill Hickok after only eight months in office on the grounds that the town no longer needed his services. There would be no need for high-profile lawmen until the Texans came up the Chisholm Trail the following spring—if, indeed, they came at all. Events of the past few months had raised serious questions about the cattle trade in Abilene.

Even before Wild Bill's sudden departure, a *Topeka State Record* reporter described Abilene as a town "divided by the railroad into sections . . . the north side is literary, religious and commercial and possesses the churches, the banks, and several large stores of various description; the south side of the road is the Abilene of 'story and song,' and possesses the large hotels, the saloons, and the places where the 'dealers in cardboard, bone and ivory' most do congregate. When you are on the north side of the track you are in Kansas; when you cross to the south side you are in Texas."

Both sides tended to respect the boundary, but crossovers and clashes inevitably occurred. During the early summer of 1871 a school program attracted a number of unruly Texans as well as parents and other respectable citizens. Two noisy and offensive cowboys sat in front of Theophilus Little, the lumberyard operator, his wife, and two sons. When Little remonstrated with them quietly, the cowboys turned and asked "what in hell" he was going to do about it. Then they stood up in front of him laughing and swearing. Little later recounted how he "jumped up and caught one of them by the throat" and choked him "till he gurgled." He then grabbed the other cowboy and "choked him until his Texas tongue ran out of his mouth, jammed him into a chair and hissed into their ears, 'another word out of you tonight and I'll smash every bone in your bodies.' " Afterward, Little admitted it was "a wonder that I was not shot to pieces. They were so utterly astounded at the audacity and foolhardiness of the act that they were cowed and helpless." All the same, Little was relieved when Marshal Hickok walked up the aisle after the program and escorted him and his family home.

But Hickok could not be everywhere, nor could he have prevented the kind of incident in which Phil Coe was gunned down and Mike Williams was accidentally killed. Such incidents exacerbated the rising resentment of the townspeople, which was also being fueled by the city's new weekly newspaper, the *Abilene Chronicle*. The newspaper's founder and editor was Vear P. Wilson, an Ohio journalist and a Universalist preacher.

After McCoy was elected mayor, Vear Wilson used the *Chronicle's* columns to make him the scapegoat for all the town's troubles. Wilson blamed him for "high salaries, high taxes and high foolishness" and hurled such unflattering words as "corrupt, contemptible, unscrupulous and unprincipled." After McCoy took the sensible step of moving the red-light district outside town, the newspaper branded it McCoy's Addition. Although the mayor was generally considered an upstanding family man, the *Chronicle* printed an anonymous letter accusing him without evidence of patronizing the prostitutes there: "On last Saturday night he was seen there with two harlots at once on his lap, one on each knee." For his own part, McCoy labeled Wilson "a

Photographed in the early 1860s, Wild Bill Hickok sported checked trousers, a Prince Albert coat, a silk vest, a cape with flowered silk lining, and hand-tooled boots that cost $60 a pair—twice a cowboy's monthly wage. Before his tenure as Abilene's marshal, Hickok was a Union army scout, an Indian fighter, and a stagecoach driver.

biped of the genus editor; although but a feeble and doubtful specimen."

Vear Wilson represented a new wave of settlers who arrived from his home state of Ohio in 1870. Their so-called Buckeye Colony helped double the population of Dickinson County, in which Abilene was located, to more than 3,000. The Buckeyes, like other puritanical newcomers in and around Abilene, adamantly opposed the consumption of whiskey and other forms of vice. These farmers resented the annual invasion of beeves that tore down their fences, trampled their crops, and threatened to infect their own cattle with Texas fever. The invention of barbed wire was still several years in the future, and few newcomers could afford the kind of board fence with which old settler James Bell enclosed his entire 240-acre farm at a cost of $1,200. As a result, cowboys and cows went where they pleased. When Almon C. Nixen of the Buckeye Colony asked cowboys to guide their herd around his 40-acre meadow, he was told to "go to hell." When a herd destroyed Jacob Schopp's cornfield, he captured two Texas horses and held them for damages. After the cowboys threatened his life, Schopp and a friend leveled a carbine and a six-shooter on the intruders and stood their ground. The Texans paid $50 in damages and complimented Schopp on his grit.

Ironically, the man who emerged as the leader of the anticattle crusade was a former McCoy ally. Theodore C. Henry had failed at raising cotton in Alabama after the Civil War and moved to Springfield, Illinois, where in 1867 Joe McCoy had urged him to seek his fortune in Abilene. Then in his mid-twenties, Henry worked first writing advertising copy for a local land speculator. In those early days in Abilene he even obligingly helped his friend McCoy pacify settlers upset at the cattle trade.

Henry then got into real estate, and his attitude changed. He joined James B. Shane, a partially disabled war veteran who was agent for some 200,000 acres of land opened to settlement by the Kansas Pacific Railroad. In real estate Henry found his call-

These handcuffs tamed many unruly Texans arrested in Dodge City in the days when it often teemed with cowboys. A lawman recalling the practices of the 1870s wrote, "A policeman didn't make an arrest . . . as he does today. None of the boys in those days would have stood while a warrant was being read to him. We had to throw them down and tie them, and read the warrants for their arrest."

ing: He was, by one account, "a hustler." Another prominent local figure, S. A. Burroughs, came into the firm as a secret partner, and the trio carefully positioned themselves politically. Henry became chairman of Abilene's board of trustees and then county registrar of deeds. Shane was elected county treasurer. Burroughs, in addition to service on the city council in Abilene, became county attorney. According to McCoy, the trio formed a "ring, or clique, which, with consummate presumption, undertook to manipulate all public matters," the first of which was to stop the cattle trade. They opposed it for the simple reason that it restricted agricultural development—and hence their real-estate profits. Coming from a New York State farming family, Henry was convinced that the Kansas prairie would be ideal for raising winter wheat—and lots of it. To demonstrate the crop's suitability, he planted a five-acre field in 1870 and several hundred acres the following year, with excellent results.

Delivering the main speech at the first Dickinson County Fair in October 1870, Henry suggested that the cattle trade deterred "settlement and cultivation." The time is "very near at hand," he said, when it ought to be abolished. As a first step, he called for a law requiring livestock owners to fence or herd their animals, thereby freeing farmers—including his own winter wheat enterprise—from the need to fence their own fields.

Joe McCoy counterattacked, arguing that the cattle trade brought Abilene merchants ready cash and local farmers a market for their grain, poultry, and other products. As for the town's sullied reputation, McCoy declared, "By a proper effort of the law-abiding men, good order can be maintained and lawlessness suppressed, and immorality of every description so regulated."

In April 1871 county voters had a chance to approve a herd law measure, exempting the county from a state law requiring settlers to fence their fields in order to collect damages from the owner of stock that trespassed on private land. In place of a fence, settlers needed only to plow a furrow a rod wide—16½ feet—around their properties. The herd law lost in Dickinson County, but the margin of only 123 votes reflected the growing disenchantment with the cattle trade.

Under the leadership of Theodore Henry and his partners, Shane and Burroughs, the settlers banded together in the Dickinson County Farmers' Protective Association and joined forces with leading townspeople from Abilene who were tired of the atmosphere of vice and lawlessness. At a convention called by the association in October 1871 and attended by delegates from all over the county, spirited speeches by Henry and Burroughs whipped anti-cattle sentiment to a peak. Out of this fervor emerged a decisive manifesto written by Henry, signed by 52 citizens, and published in the *Abilene Chronicle* on February 8, 1872: "We the undersigned members of the Farmers' Protective Association and Officers and Citizens of Dickinson county, Kansas, most respectfully request all who have contemplated driving Texas Cattle to Abilene the coming sea-

son to seek some other point for shipment, as the inhabitants of Dickinson will no longer submit to the evils of the trade."

The manifesto was run three more times in the *Chronicle,* and a final version, with 366 signatories, was mailed to post offices throughout Texas. The end came in April, as nearly 94 percent of the county's voters cast their vote on a new, tougher herd law that would effectively prevent animals from running at large: The voters supported the ban by a margin of more than two to one. Even in Abilene the ballot went against the cattle trade.

Texas drovers took Abilene at its word. Herds coming up the Chisholm Trail in the spring of 1872 were met by agents from other Kansas cattle markets in Newton, Ellsworth, and Wichita. The only cattle shipped from Abilene in the summer of 1872 were those left over from the last season, when a record drive of more than 600,000 Texas beeves had overloaded the Kansas market and depressed prices. To make matters worse, a winter of severe cold and blizzards left scarcely 1 beef in 10 alive. Yet during Abi-

lene's first cattle-free summer in five years, the *Chronicle*'s Vear Wilson happily noted that "citizens have the satisfaction of knowing that hell is more than sixty miles away"—in Ellsworth. And as the railheads moved west in the mid-1870s, other towns—even the notorious Dodge City, famed as "Queen of Cow Towns"—repeated Abilene's experience of sudden prosperity, a period of lawlessness, and the eventual decline typical of the pattern begun by Abilene.

The irrepressible Joe McCoy had seen the handwriting on the wall. As early as the spring of 1871, while he was serving as Abilene's mayor, he was designing stockyards and a siding at Newton, 65 miles to the south, for the Atchison, Topeka & Santa Fe Railroad. In 1872 he was selling wrought-iron fence—"the most durable and cheap fence ever invented"—and vigorously promoting Wichita as the next boom town for prospective cattle buyers. Even then the days of the great cattle drives Joseph Mc-Coy had helped pioneer were numbered. The Chisholm Trail and other longhorn highways were soon blocked by barbed wire fences, and a network

Dodge City, a sleepy village of 500 in 1872 *(below)*, was transformed by the arrival of the Santa Fe Railroad into the premier cow town in Kansas. In its peak year, nearly 500,000 cattle and their trail-weary drovers arrived in town. Among the well-known officers charged with keeping the peace in Dodge City were Sheriff Bat Masterson and Marshal Wyatt Earp.

of rail lines began to take shape in cattle country. While his former friend T. C. Henry became one of the first large-scale wheat growers on the Great Plains, and the precocious Jim Daugherty put together one of the largest ranches in Texas, Joe McCoy took jobs as a grocer, livestock dealer, real-estate salesman, and even recorder of livestock statistics for the U.S. Census Bureau. He never recovered the fortune he lost building up Abilene.

The homesteaders who had tamed the unruly cow town found no gold at the end of their rainbow. Abilene soon bore the look of just another struggling rural community. "Four-fifths of the business houses became vacant," wrote McCoy later, "rents fell to a trifle, and many of the leading hotels and business houses were either closed or taken down and moved to other points. Property became unsalable. The luxuriant sunflower sprang up thick and flourished in the main streets, while the inhabitants, such as could not get away, passed the time sadly contemplating their ruin. The whole village assumed a desolate, forsaken, and deserted appearance." ◆

A WESTERN LEGEND

Even in his teens, James Butler Hickok displayed a high regard for justice and fair treatment: He was fired from his job on the Illinois and Michigan Canal after throwing his boss into the canal for abusing his mule team. Perhaps it was just as well, for a canal job couldn't have satisfied a lad like James. In 1856, the 19-year-old left Illinois for the Kansas Territory, where he sharpened his skill with a pistol. A neighbor, perhaps given to exaggeration, recalled: "It was a common feat with him to take a stand at a distance of a hundred yards from an oyster can, and with a heavy dragoon revolver send every bullet through it with unerring precision.

He had not then commenced his practice upon human beings."

Practice paid off. Hickok was working at an overland stage station in the Nebraska Territory in 1861 when he got into a row. Exactly what happened in the course of it is unclear, but a local named David McCanles and several other men appeared at the station, shooting erupted, and when the smoke cleared, McCanles and two others were dead. Some labeled it murder; others insisted it was self-defense. Whatever the truth, Hickok was arrested but soon released.

Hickok's gunfighting prowess earned him further notoriety after a game of poker in

Springfield, Missouri. He had set his prized watch down on the table, and another player, a man he'd had trouble with before named Dave Tutt, picked it up, claiming it as payment for an alleged gambling debt. When he refused to return it, a duel ensued in the town square, and Tutt was shot dead. Hickok was acquitted of manslaughter.

By now people had taken to calling Hickok Wild Bill. Famous in his corner of the world, he stepped into the national limelight when in 1867 *Harper's New Monthly Magazine* published an article, liberally laced with heroic fancies, about his exploits. Other periodicals soon jumped on the Hickok bandwagon.

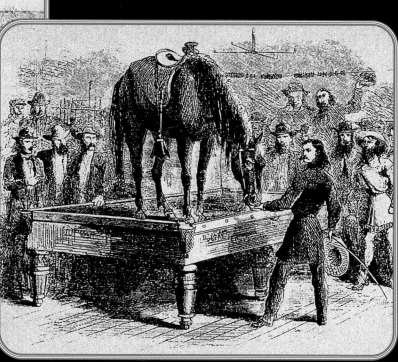

The illustration above for George Ward Nichols's article in *Harper's* shows a heroic Hickok single-handedly battling David McCanles and a band of ruffians. In another scene *(right)*, Hickok's horse, Black Nell, stands obediently on a pool table. The extraordinary abilities Nichols attributed to Nell enhanced her master's legendary status.

"...there is no Common Law here now hardly at all. a man Can do what he pleases without fear of the Law or any thing els. thare has been two awful fights in town this week. you dont no anything about sutch fighting at home as I speak of, this is no place for women and children yet."

JAMES HICKOK DESCRIBING KANSAS
IN A LETTER IN 1858

Monthly.] [Number 10

DE WITT'S TEN CENT ROMANCES

Wild Bill's First Trail.

For Sale by "The New York News Co."
8 SPRUCE STREET,
(Opposite Tribune Buildings,) New York.

The cover of the December 1867 issue of *De Witt's Ten Cent Romances* featured an Indian-fighting Hickok. The July issue of the magazine had glorified him in a story entitled "Wild Bill, the Indian-Slayer." Several years later, with his fame well established, Hickok sat for the formal portrait at right.

"His influence among the frontiersmen was unbounded; his word was law, and many are the personal quarrels and disturbances which he has checked among his comrades by his simple announcement that 'This has gone far enough.'"

GEORGE ARMSTRONG CUSTER

CAVALRY SCOUT

By 1866 the Plains Indians were in full revolt over the intrusion of whites. Among the army units that were sent to subdue them was the 7th Cavalry, which was led by General George Armstrong Custer. Ever drawn to the fringes of civilization, Hickok signed on as a scout and dispatch rider for Custer. The general's wife, Elizabeth Bacon Custer, was greatly impressed by the scout and said that "the manly, frank expression of his fearless eyes and his courteous manner gave one a feeling of confidence in his word and in his undaunted courage." Years later she wrote of Hickok: "I remember watching Wild Bill, as he reported at the commanding officer's tent to get despatches for my husband, and wishing with all my heart that I could go with him. I know this must seem strange to people in the States, whose ideas of scouts are made up from stories of shooting affrays, gambling, lynching and outlawry. I should have felt myself safe to go any distance with those men whom my husband employed as bearers of despatches."

Accounts of the adventures of these scouts, particularly those of Wild Bill, appeared frequently in the press, bringing him more and more into the public eye. Henry M. Stanley, who was special correspondent for the *Weekly Missouri Democrat,* described Wild Bill: "He is brave, there can be no doubt; that fact is impressed on you at once before he utters a syllable."

George Custer's adventurous wife, Elizabeth, lived with her husband at a succession of rugged western army posts until his death in the 1876 battle with the Sioux that took place at the Little Bighorn.

COW TOWN LAWMAN

When Wild Bill became marshal of Hays City, Kansas, in 1869, he found himself in the middle of a volatile situation: "There were twenty-two saloons, three dance halls, one little grocery and one clothing store. We did not think anything of having one or two dead men on the streets nearly every morning," recalled an early citizen of Hays City. About a mile from the city lay Fort Hays, a supply depot for the army. The post's commandant reported that there were often 300 or 400 wagon masters and mule skinners congregated at one time, and "...what with the use of whisky and their revolvers, the town was rendered very uncomfortable for the better class of citizens."

Bill took to wearing a Prince Albert coat and cape, and his passion for hot baths started a trend among the menfolk of the town. His reputation and position as marshal made Wild Bill a target for fame seekers and desperadoes. After several attempts were made on his life, he acquired the habit of walking down the center of the street to keep from being ambushed.

In 1871 Hickok was offered a promotion of sorts: the job of marshal of Abilene, Kansas. The town's booster, Joseph McCoy, declared, "... he was the squarest man I ever saw. He broke up all unfair gambling, made professional gamblers move their tables into the light, and when they became drunk stopped the game." With only three deputies to help him control the cowboys who were driving cattle from Texas to the railhead in Abilene, it was necessary for Hickok to stay on his toes. "It was a very common sight," noted John Conkie, the city jailer, "... to see Wild Bill sitting in a barber's chair getting shaved, with his shotgun in his hand and his eyes open."

One night Hickok ordered a drunken mob of Texans, including one Philip Coe, to disarm and leave town. Coe and Hickok exchanged shots just as policeman Mike Williams dashed around a corner into the fray. Both Coe and Williams were killed by Hickok's bullets.

In Abilene, Hickok carried this Remington Army revolver *(right)*. In place of a holster, he preferred a belt, sash, or just his waistband. For a speedier draw, he wore his guns with their handles forward.

"Young man, never run away from a gun. Bullets can travel faster than you can. Besides, if you're going to be hit, you had better get it in the front than in the back. It looks better."

WILD BILL HICKOK

"There is no Sunday west
of Junction City, no law
west of Hays City, and no
God west of Carson City."

WILD BILL HICKOK

N. C. Wyeth's drawing captures the popular conception of Hickok. Asked how he stayed calm in a gunfight, Hickok said, "When a man really be-
lieves that a bullet isn't moulded that is going to kill him, what in hell has he got to be afraid of?" A receipt for his services is shown (above, right).

WILD WEST SHOWMAN

Early in 1873, Hickok's longtime friend William F. Cody organized "Buffalo Bill's Combination," a theater troupe presenting the drama of life on the plains. In their second season, Cody and his partner, Texas Jack Omohundro, persuaded Hickok to join, playing himself, the legendary persona Wild Bill.

One scene required that the characters sit and swap stories while sharing a bottle of whiskey. Hickok took a large swig, then froze with a look of horror on his face. He spat the mouthful toward the wings and shouted, "... Cold tea don't count—either I get real whiskey or I ain't tellin' no story!" The response from the audience was tremendous; it is said that Cody left the scene permanently in the play.

In spite of the show's popularity, Hickok was uncomfortable on the stage. He thought that the make-believe fighting, killing, and dying made them all look ridiculous. The rough frontiersman was just not cut out for the stage; in Rochester, New York, he left the tour and wandered back to his beloved West.

As a member of Buffalo Bill's troupe, Hickok wore a plainsman's traditional costume similar to the one he wears in the photograph at right. His belt holds a hunting knife and his two Colt revolvers, handles forward.

In a photograph taken when the troupe was performing in New York City, Wild Bill

appears second from the left. Buffalo Bill Cody stands in the center, between Wild Bill and Texas Jack.

OPERA HOUSE!
KEOKUK.
Fri. & Sat. April 17 & 18
LINKS BETWEEN CIVILIZATION AND SAVAGERY
ON THE TRAIL!

THE Originals!

LIVING HEROES!

BUFFALO BILL
Hon. WM. F. CODY.

BORDER PERILS!

INDIAN FIGHTS!

TEXAS JACK!
J. B. OMOHUNDRO.

DARING DEEDS!

Representative Men!

WILD BILL!
J. B. HICKOK.

DANGER!
PEACE CONFERENCES!

TREACHERY!
INDIAN POLICY

THE PEERLESS
MORLACCHI!

Scouts of the Plains!
FULL DRAMATIC COMPANY!
Elaborate Dresses.
HARRY MINER, Business Manager.

DEAD IN DEADWOOD

Hickok met Agnes Lake, a widow from Cincinnati, in Abilene in 1871. The relationship was slow to mature, however, for the prospect of being tied down was unthinkable to the free-spirited Hickok: "I don't want any paper collar on, it's me for the West. I would be lost back in the States." But after years of letter writing, the pair married in Cheyenne on March 5, 1876. Domestic life was no match for Hickok's wanderlust, however, and after a two-week honeymoon back east he set out for the Black Hills in the Dakota Territory hoping to strike it rich. With the discovery of gold there in 1874,

mining camps had sprung up rapidly. The town of Deadwood consisted of one main street lined with hotels, saloons, and gambling dens. In the first flush of gold fever, the town was virtually lawless.

Hickok staked a small mining claim, but he spent most of his time gambling. Evidently he lost more than he won, and this may have contributed to his growing depression. He spoke repeatedly of death: "I feel this is going to be my last camp, and I won't leave it alive."

On August 2, Hickok joined a poker game in Deadwood's Saloon No. 10 and asked

for his usual place, where he could sit with his back to the wall. A friend was already sitting there, and he only laughed and teased Hickok for being overcautious. They were still playing when a man named Jack McCall entered the saloon. Just what his grievance with Hickok was remains a matter of dispute. Some believe that he was looking to avenge a brother allegedly killed by Wild Bill; a more chilling suggestion is that McCall was simply trying to make a name for himself. Whatever the motive, he walked up behind Hickok and without warning shot him in the back of the head, killing him instantly.

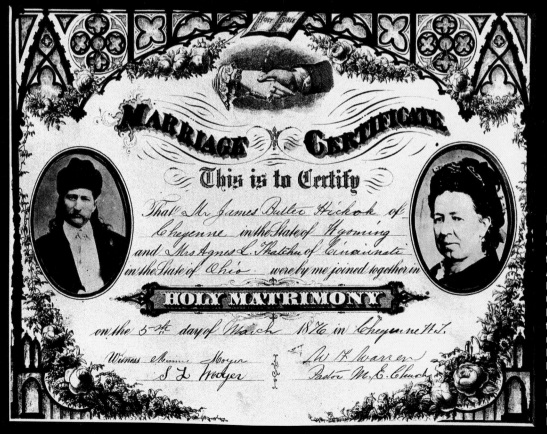

In a letter to Hickok's mother, Agnes wrote: "Dear Mother I want you to give me James exact Age as I want to put our Berths on our Marriage Certificate he plays the Larkes with me so much that I wont put it down until I git it from you." Hickok was actually 39 but told the clerk he was 45, perhaps out of gallantry: Though claiming to be 42, his bride was probably 50.

On the way to Deadwood, Hickok's party of gold seekers was joined by a group that included the flamboyant frontierswoman Calamity Jane *(right)*. She later claimed that she and Wild Bill married, but others said her story was fabricated, and that little of what she said could be believed.

In his last card game, Wild Bill Hickok, shown above with his back to Jack McCall, held two black aces, two black eights, and the jack of diamonds—a combination known ever since as "Aces and Eights, the Dead Man's Hand."

"Agnes, Darling, if such should be that we never meet again, while firing my last shot, I will gently breathe the name of my wife—Agnes—and with wishes even for my enemies I will make the plunge and try to swim to the other shore."

HICKOK IN A LETTER WRITTEN THE DAY BEFORE HIS DEATH

A Gallery of Frontier Rogues

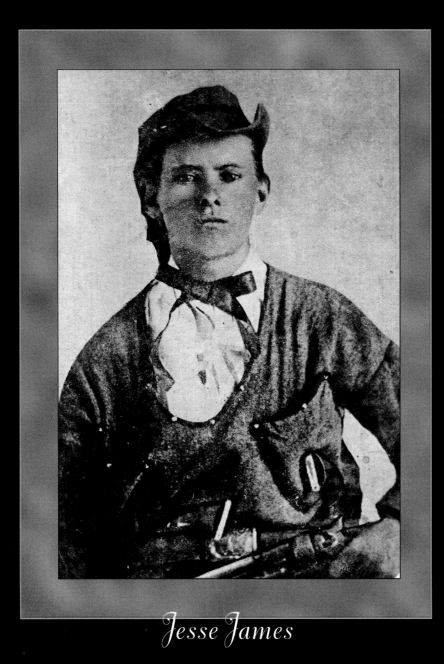

Jesse James

When Jesse James walked into a Missouri bank in 1866 and robbed it in broad daylight, a post-Civil War boom time for outlaws was ushered in. The unprecedented heist was the first of many audacious exploits that made James a scourge to some and a folk hero to others. In 1872, after the James gang looted the ticket booth at the Kansas City fair, getting away with almost $1,000, the *Kansas City Times* declared that men "who can so daringly execute a scheme in the light of day, in the face of authorities, deserve at least admiration for their bravery and nerve."

Much of this misplaced admiration stemmed from James's stint with the bushwhackers, the Confederate irregulars who engaged in notoriously brutal guerrilla warfare against the Jayhawkers, their Union counterparts, along the Missouri-Kansas border. In the eyes of many Southern sympathizers, James, seen here as a 17-year-old bushwhacker, was a war hero. His 15-year postwar career as a criminal Robin Hood ended in 1882 when Bob Ford, a recent recruit to the gang, shot him in the back.

Clay Allison was a paradox. A Tennessean who became a prosperous rancher in New Mexico after the Civil War, he was also a menace to society noted for often-drunken violence. Shown in 1870 after shooting himself in the foot in a mule stampede, Allison killed several men in barroom shootouts but had a macabre talent for variety. He once hanged a man accused of murdering his own infant daughter, decapitated him, impaled the head on a pike, and carried it to a saloon. He repaid a dentist who had failed to cure Allison's toothache by extracting one of the dentist's teeth.

The Confederate army doctors who discharged Allison after only three months of service said he had a mental disorder described as "partly epileptic, partly maniacal." Allison, however, always rationalized his actions. When a Missouri newspaper accused him of 15 killings, he responded indignantly that he protected "the property holders and substantial men of the country from thieves, outlaws and murderers, among whom I do not care to be classed." He died in 1887 when he fell off a wagon and was crushed under the wheels.

Clay Allison

Billy the Kid

With his good humor, obliging ways, and innocent grin, Billy the Kid did not project the image of a killer. More formally known as William Bonney, he became a saddle tramp and odd jobber after being orphaned at 14. He first killed at age 17, shooting a bullying blacksmith at an army post in Arizona. He drifted on to Lincoln County, New Mexico, where he got involved in a local war pitting cattlemen against traders supplying beef to the government. When his cattleman boss was murdered, Billy became obsessed with avenging his death, and did so ruthlessly, slaying two of the culprits after they had been captured and had surrendered their arms.

Twice Billy was caught and jailed for murder, and twice he escaped. In 1881, at 21, he was shot and killed by Lincoln County sheriff Pat Garrett. Within the year Garrett published a novel about the Kid that he billed as an authentic account but was a tissue of fantasies. Nor was Garrett alone, for seven other books romanticizing Billy appeared in short order; all told, an eager public quickly snapped up one million copies.

The precocious John Wesley Hardin was only 11 when he stabbed another boy during a quarrel. At 15, seething with the rage that many other Southerners felt after the abolition of slavery and the Union victory, he fatally shot a former slave, then gunned down the three men who came to arrest him. By the time he was 25, he was a seasoned killer, with 39 deaths charged against him.

A native of Texas, Hardin spent much of his time on the run and, like Jesse James, was often protected from the law by Confederate sympathizers and relatives. He was finally tracked down and arrested by the Texas Rangers in 1877 for the murder of a sheriff. While in prison Hardin studied law, and when he was pardoned in 1894 after serving 15 years, he opened a law office in El Paso. But apparently his temper had not mellowed, for the next year he was overheard threatening a police officer named John Selman. A few days later, Selman shot Hardin in cold blood. He was acquitted by a jury.

John Wesley Hardin

Belle Starr

$\mathcal{B}$elle Starr was the darling of newspaper journalists with romantic notions about desperadoes. The femme fatale of the Indian Territory, she dallied with badmen such as James gang member Cole Younger; a daughter was the product of that liaison. Boldly taking her stand on the wrong side of the law, she once declared to a reporter, "I am a friend to any brave and gallant outlaw. There are three or four jolly good fellows on the dodge now in my section, and when they come to my house they are welcome, for they are my friends."

A good organizer, Starr managed the operations of rustlers, horse thieves, and bootleggers. When friends were arrested, she used money or seduction to buy their freedom. In 1886 her lawyers persuaded President Grover Cleveland to commute the death sentence of her lover, Blue Duck; two years later Cleveland pardoned Starr's horse thief son. The Bandit Queen's luck ran out in 1889 when she was ambushed by a gunman never identified—though her third husband reportedly had threatened her life.

Butch Cassidy's Wild Bunch was the last of the storied outlaw gangs. Like the James gang, the Wild Bunch robbed banks and trains for a living; and like Jesse James, Cassidy, along with his confederate Harry "Sundance Kid" Longbaugh, has been enshrined in western lore as a folk hero.

Cassidy may not have been dangerous—his claim that he never killed anyone appears to be true—but he was certainly a nuisance. When his gang repeatedly robbed Union Pacific trains, the company tried to stop him by offering him a high-paying job as a guard. Cassidy stuck to robbery. After robbing a bank in Winnemucca, Nevada, in 1900, the Wild Bunch sat for the portrait below, with Butch shown front right and Sundance front left, then sent the photo to the bank with thanks for its contribution.

With the Pinkerton Detective Agency on their trail, Butch and Sundance fled to South America in 1902. Some reports say that the pair was killed there by Bolivian troops, but a more prosaic story has it that both returned to the United States and lived on for many more years.

The Wild Bunch

CHAPTER 3

THE GOLDEN SPIKE

"The transcontinental railroad will be built, and I will have a part in building it." THEODORE JUDAH

Promontory, Utah, had never seen such excitement, and never would again. Situated at the crest of a broad, arid pass through the Promontory Mountains north of Great Salt Lake, it had long been a province of sagebrush, dry winds, and wheeling buzzards. Then, in the mid-1860s, occasional teams of surveyors had appeared, sighting and staking their way across the desert. By 1869 rival armies of laborers had swept in from east and west, building roadbeds that seemed to stretch away to infinity. That spring another two armies approached from opposite directions, laying down track. Now it was May, and the work was nearly done. The crews were poised to join the bands of iron and thus connect, for the first time, the Atlantic and Pacific coasts of America by railroad.

The climactic ceremony—the driving of the last spike—was scheduled for noon on May 8 at the makeshift town of Promontory, where a row of shops and saloons had sprung up in order to cater to the construction crews. When the rails were joined there, cities across the country would mark the dawn of a new American era of unimaginable prospects with speeches, parades, and 21-gun salutes. But the ceremony at Promontory did not take place on May 8, and nearly did not take place at all.

The train bearing the dignitaries of the Central Pacific Railroad traversed its 690 miles of track from Sacramento, California, and arrived in good time. But there was no sign of the delegation from the Union Pacific Railroad, which had set out from Omaha, Nebraska, 1,086 miles to the east. The announced reason for the delay was that heavy rains had washed out the track in several places. The real reason, admitted much later, was that the train carrying the Union Pacific officials was being held near the Wyoming-Utah border by a mob of tie cutters who had not been paid for four months. Not until the angry workers received their pay on May 8 did they release the train, which then was further delayed by a flood-damaged bridge.

While the Central Pacific party killed time by visiting the nearby town of Ogden, a newspaper reporter at Promontory recorded a historic moment. Wells Fargo's Overland Stagecoach Number Two rattled up from the east carrying the last shipment of mail for the West Coast ever to be transported by horses. "The four old nags were worn and jaded," the reporter wrote, "and the coach showed evidence of long service." The drivers handed the mail over to the railroad, and "the old order of things passed away forever."

For most of his adult life Theodore Judah *(left)* single-mindedly pursued his dream of a transcontinental railroad. Another of his passions was music. He especially enjoyed playing the organ and, his wife Anna said, "poured out his soul in song and harmony."

THE FIRST TRANSCONTINENTAL CONNECTION

With the U.S. acquisition of California in 1848 and the ensuing gold rush, a burgeoning western populace demanded an overland alternative to the long sea voyage from the East. In 1857 John Butterfield founded the Butterfield Overland Mail Company, offering coach service for passengers, mail, and freight from Memphis and Saint Louis to San Francisco. The route, which ran through present-day Texas, New Mexico, and Arizona, was a victory for the South, wanting to strengthen ties to the West as tensions grew on the eve of the Civil War.

The fare for the journey—$200 from end to end or 10¢ a mile—did not include the often nauseating meals served during 10-minute stops at the route's nearly 200 relay stations. Butterfield's service ceased with the outbreak of war. The newly established Pony Express and, after the war, the transcontinental railroad followed a more northerly route.

No. 2.	GOING WEST.				Jan. 1859.
LEAVE.	DAYS.	Hour.	Distance, Place to Place.	TIME ALLOWED
St. Louis, Mo., and Memphis, Tenn.,				Miles.	No. Hours.
Tipton, Mo.	Monday and Thursday,	8.00 A.M		
Springfield, "	Monday and Thursday,	6.00 P.M	160	10
Fayetteville, Ark.	Wednesday and Saturday,	7.45 A.M	143	37½
Fort Smith, "	Thursday and Sunday,	10 15 A.M	100	26¼
Sherman, Texas.	Friday and Monday,	3.30 A.M	65	17¼
Fort Belknap, "	Sunday and Wednesday,	12.30 A.M	205	45
Fort Chadbourne, "	Monday and Thursday,	9.00 A.M	146½	32½
Pecos River Crossing,	Tuesday and Friday,	3.15 P.M	136	30¼
El Paso,	Thursday and Sunday,	3.45 A.M	165	36½
Soldier's Farewell,	Saturday and Tuesday,	11.00 A.M	248½	55½
Tucson, Arizona	Sunday and Wednesday,	8.30 P.M	150	33½
	Tuesday and Friday,	1.30 P.M	184½	41
Gila River,* "	Wednesday and Saturday,	9.00 P.M	141	31½
Fort Yuma, Cal.	Friday and Monday,	3.00 A.M	135	30
Los Angelos, "	Sunday and Wednesday,	8.30 A.M	254	53½
Fort Tejon, "	Monday and Thursday,	7.30 A.M	96	23
Visalia, "	Tuesday and Friday,	11.30 A.M	127	28
Firebaugh's Ferry, "	Wednesday and Saturday,	5.30 A.M	82	18
(Arrive) San Francisco,	Thursday and Sunday,	8.30 A.M	163	27

* The Station referred to on the Gila River is 40 miles west of the Maricopa Wells.

This Schedule may not be exact—all employes are directed to use every possible exertion to get the Stage through in quick time, even though ahead of this time.

No allowance is made in the time for ferries, changing teams, &c. It is necessary that each driver increase his speed over the average per hour enough to gain time for meals, changing teams, crossing ferries, &c.

Every person in the Company's employ will remember that each minute is of importance. If each driver on the route loses 15 minutes, it would make a total loss of time, on the entire route, of 25 hours, or, more than one day. If each one loses 10 minutes, it would make a loss of 16½ hours, or the best part of a day.

If each driver gains that time, it leaves a margin against accidents and extra delays.

All will see the necessity of promptness; every minute of time is valuable, as the Company are under heavy forfeit if the mail is behind time.

JOHN BUTTERFIELD, President.

The westbound schedule for Butterfield's stagecoaches indicates two departures a week from each station on the 2,700-mile route. A one-way trip between Memphis or Saint Louis and San Francisco took approximately 24 days.

The luxurious Concord coach *(sketch, far right)* transported passengers within towns and cities and was exchanged for a lighter vehicle such as the so-called celerity wagon *(center)* in rougher terrain. Describing the ride, journalist Waterman Ormsby wrote, "To feel oneself bouncing—now on the hard seat, now against the roof, and now against the side . . . was no joke."

The shriek of an approaching whistle on Monday morning, May 10, signaled at last that the Union Pacific train was coming in. Leland Stanford, president of the Central Pacific and former governor of California, led his colleagues over to meet the arriving party of Thomas C. Durant, vice president of the Union Pacific. The two sides promptly got into an argument over the details of the ceremony and at one point threatened to withdraw.

After haggling some more over protocol, they reached agreement and strode out to where the last rail ends lay on the last tie, made of polished laurel wood and decorated with a commemorative silver plate. Gold spikes were set in predrilled holes in the tie for the officials to tap into place. When Stanford's silver-plated sledgehammer touched gold, a telegraph signal flashed across the United States. From New York City to San Francisco, church bells began to ring, cannons fired salutes, tugboats and locomotives opened their steam whistles, bands struck up, and celebratory parades stepped off. It was the greatest outpouring of national pride and optimism since the end of the Civil War four years earlier. The event at Promontory marked one of the grandest engineering feats of the 19th century, and bound east and west together as never before.

As proud Americans celebrated that day, there was one person far from Promontory who saw the driving of the last spike as the triumph not of a nation but of an individual. Fifteen years earlier the idea of a transcontinental railroad had been just a dream, incomprehensible to all but a few visionaries. It proved to be a powerful dream, capable of making men and breaking them. Its realization had required unprecedented amounts of raw materials, labor, and capital. Beyond that, it had required a champion of intense determination. For only a true believer could have rallied the nation's leaders in support of a railroad over the Rocky Mountains and the Sierra Nevada.

Anna Judah, who spent the day of celebration quietly at her home in Massachusetts, knew that one man had believed in this dream from the start and sustained it. He did not live to witness the driving of the last spike, nor was his name mentioned by the dignitaries at Promontory. Yet Anna was certain that, more than any other person, her husband, Theodore D. Judah, had made it happen.

The adventure had begun on a late winter morning in 1854 with a cryptic message. All Anna Judah knew was that her husband had received a telegram asking the young railroad engineer, then in his late twenties, to "come to New York city at once" to confer with the state's governor and other prominent figures. In the seven years since marrying Anna, Theodore Judah had achieved much, and she had come to know him as a driven man with large visions. She had met him shortly after he started work as a surveyor helping to build a railroad between Springfield, Massachusetts, and Brattleboro, Vermont. Now, in March 1854, they were living in Buffalo, New York, where he was in charge of construction for the Buffalo & New York City Railroad.

Those who knew the couple expected remarkable things of them. The former Anna Pierce of Greenfield, Massachusetts, was a green-eyed, auburn-haired beauty who possessed all the grace that a wealthy family and a first-class education could bestow. Theodore, born in Bridgeport, Connecticut, to an Episcopal clergyman, was a short, handsome, curly-haired, intense young man. He paid close attention to his manners, his clothes (he favored elaborately embroidered waistcoats), and his carefully trimmed goatee.

It was no surprise to Anna that her accomplished husband had been summoned to a mysterious conference with the governor of New York. But nothing could have prepared her for the telegram that arrived a few days after Theodore departed. "Be home tonight," her husband informed her. "We sail for California April Second."

"You can imagine my consternation," Anna would write years later. Theodore had made his name as a builder of railroads, but there were no railroads in

For a Victorian woman of her respectable station, Anna Judah's preparations for a lengthy stay in California required packing cumbersome clothing such as the crinoline hoop skirt she wore for this photograph. "My good mother and father," she later wrote of the impending journey, "gave us all their energies, though with full hearts, for it was a hard thing to send an only daughter so far away and it was a great undertaking in those days."

California. For that matter, there were no railroads west of Texas. Anna knew about California, the site of the great gold rush of 1849. But that recently admitted state was as remote to a well-bred lady of Massachusetts as any fabled spot in farthest Cathay. She must have wondered, as she awaited her husband's return and explanation, what California could offer a builder of railroads.

Everything, as it turned out. Theodore had been offered the position of chief engineer for the upstart Sacramento Valley Railroad. Charles L. Wilson of San Francisco had taken charge of the railroad the previous year when it was little more than an idea, and now he needed someone to build it. He had come east to buy materials and hire people. On both counts he had looked to Silas Seymour, a consulting engineer who would soon organize the firm of Robinson, Seymour & Company to supply Wilson's line with rails and rolling stock. Silas, whose brother Horatio was governor of New York, had worked with Theodore Judah, and both Seymours heartily recommended the young man to Wilson.

Wilson hoped to profit handsomely by transporting men and equipment to the gold fields in the Sierra Nevada foothills. Many prospectors reached California by ship, arriving at the port of San Francisco and traveling by riverboat to Sacramento, in California's Central Valley. From there, however, the trip north or east to the Sierra foothills had to be made by foot or horse-drawn wagon over terrible roads. Five years of prospecting had gleaned the easily found gold, and mining now required heavy equipment and large crews to wash gold out of gravel banks or dig it out of deep hard-rock mines. The Sacramento Valley Railroad would move everything the miners needed faster and cheaper.

Theodore Judah explained all this to his skeptical wife on his return from New York. Even at this early time, she recalled, Judah had a dream that went far beyond California. He would become the "pioneer railroad engineer of the Pacific coast," then he would turn his attention to a transcontinental railroad. "It will be built," he told Anna, "and I am going to have something to do with it."

Judah had booked passage to San Francisco on a route that combined travel by steamship with an overland journey across Nicaragua. Although shorter and safer than either the four-month ocean voyage around Cape Horn or the alternate sea and land route across the rugged Isthmus of Panama, the trip was still subject to unpredictable storms, landslides, and fevers. "It was a sad parting," Anna wrote of leaving her worried parents behind in New York, "but we were full of youth and hope."

Nearly six weeks later, the young couple arrived in Sacramento, which would be Anna's home for much of the next decade while Theodore spent months on end in the field. Although Sacramento was designated the capital of California the same year they arrived there, it retained the raw ener-

gy of a gold rush boom town. Its streets, saloons, and dance halls pulsed with the round-the-clock activities of muleteers, longshoremen, cardsharps, failed and future prospectors, thieves, and whores. The town's principal businesses were arrayed along Front Street in rambling two-story buildings of clapboard and brick, facing a thoroughfare alternately whipped by windblown dust or mired in soupy mud. How she was going to deal with this, Anna would have to determine on her own. Theodore installed her in rented rooms and threw himself into his work.

After just two weeks, on May 30, Judah presented the company's directors with a plan for building the Sacramento Valley Railroad. His first report was preliminary, covering only part of the proposed 40-mile route from Sacramento to Marysville, the gateway to the northern foothills. Nonetheless, the plan was remarkably detailed. It laid out the precise course and grade of the roadbed, identifying the owner of each piece of property along the route and estimating

This late-1850s lithograph depicts Sacramento's bustling waterfront at the time Theodore and Anna Judah lived there. Prospectors traveled by steamboat from San Francisco to Sacramento, then continued to nearby mining regions aboard the Sacramento Valley Railroad (far right).

A SPRINTING COURIER ON HORSEBACK

On April 3, 1860, Pony Express riders simultaneously left Saint Joseph, Missouri, and Sacramento to inaugurate mail service between those points. It was a victory for proponents of a central overland route, which would be followed nine years later by the Central Pacific Railroad.

The riders' parcels included newspapers, mail, and urgent messages—as of yet, there were no transcontinental telegraph lines. Local newspapers *(below, left)* marveled that dispatches could be sent from Saint Joseph through a series of relay stations and arrive in Sacramento in a mere 10 days—a vast improvement over the amount of time taken by the Butterfield stage line *(page 98)*.

Daring young riders like "Ras" Egan *(below)* overcame the perils of harsh, lonely terrain, bad weather, and bandits. Two days after the completion of transcontinental telegraph lines in October 1861, the Pony Express went out of business.

NEWS!!

PONY EXPRESS AT CARSON CITY.

[SPECIAL DISPATCH TO THE ALTA CALIFORNIA.]

TEN DAYS LATER.

St. Louis Dates to 12th April.

Eight Days and Nineteen Hours on the Way......... Rhode Island Democratic.........Row in Congress ....American Vessel Stopped by a Spanish Steamer......Siege of Vera Cruz Abandoned...... Eight Days Later from Europe.........Liverpool Dates to March 29th......The Two Annexations Finished......Excommunication of Victor Emanuel......An Occasion of National Rejoicing.... End of the Moorish War.

[Prepared by our Special Correspond— thence by Express to St. Joseph's, t— to Carson City, thence by tel— the Alta Californi—

Richard Erastus "Ras" Egan, an 18-year-old Pony Express rider, once found himself riding at night through a knee-deep snowstorm between Fort Crittenden and Rush Valley in Utah Territory. He tried to navigate through the darkness by keeping the wind on his right cheek. But as the night wore on he failed to notice that the wind changed direction, and he ended up back at Fort Crittenden at daybreak. He quickly changed horses and sped to Rush Valley, having ridden 150 miles without rest or relief.

closely not only construction costs but the freight traffic to be expected. Judah concluded that the railroad would be easy to build, with no steep grades or difficult obstacles, and thus easy to run. "With such a road and such a business," he wrote, "it is difficult to conceive a more profitable undertaking."

The directors told Judah to go ahead with the final survey, a work of several months. Anna, meanwhile, did what she could to fill the time. She took up sketching, joining Theodore on weekends to capture views of the landscapes and share a picnic lunch with him when he took a break from his feverish recording of measurements and calculations for the final survey. Mostly, she listened. He raved not only about the prospects for this railroad, but also about its potential as the first link in a vast transcontinental system.

Judah finished the final survey and cost estimate in late summer, projecting expenses of $45,000 per mile, or $1.8 million in all. In February 1855, 100 men wielding picks and shovels began grading the roadbed from Sacramento. Another 400 men joined them in March. In June, straining winches eased a 15-ton locomotive and 400 tons of rails from a riverboat onto the Sacramento levee. In August, Judah and three other men took the first trip on the new railroad, by handcar, for about 100 yards.

Once two miles of track had been laid, from the levee to the outskirts of Sacramento, Judah began running a locomotive and three flatcars along the spur, conducting tours for the press and public. He was intent on keeping enthusiasm for the railroad at a fever pitch, even as the project became enmeshed in financial problems. A gold panic depressed the California economy in the summer of 1855 and led to bank failures. The railroad began missing payments on its debt and was forced to shorten the length of the line under construction. The tracks would end at Folsom, 22 miles northeast of Sacramento, instead of at Marysville.

In the midst of this crisis, the company reorganized, removing Wilson as president and adding to the board of directors a former army officer from Ohio named William Tecumseh Sherman, who had ventured to California and was trying his hand as a banker. Sherman would soon come to share Judah's conviction that building a transcontinental railroad required support from the U.S. government. Spanning the continent with rails was the "work of giants," Sherman would declare, adding that "Uncle Sam is the only giant I know who can grapple with the subject."

The reorganized Sacramento Valley Railroad, meanwhile, set its construction crews laboring long hours, while Judah continued to promote its services. He led excursions along the finished track, always including any available newspaper reporters. By January 1856, 18 miles of track were in regular operation, bringing in more than $200 per day. Once the line to Folsom was completed in February, the railroad began shuttling overcrowded passenger cars and heavily laden freight cars back and forth. But the cost of construction had been greater than Judah anticipated, and the railroad still owed Robinson, Seymour & Company $700,000 at annual interest rates of up to 30 percent. As railroad officials struggled with the debt, it dawned on them that they had built the line too late. The Sierra gold mines were playing out, and the miners were moving on to new strikes in Nevada.

With the Sacramento Valley Railroad barred from expanding by its financial plight, Judah had no work to do and needed a new challenge. He decided that private investors were not equal to the task of building a railroad, certainly not the transcontinental line he dreamed of. The government would have to help. He would go to Washington.

Washington, D.C., had a great deal in common with Sacramento in 1856, laying plans with limitless optimism amid unpromising surroundings. Along the Potomac River, between the stubby beginning of a monument to George Washington and a truncated, domeless Capitol, ran open sewers, dirt roads, and grazing animals. Washington buzzed with talk of power and America's manifest destiny to bestride the continent, just as Sacramento pulsed with dreams of gold and sudden wealth. But when

Theodore Judah arrived in Washington, after escorting Anna to her family home in Massachusetts, he encountered something he had not seen in New England or California: black slaves tending to the legislators and dignitaries of the South. Slavery offended him, and the tensions it created between North and South threatened his dream by making it hard for legislators to agree on a transcontinental route.

Railroad projects were not new to Washington. In 1853 Congress had instructed the secretary of war, Jefferson Davis, to dispatch army engineers to survey several promising railroad routes across the continent. One of those was the central route Judah advocated, which would follow the existing Mormon Trail from Nebraska to Utah and continue on across the Great Basin and the Sierra to the heart of California. But there were strong partisans of other options, including a northern route that would link the upper Midwest with the Northwest coast, and a southern line that would run from Texas to Los Angeles.

The army's two-year survey of the various options had yielded a 12-volume report on such things as the weather along the proposed routes, the flora and fauna encountered, and the abundance or scarcity of grass and buffalo. In Judah's view, all this was beside the point. Someone who was considering investing in a railroad, he insisted, needed detailed estimates of the construction costs and the expected revenues. None of this was to be found in the army's 12 volumes. Congress could have an "actual and reliable" survey of the central route, he said, for only $200,000.

To his immense frustration, Judah found the members of Congress indifferent to his arguments. They were caught up in the worsening strife between North and South. Northerners feared that a southern railroad would carry slaves and their masters westward into the territories of New Mexico and Arizona and lead to the creation of more slave states. Southerners believed that a northern or central route would help populate more free states and leave the slave states hopelessly outnumbered in Congress.

When Judah rejoined Anna in Massachusetts he was raging with disappointment and anger. But he

ORDEAL IN A MOUNTAIN PASS

The emigrant party of 87 organized by Illinois farmer George Donner set out for California with high hopes in April 1846. But a series of mishaps slowed their progress, and time was of the essence if they were to cross the Sierra Nevada before snow made the mountains treacherous. A guidebook the party was using described a trail that promised to shave many miles, and presumably days, from the trek. At the urging of James Reed, a party leader, the wagon train left the well-traveled California Trail in southwestern Wyoming and struck off on the shortcut.

The decision cost precious time, for the trail had to be widened to accommodate Reed's oversize custom-built wagon. In late summer the party ran into ominously e[ ] snow in Utah's Great Salt Desert. More[ ] fronted them in the Sierra in October, [ ] November they were immobilized in a clogged pass that would one day bear Donner's name. With only makeshift sh[ ] and dwindling provisions, the travelers found themselves in a perilous situatio[ ]

On December 16, 15 adults set ou[ ] snowshoes to seek help. A month late[ ] women and two men reached Sutter's at present-day Sacramento. Rescue p[ ] found 46 survivors, many of whom ha[ ] resorted to cannibalism. The Reed fa[ ] did not, but 13-year-old Virginia reca[ ] how they ate the family dog—"his he[ ] and feet & hide & evry thing about hi[ ]

JAMES AND MARGARET REED

Eight-year-old Patty Reed, shown here in her teens, was separated from her mother by rescuers intent on saving the children first. "If we never see each other again," Patty told her, "do the best you can, God will take care of us."

Young Virginia Reed wrote, "We went over great hye moun-tai . . . in snow up to our knees litle James walk over the hole way . . . in snow up to his waist, he said every step he took he was a gitting nigher Pa and something to eat."

Years after the ordeal, Virginia Reed recalled that her sister Patty kept the doll below "hidden away in her bosom" and carried it "day and night through all of our trials."

was not defeated. During the voyage back to San Francisco he devised a new strategy for promoting a railroad across the continent. Congress might ignore the arguments of one man, he reasoned, but it could not long ignore the demands of an entire region.

Even for San Francisco, the major metropolis of the West Coast, the meeting convened in Assembly Hall on September 20, 1859, was of unusual interest and import. More than 100 official delegates, from every California county and from Oregon and Washington as well, gathered to urge Congress to support a transcontinental railroad. Theodore Judah held no official title other than that of delegate from Sacramento. But those on hand understood that after his mission to Washington three years earlier, he had promoted this railroad convention and would have a great deal to say about its outcome.

The prospects for linking the Pacific to the Atlantic by rail looked bleak. Another financial panic had recently swept the country, the production of the California gold fields continued to slacken, and competition from steamship, stagecoach, and freight wagon companies was fierce. Yet Theodore had pressed for a transcontinental railroad with such zeal that weary listeners had begun referring to him as Crazy Judah. Partly at his urging, California state legislators had passed a resolution calling for the railroad convention that September.

Many of the delegates who assembled in San Francisco came to promote railroad routes that would benefit their communities at the expense of others. It would be a daunting task to build a consensus, but Theodore and Anna Judah came equipped to try. Anna had spent the summer compiling maps, charts, graphs, and sketches that supported in a concise and visually memorable way the arguments for a railroad across America. At the convention she set up an exhibit of her material, then circulated among the delegates, indulging in what

This transit compass belonging to Theodore Judah was probably among the equipment he used when he surveyed the Donner Pass region in 1861. In a letter to Anna describing the survey, Judah's exhaustive schedule is apparent: "I get my breakfast and am off by sunrise every morning—and in the saddle all day long over hills mountains ravines and etc. And come home tired out—then in evening I have four men at work till after ten PM plotting up work. . . ." He added regretfully that there was "no time" for him to visit her.

seemed to be social chatter. In fact, she was keeping a constant tally of votes and opinions.

Theodore, for his part, deftly skirted the divisive issue of which route to select by proposing to delegates that the matter be left to "those capitalists who are willing to embark their money in the enterprise." The important thing, he argued, was to attract major investors to the project by persuading Congress to provide financial incentives to companies engaged in surveying and building a transcontinental railroad. The convention endorsed that idea and appointed Judah to carry the message to Washington. On October 20, mandate in hand, Theodore and Anna once again boarded a ship for the East. The journey itself was to offer Judah a crucial opportunity.

Traveling on the same ship, as Judah well knew, was the newly elected congressman from California, John A. Burch. A captive, albeit willing, audience, Burch later recalled that "no day passed on the voyage to New York that we did not discuss the subject, lay plans for its success and indulge pleasant anticipations of the wonderful benefits certain to follow that success." Burch would go on to lead the fight for the legislation Judah proposed on the floor of the House.

In the capital, Judah found the North-South antagonism worse than it had been on his previous visit. Just 55 miles away, at Harpers Ferry, Virginia, the abolitionist John Brown had attacked the Federal arsenal in search of guns to arm an insurrection of slaves and was on trial for his life. Appalled Southerners were clamoring for his execution, while abolitionists declared him a hero. Congress was consumed with talk of disunion, insurrection, even civil war. It had no time for Judah's railroad. In desperation, he obtained an audience with the aging President James Buchanan, who was rumored to be so distraught by the fracturing of his country that he spent his days weeping and praying. At the close of their brief conversation, the saddened president told Judah, "For-

During his 1861 surveying trip to Donner Pass, seen here overlooking Donner Lake, Judah wrote his wife urging her to join him "and try camp life a while." Anna arrived with the items her husband had suggested: a pillow, two pillowslips, two sheets, a large comforter, reading matter, a book to press flowers, and needlework.

get the railroad, young man, until we see what is going to happen to the country."

Rebuffed at the White House, Judah at least got permission to display in a room at the Capitol the maps and other materials that Anna had compiled for the railroad convention and brought east, along with samples of California's minerals, fossils, and flora. This exhibit appealed to Washingtonians, who were intrigued by the West and relieved to have something to discuss other than sectional strife. Hundreds of people toured the display, and few escaped being subjected to Judah's courteous but impassioned advocacy.

In December, John Brown was convicted and hanged. After Christmas, Congressman Burch introduced the legislation requested by the railroad convention. Confident that his recent efforts had prepared the way for passage, Judah watched in dismay as Congress tabled the bill for future consideration. He closed the railroad exhibit and returned with Anna to California. As in the past, his deep discouragement soon gave way to renewed optimism. Congress would come through with financial support, he believed, once a route across the Sierra had been surveyed and powerful investors had agreed to back the railroad. In this confident frame of mind he prepared a bill for his expenses as the convention's delegate to Washington, listing only $40 for printing circulars. When Anna pointed out that the cost of travel brought their expenses to at least $2,500, he simply smiled and told her, "The transcontinental railroad will be built, and I will have a part in building it." Anna wondered wistfully whether she was "married to a man or a railroad."

The silence itself may have awakened him. The myriad small sounds of the night creatures, the lullaby that usually soothes wilderness campers, had ceased. Daniel "Doc" Strong sat up, careful for the moment not to awaken Theodore Judah, who lay snoring next to him in their hut. It was October 1860, and the two men were high in the mountains, 90 miles northeast of Sacramento, searching for a path that would carry a railroad through the heart of the Sierra.

Strong, the pharmacist and medical practitioner of Dutch Flat, a small town roughly midway up the western slope of the Sierra, was no stranger to conditions in the high country, having explored its passes as an amateur surveyor. But as he peered out into the darkness, he met with a startling sight. It was snowing. Already a thick blanket lay on the trees and ground. That was why there were no night sounds. The sight was beautiful, and deadly. The two men had assumed that the weather would remain fine until later in the fall, as it sometimes did. They were not equipped nor supplied for a long stay in snow and cold, and no one knew where they were. They had to get out, and fast.

Doc Strong awakened Judah, and together they hastily struck camp and loaded their packhorses. As they prepared to leave, they may well have reflected on the misfortune that befell another party stranded in the vicinity by unforeseen storms. In October 1846 a group of emi-

A GLIMPSE OF THE SIERRA NEVADA

An exhibit that Anna Judah assembled to promote her husband's plan for a transcontinental railroad was put on display at the U.S. Capitol in 1862, when Theodore returned to Washington to lobby for passage of the Pacific Railroad Act. Designed to represent California's natural beauty, the exhibit included pressed wildflowers that Anna had gathered near Donner Pass (below), a herbarium of live mountain plants, and her sketches and paintings of the region.

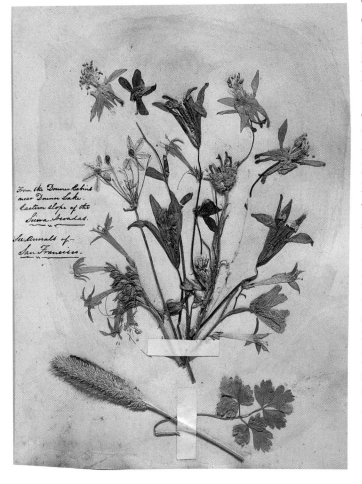

grants bound for California had become snowbound in a nearby pass with little food or shelter. By the time they were rescued more than two months later, roughly half of their number had died, and the desperate survivors had resorted to cannibalism. The tragedy had become a legend of the West, and the pass would later bear the surname of the two brothers who had organized the ill-fated party—Jacob and George Donner.

As the Donner party discovered, the Sierra Nevada posed a formidable obstacle to east-west travel. Extending northwestward from the Mojave Desert for nearly 400 miles, the range of steep granite peaks included some of the loftiest mountains in America. Mount Whitney in the south would be designated in 1864 as the nation's highest, at an elevation of 14,494 feet. From late fall through early spring, prevailing winds shoved moisture from the Pacific Ocean against the mountaintops, producing blinding snowstorms that transformed inviting gaps in the range like Donner Pass into deathtraps.

Doc Strong and Theodore Judah escaped before the deepening drifts made travel impossible. Floundering through the night and well into the next day, relying often on the judgment of their horses, they struggled back down the west slope of the Sierra to Dutch Flat, about 25 miles from their campsite.

Judah had Doc Strong to thank for the adventure. Earlier in the fall, Judah had just returned to Sacramento from one of many fruitless searches for a Sierra pass suitable for a railroad when he found a letter waiting for him from Strong. The pharmacist reported that while investigating a path that might carry wagons over the Sierra to Dutch Flat, he had come upon a route he thought would serve well for a railroad, which required a gentler incline than a wagon trail. Judah caught the next stage to Dutch Flat, met the sunburned, muscular Strong—who looked to Judah more like a prospector than a doctor—and followed him into the high Sierra.

The climb began like a railroader's dream, a long, easy slope up from Dutch Flat between the south fork of the Yuba River and the north fork of the American River. And it continued like that much of the way to Donner Pass. To be sure, there were gaps and cliffs to be negotiated, but as Judah noted altitude readings and the requirements for trestles and tunnels, he grew ever more hopeful. He was experienced enough, however, to restrain his excitement until he could see how the route ran down the eastern slope of the Sierra.

When Judah and Strong reached the crest of Donner Pass, roughly 7,000 feet above sea level, they looked out on an exhilarating view. To the south, Crested Peak rose another 2,000 feet into the sky.

Ever attuned to finances, Judah appraised the business potential as favorable. The discovery in the late 1850s of the fabulous Comstock Lode of gold and silver in western Nevada, near the California border and the proposed railroad, would generate freight revenues that he projected at five million dollars a year. In his enthusiasm, he underestimated both the cost of building the line and the problems that would confront the construction crews. But his calculations demonstrated that the route was feasible. Judah gathered his papers, slapped down his pen, and announced his conclusion to Doc Strong: As far as he was concerned, the transcontinental railroad would cross the Sierra by way of Dutch Flat and Donner Pass.

Judah wrote up a brochure and shared his findings with the *Sacramento Union,* which ran the story on November 9, three days after the election of Abraham

"Everything he did from the time he went to California to the day of his death was for the great continental Pacific railway. Time, money, brains, strength, body and soul were absorbed." ANNA JUDAH, OF HER HUSBAND, THEODORE

Below them to the east, they saw the gleam of Donner Lake. Beyond the lake lay the Truckee River, which descended gradually to the Nevada desert. The snowstorm hit before the two men could explore the steep terrain from the crest of the pass to the banks of the Truckee, but Judah was confident that a railroad could be built there.

After struggling back from the camp to the safety of Doc Strong's store in Dutch Flat, Judah was too excited to take more than a brief rest. Then he spread out his notes and maps and began working feverishly on the new route, a project that absorbed him for hours. The distance from Sacramento to the crest of the pass Judah figured to be 102 miles; from there, he estimated, it was only another 13 miles to the Nevada line. The ascent to the pass was remarkably steady, rising at a maximum rate, he later calculated, of 105 feet per mile—acceptable for a locomotive. Although a number of trestles and tunnels would have to be built, he saw no insuperable obstacles along the way.

Lincoln as president. Judah then drew up articles of incorporation for the Central Pacific Railroad of California. The company's initial objective, and an ambitious one, was to lay down rails from Sacramento to the Nevada border. From there, Judah hoped, the Central Pacific might link up with a railroad to the east and complete the transcontinental route.

First, however, serious financial obstacles had to be overcome. By 1860 there had been so many railroad scams in California that the state required capitalization of $1,000 per mile of track before it would incorporate a railroad company. In three days Judah and Strong received pledges of nearly $50,000 from investors in Dutch Flat and four other towns along the proposed route, but that was not even half what they needed to cover the 115 miles of track from Sacramento to the Nevada border. Judah thought he knew where to get the rest—San Francisco.

Encouraged by the city's financial elite, he invited potential investors to an organizational meeting.

"I have struck a lucky streak," he wrote Doc Strong beforehand, "and shall fill up the list without any further trouble." But as the meeting progressed, the businessmen of San Francisco raised serious questions: Would Congress pass legislation providing financial support for the railroad? Could the line really make money? Would the Comstock Lode play out, leaving the railroad short of customers? Would civil war erupt and drain the resources needed to complete the project? To men without Judah's emotional stake in the project, the risks seemed too great. They would not invest in his railroad.

Judah made a defiant prediction. Within two years, he told Anna, the men who had rebuffed him would give "all they hope to have from their present enterprises to have what they put away tonight."

The next time Judah made his presentation, it was in the familiar surroundings of Sacramento, among businessmen who knew him well. But the outcome was the same: His listeners would not part with their money. Judah, dejected, was watching

In his survey of the region between Dutch Flat and Donner Pass, Theodore Judah paused every mile or so to take readings of temperature and atmospheric pressure, which he compiled in his notebook under columns headed "Therm" and "Aneroid." He used the changes in atmospheric pressure, which was measured with an aneroid barometer, to determine changes in altitude.

them file out of the room when Collis P. Huntington sidled over and murmured: "You are going about this thing in the wrong way. If you want to come into my office some evening I will talk to you about the road."

Huntington had become a legend in Sacramento for his tight-fisted business acumen. A lean, hard-muscled man, six feet two inches tall, with clear, blue gray eyes, he was reserved and forceful. And he never missed an opportunity to turn a profit. At the age of 14 he had run away from his Connecticut home and spent more than a decade working as a farm hand, clerk, and grocer in upstate New York. He saved his money nickel by nickel, putting together enough to buy a shipment of dry goods for resale and then heading with the merchandise for California in 1849.

Leaving the chancy hunt for gold to others, Huntington set out his goods under a tent in Sacramento. When it came time to renew his stock, he would back the next step toward creation of the railroad—a complete survey of the Dutch Flat route.

To help fund that survey and provide the tens of thousands of dollars the railroad still needed from investors to incorporate under state law, Huntington induced Hopkins to join him in the venture and also recruited two other wealthy friends. One was Leland Stanford, a Sacramento dealer in oil and groceries with powerful political ambitions. He had grown up near Albany, New York, which had been transformed by the opening of the Mohawk & Hudson Railroad. Stanford's father had opened a hotel along the line and set his seven sons to work cutting wood for the locomotives. Stanford himself was a large, beefy man, with a dark and determined visage. Like Huntington, he was laconic, but he did not share Huntington's aversion to public attention. Since arriving in California in 1852, he had become

"We could not borrow a dollar of money on the faith of the company. Mr. Stanford, Mr. Huntington, Mr. Hopkins, and myself had to give our personal obligations for the money necessary to carry us from month to month....Those were the responsibilities we took, and if we had not done it, there would have been no railroad." CHARLES CROCKER

made it a policy to buy low and sell as high as possible. "I'll never be remembered," he once said, "for the money I've given away." Soon he had five tents. By the time Judah met him he was part owner of Huntington & Hopkins Company, a hardware store that was one of Sacramento's leading businesses. Although not yet 40, he was known as Old Huntington, no doubt in recognition of his humorless, parsimonious ways. He was as careful with words as he was with a dollar, and thus his laconic invitation to Judah carried all the more promise.

With hopes high again, Judah spent an evening explaining the whole project to the silent Huntington. Then he spent another evening facing a barrage of questions from Huntington's friends, including his partner in the store, Mark Hopkins, a thin, sad-eyed bookkeeper who detested risk taking. At the end of the session, Huntington announced that he

a prominent figure in the state's Republican party. He had lost in his first bid for governor in 1859, but he would soon try again.

The other recruit, Charles Crocker, provided a marked contrast to the three quiet businessmen he joined. Wielding a hard stare, a loud voice, a profane vocabulary, and a bottomless appetite for hard work, the 250-pound Crocker relished his nickname, Bull. At the age of 10 he had peddled newspapers on a New York dock. Later, as a teenager, he dug stumps from a hardscrabble Indiana homestead, then made his way overland to California to open a grocery store that served the goldminers. Since 1852 he had prospered as a dry-goods merchant in Sacramento, but he was less proud of his wealth than of his status as a rough leader of rough men.

When Judah met with Stanford and Crocker, he set aside talk of the larger ideas of national union

LELAND STANFORD

CHARLES CROCKER

MARK HOPKINS

COLLIS P. HUNTINGTON

and Manifest Destiny and spoke instead to their wallets: "You are tradesmen of Sacramento city; your property, your business is here. Help me to make the survey. I will make you the company." Once Congress had come through with financial backing for the line, Judah added, "you will have control of business interests that will make your fortune in trade." Then, in an effort to make their investment seem safe, he added words he would later regret: "Why, you can have a wagon road if not a railroad."

After the meeting, Judah returned to Anna, awaiting him in their Sacramento apartment. This time, he was jubilant. "Anna," he proclaimed, "the door has opened up for us." Huntington, Hopkins, Stanford, and Crocker—the men who would be known to history as the Big Four of the Central Pacific Railroad—had each subscribed for 150 shares of the new company at $100 a share, as had a fifth investor who was not closely aligned with the others, James Bailey. Judah, for his part, was assigned 150 shares without having to offer even the minimum 10 percent down payment expected of stockholders. He understood that the shares were offered as compensation for his work and expenses in advancing the project thus far.

By March 1861, Judah was ready to start the survey from Sacramento to the Truckee River. "If you want to see the first work on the Pacific Railroad, look out of your bedroom window," he told Anna. "I am going to have these men pay for it." Even in the worst times, Anna had never been as depressed as her husband. Now, she was not as exultant. She worried about the reputations of the big investors for hard business dealing, and she noted that their commitment to Judah was merely verbal. But she managed to say, "I am glad, for it is about time somebody else helped."

Three events of great significance for the railroad, the state of California, and the nation followed in the months to come. On April 12, 1861, Confederate forces fired on the Federal garrison at Fort Sumter, South Carolina, beginning the Civil War. In mid-June, Leland Stanford was nominated as the Republican candidate for governor of California. And on June 28, the Central Pacific Railroad was formally incorporated, with Stanford as president, Huntington as vice president with considerable responsibility for running the company, Hopkins as secretary and treasurer, Crocker as a director, and Judah as chief engineer.

If Judah had thought that his knowledge of railroad building would give him a free hand, he was mistaken: He soon learned that he was working for strong, opinionated men not in the habit of deferring to others. The directors of the Central Pacific wanted the Donner Pass route surveyed, but they also wanted to evaluate other possible routes through the Sierra before beginning construction. Huntington would accompany Judah on an exploration of one alternative, along the Feather River, which proved to be impracticable. After lengthy investigation, the directors would conclude that the route from Dutch Flat through Donner Pass was indeed the most promising path.

Before a route could be pinned down and construction could begin, however, the Central Pacific needed backing from Congress. Without it, no banks would lend to the fledgling railroad, and it was unlikely that individual investors would come forward in sufficient numbers to provide the estimated $12 million needed to build the road. Thus, in October 1861 Judah again traveled to Washington to lobby for a railroad bill. Three months earlier a Confederate army had routed Federal forces at Bull Run, not far from Washington, D.C. Getting Congress to focus on a railroad project under such trying circumstances would be a challenge. But Judah and his backers among the California legislators shrewdly tailored their arguments to suit the crisis. They talked of binding the Far West to the Union with bands of iron track, of assuring timely delivery of the gold and silver that the war effort would require, of defending loyal California from secessionists within the state's borders and beyond. Other members of Congress began to see a need for the railroad

At a historic meeting on April 30, 1861, on the second floor of the Huntington & Hopkins hardware store *(left)* the businessmen shown above—later known as the Big Four—became directors of the Central Pacific Railroad, which was formally incorporated two months later. Once used as Huntington's living quarters, the second floor served as the headquarters of the railroad between 1862 and 1873.

and to consider the details. With no representatives from the slave states to contend with, Judah found it easier to build support for the central route.

The matter was referred to three committees for study, and Judah managed to have himself appointed to the staff of each one. In the end he virtually wrote the legislation, which called for the construction of railroad and telegraph lines from the "Missouri River to the Pacific Ocean." This railroad act eventually passed both houses of Congress and was signed into law by President Lincoln on July 1, 1862.

The act commissioned two companies to build 1,800 miles of track. The Central Pacific would build eastward from Sacramento while the Union Pacific Railroad, which had yet to be incorporated, would head west from Omaha, Nebraska. The Union Pacific would soon attract prominent investors, for the terms of the railroad act appeared generous. It promised the two companies government loans ranging from $16,000 to $48,000 per mile, depending on the terrain traversed, after completion of each 40-mile segment or, in mountainous

terrain, after each 20-mile segment. Furthermore, each company was granted a 400-foot-wide right of way through public lands and up to 10 square miles of additional public land for each mile of track laid.

To Huntington and his partners in Sacramento the act offered hefty incentives. But they first had to lay down enough track to capitalize on the opportunity. Huntington reportedly likened the legislative victory to cornering an elephant: "Now let us see if we can harness him up."

January 8, 1863, dawned clear and mild in Sacramento, a welcome change after three weeks of frequent heavy rains. The streets were a quagmire, and the Sacramento River was running out of its banks. During the late morning, townspeople and visitors began to assemble on Front Street before a bunting-draped platform. Most of the ladies stayed in their carriages, sunk hub deep in mud, or watched

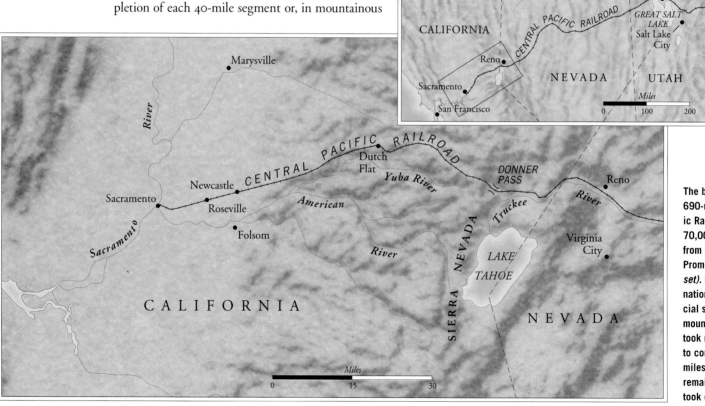

The builders of the 690-mile Central Pacific Railroad laid some 70,000 tons of rail from Sacramento to Promontory, Utah (inset). Due to the combination of early financial setbacks and mountainous terrain, it took nearly five years to complete the 154 miles to Reno (left); the remaining 536 miles took only 10 months.

from second-floor balconies. Men and boys perched on hay bales thrown down in the muck.

At noon, Charles Crocker, now bearing the title of General Superintendent of the Railroad, bellowed at the crowd to be silent, introduced a minister who intoned a lengthy invocation, and then proclaimed: "The Governor of California, Leland Stanford, will now shovel the first earth of the great Pacific Railroad." After that ritual, Stanford and six other notables made lengthy speeches, laden with optimism. A band played, and the crowd raised nine hearty cheers. "This is no idle ceremony," insisted Crocker as he concluded the celebration. For even then, he announced, railroad workers were "driving piles for the foundation of the bridge across the American River," at the eastern end of town.

Through all this, Judah stood quietly by the platform, harboring more than a few misgivings. The day's forced enthusiasm masked serious troubles and deep divisions within the young railroad company. Judah had worked through the summer and fall of 1862 to complete the final survey for the road, write specifications for each job, and investigate all bidders to make sure they had the necessary manpower and resources. In December he had presented the first set of contracts, ready to let, to the board of directors, only to discover that the Big Four, who dominated the board, had ideas of their own. They would be in tight financial straits until the first 40 miles of track were completed and federal loans were forthcoming. The only people who could conceivably make money from the Central Pacific in the short term would be the contractors paid to build it. At the December meeting, the directors preempted Judah by taking up a motion to award the building of the first 18 miles of the railroad to Charles Crocker & Company, in which the other members of the Big Four allegedly had a stake.

Judah protested that it would be unethical for the company to award the costly job to one of its own directors. The response was well rehearsed. Crocker cheerfully resigned as a director to devote himself to the contracting company, nominating as his replacement on the board his brother, Edwin B. Crocker, the company's attorney. Still Judah objected. He was the railroad builder, he pointed out, and the chief engineer. Surely it was only sensible to let him oversee the details of the contracts. No one argued with his assertion that Charles Crocker had no experience whatsoever in railroad building. As the merchant himself would say later, "I could not have measured a cut any more than I could have flown." The directors listened patiently to Judah's arguments, then ignored him, voting to give the contract to Crocker's company.

The company was paid $350,000 in cash and $60,000 in stock and bonds—not nearly enough, it turned out, to cover the cost of building the first 18 miles. Charles Crocker could not be faulted for lack of effort. He sold his dry-goods business and plunged into his railroad work, bullying, yelling, racing from place to place, often flinging off his coat and wielding a shovel to demonstrate how he wanted earth moved. Despite his energy, the work got off to a bad start. Although the first stretch of tracks was across level ground, the roadbed had to be raised to guard against flooding. And the earth was hard to move, with only one foot or so of topsoil overlying a hard conglomerate of rock, pebbles, and sand. After a few weeks 200 workers had created not a continuous roadbed but a series of disconnected mounds across the floor of the valley. Many of the men had drifted off in search of easier money in the mines.

Judah was tempted to step back and let Crocker fail in order to regain control of the contracting process. But the consequences for the railroad would have been grim. Instead, Judah exercised his authority as chief engineer to insist that the construction work be done properly. The directors soon realized that they would need more cash, and quickly. Local investors remained wary of the Central Pacific, and Huntington went east to see if he could stir up interest among financiers in Boston and New York.

Governor Stanford, meanwhile, improved the railroad's prospects somewhat with a little creative geography. Although the directors had originally agreed to pay the Crocker construction company some $23,000 per mile to build the first stretch of railroad and would spend far more than that before the task was done, the railroad act offered reimbursement of only $16,000 per mile for such "easy ground." Once the tracks reached the foothills, some 20 miles east of Sacramento, the reimbursement rate would climb to $32,000 per mile. Stanford brought the hills closer with a stroke of the pen. Citing the testimony of the state geologist and other experts that the terrain began to ascend ever so gently seven miles east of Sacramento, he argued that the foothills began there and referred his case to Washington. Judah denounced what he considered a flagrant act of deception, insisting that "President Lincoln will never consent to such a scheme." But Lincoln wanted the railroad built and sided with Stanford. As California congressman Aaron Sargent put it wryly, "Abraham's faith has moved mountains."

Huntington, for his part, failed to move many East Coast financiers. He returned to Sacramento in June 1863 virtually empty-handed, but he retained high hopes for another money-making plan that had been in the works for a while. The plan went back to something Judah had said in persuading the Big Four to invest in the project: "You can have a wagon road if not a railroad." Judah had meant a road that, although built for the purpose of carrying materials to the railroad crews, could incidentally bring in some revenue. But Huntington and his colleagues had since invested in the Dutch Flat and Donner Lake wagon road to the boom town of Virginia City, Nevada, near the Comstock Lode, so that they could collect tolls on freight and passenger traffic moving to and from the mines while the railroad was still under construction. Once the tracks reached Dutch Flat,

DUTCH FLAT WAGON ROAD.

This new route over the Mountains, by way of Dutch Flat and Donner Lake, can now be traveled by Teams without load, and will be open for loaded Teams

JUNE 15th, 1864.

IT IS

The Shortest, Best and Cheapest Route to Washoe, Humboldt and Reese River.

Its grade going East at no place exceeds ten inches to the rod, and it is wide enough for Two Teams to pass without difficulty. All teams coming West, without load, can travel the New Road FREE OF TOLL until further notice. All those taking loads at Newcastle, the terminus of the Central Pacific Railroad, three miles from Auburn, can travel the New Road going East, Free of Toll, up to July 1, 1864.

Teams starting from Virginia City will take the Henness Pass Road to Ingram's, at Sardine Valley, where the New Road turns off to the left.

CHARLES CROCKER,

Sacramento, June 6, 1864   Pres't of the Co.

Charles Crocker issued this notice touting the new Dutch Flat Wagon Road, which carried toll-paying travelers over the Sierra to the Nevada mining town of Virginia City. One rider recalled the toll road, shown opposite, as "wide, well watered, and with a stream of prairie schooners and wagons passing over it in both directions."

travelers could transfer there from trains to wagons, and the revenues would help offset the steep cost of building the railroad over the high Sierra.

It was a sound business proposition, but Judah opposed it, fearing that it would hurt rather than help the railroad. He suspected that the money for completing the wagon road would come from funds paid to Charles Crocker for railroad construction, and he worried that if the wagon road proved profitable, the Big Four might never lay tracks east of Dutch Flat. Newspapers in San Francisco were charging as much in articles that referred ominously to the "Great Dutch Flat Swindle." The press alleged that the greedy moneymen in Sacramento had no intention of building a railroad beyond Dutch Flat once the federal government reimbursed them for reaching that town, 65 miles from the state capital.

In fact, the Big Four still had much to gain by completing the railroad to the Nevada border and beyond. But Judah's relations with them had so deteriorated that he no longer trusted in them to see the project through. "I had a blow out about two weeks ago," he wrote to Doc Strong after one board meeting, "and freed my mind, so much so that I looked for instant decapitation. I called things by their right names and invited war; but council of peace prevailed and my head is still on; my hands are tied, however."

Weary of Judah's constant carping, the Big Four took to gathering on their own. That summer they moved to shore up the financial condition of the Central Pacific by raising cash from stockholders. Small investors who had signed up for shares with down payments were required to pay up in full, and those who failed to do so forfeited their holdings. In Judah's case, the Big Four asked that he make the 10 percent down payment he had earlier been exempted from. Judah protested that he owed nothing, because his stock had

been offered to him in payment for his work. But as Anna had pointed out at the time, he had only a verbal agreement to that effect. This was how business was done, Huntington now informed Judah.

At least one other member of the board resented the way business was being done, however, and sided with Judah. James Bailey, now serving as secretary of the company, balked when the Big Four resolved at a subsequent board meeting that the expenses of the railroad would have to be borne equally by the remaining stockholders. Bailey and Judah preferred to raise cash by mortgaging the railroad's equipment and roadbed, but Huntington spoke for the Big Four in rejecting that option. "Let's go slow and steady and own what we build," he insisted.

Huntington then moved to resolve the bitter boardroom dispute by demanding that Bailey either sell his stake in the company or buy out the Big Four, who were prepared to unload the troubled company provided that the terms were right. Bailey responded that he was neither buying nor selling. "Then there's only one alternative," Huntington shot back. "The work must stop at once." He left the meeting, rode out to the construction site, and brought the project to a halt. The standoff continued for two weeks while Bailey desperately tried to raise the money needed to buy out the Big Four. He could not do it, and had no choice in the end but to yield and sell.

With Bailey on the way out, Judah was eager to be done with the Big Four. He would do well if he sold

WORKHORSE OF THE CENTRAL PACIFIC

The wood-fired *Gov. Stanford* was the first locomotive on the Central Pacific to haul passengers as well as freight. Distinctive features of the 56,000-pound engine included a large, funnel-shaped smokestack to trap sparks, an enclosed cab, and a cowcatcher. The headlight was added later, since trains did not run at night during the railroad's early years.

out to them, for despite the disagreement over the down payment for his shares, his stake in the company had grown and was now worth nearly $100,000. In the end, he agreed to sell, but he retained the option of buying out the Big Four if he could attract financiers to back him. There were no good prospects in California, so he wrote to every influential person in the East who might be of assistance. The struggle with the Big Four had exhausted him, and he was

CENTRAL PACIFIC RAILROAD.
NO. 1, TIME CARD NO. 1.
To take effect Monday June 6th, 1864, at 5 A. M.

TRAINS EASTWARD.				STATIONS.		TRAINS WESTWARD.	
Frt and Pass No 3	Frt and Pass No 2	Pass & Mail No 1.			Frt and Pass No 1	Pass & Mail No 2	Frt and Pass No 3
5 P M leave	1 P M leave	8·15 A M, 1		Sacramento..		8·45 A M arr	12 M arr.	6·40 P M ar.
5·30 }5·55 } mt frt	2·15	3·55	18	Junction....	18 4		11·20	3·55 }3·30 } mt Ft
6·09	2·38	7·05	22	Rocklin...	4 7·40	11·07	5·37
6·22	2·55	7·15 m et F	25	Pino..	3 7·15 mt pass	10·56	5·25..
6·40	3·30 P M arr	7·30 A M arr	31	Newcastle...	6 3·45 A M, L	10·30 A M, L	5 P M, L..

Trains No. 2 and 3 east, and 1 and 3 west, daily, except Sunday.
Trains No. 1 east and 2 west, daily.

LELAND STANFORD, President.

The Central Pacific's first timetable *(above)* was issued in 1864 after 31 miles of track had been completed.

near the breaking point. "You are killing yourself, dear Ted," Anna told him, "killing yourself."

Hoping to meet with potential investors, Judah and Anna sailed for New York in October, traveling via Panama, which could now be crossed by rail. Judah's goal, said one acquaintance, California congressman John Burch, "was to buy the Central Pacific Railroad and place its management in the hands of a new set of men of known public spirit who would, without other designs to hinder or obstruct them, prosecute diligently the main work of completing the

railroad from ocean to ocean." During the voyage Judah relaxed. He expressed "relief in being away from the scenes of contention and strife" and looked forward to an imagined triumph over the Big Four.

Anna hoped the trip might give him a new lease on life. Instead, it proved to be his undoing. After traveling by train across the Isthmus of Panama and transferring to a steamship at the Atlantic dockside station, he began to shiver and complain of a headache. Anna called the ship's doctor, who diagnosed Judah's illness as yellow fever and said there was nothing to be done. For the next eight days Anna sat beside her feverish, frequently delirious husband, listening to him rave about "my road." When they reached New York on October 26, Anna immediately summoned a trusted doctor friend. But he offered no hope.

That same week in Sacramento a small crowd gathered to watch workmen put in place the first rails of the Central Pacific Railroad. Someone had proposed another celebration, but Huntington did not want to "jubilate" yet, he told his colleagues: "Those mountains over there look too ugly, and I see too much work ahead of us. We may fail, and if we do I want to have as few people know it as we can. Anybody can drive the first spike, but there are many months of labor and unrest between the first and the last spike."

A week later, at dawn on November 2, 1863,

To make the 63-foot-deep, 800-foot-long Bloomer Cut *(left)*, the rock was first loosened with explosive charges, then picked and shoveled by hand into horse-drawn carts and used as fill at low points along the right of way. Leland Stanford reported to President Andrew Johnson that the grading in the Sierra was "very difficult and expensive, increasing as the line was pushed up the mountain slope. The cuttings have been deeper, the embankments higher, and more rock work encountered, as the line has progressed eastward."

On March 19, 1864, the principals of the Central Pacific Railroad, having scraped together enough cash to complete more than 20 miles of track, decided that it was time to jubilate, whether Huntington thought it appropriate or not. Shortly after 1:30 p.m., the line's first passenger-carrying locomotive, dubbed the *Gov. Stanford* and draped with bunting, chuffed out of Sacramento pulling two passenger cars crowded with officials and legislators and seven platform cars conveying other celebrators and a brass band.

The first 18 miles of the trip, across the valley to the little orchard town of Roseville, passed swiftly.

"The sun shone brightly out from among fleecy clouds," reporter Lauren Upson wrote for the *Sacramento Union*. "The vivid green of the plains was bedecked here and there with bright patches of yellow flowers, just opening in the warmth of spring-time, and the distant mountains looked darkly blue and sharp in outline." Despite the early problems and mistakes, Upson added, "everybody was pleased with the smooth and steady motion of the train, which showed how well the new track had been laid." The good condition of the road was a tribute not only to Judah but to the Big Four, who had entrusted the job of chief engineer to the capable Samuel S. Montague.

The rise in elevation was only 129 feet from Sacramento to Roseville, but thereafter, Upson noted, the topography changed. The train threaded its way "among beautifully rounded foothills, gemmed with groups of green trees—oaks, scrubby pines and buckeye clumps—with rocks picturesquely arranged in small cliffs, chasms and grottoes, while through the little valleys brooklets meandered." The excursion reached the end of the completed line four miles beyond Roseville. There the guests enjoyed a picnic of bread and cheese, accompanied by bottles "with something in them," as Upson put it. Leland Stanford and Charles Crocker made the obligatory speeches, and the train returned to Sacramento. It was all great fun, but as Huntington had predicted, hard "months of labor and unrest" lay just ahead for the Central Pacific.

Already the grading crews, who prepared the roadbed well ahead of the tracklayers, were advancing into difficult terrain. Thirteen miles beyond Roseville, near Newcastle, the rate of ascent reached the peak of 105 feet per mile, the grade it would maintain much of the way to the summit. And just beyond Newcastle, the crews confronted their first truly awesome challenge. There the route was blocked by a mound of rock that had been ground by glaciers into gravel and then compressed by natural forces into a cementlike mass. Through this barrier, the workers had to carve a path 800 feet long and 63 feet deep.

The crews attacked the Bloomer Cut, as it came to be known, with all the weapons at their disposal. They first used black-powder charges to loosen a few cubic feet of rock at a time, then hauled the debris off in one-horse carts or wheelbarrows, while others refined the cut with picks and shovels. The men put the debris to good use by dumping it in a gap up to 60 feet deep that the tracks would cross between Newcastle and the Bloomer Cut. It would take eight months of hard labor to prepare the Bloomer Cut and fill the gap for the laying of track.

The Central Pacific carried its first freight in late March 1864 and in April began regular passenger

"Now, if you want to jubilate over driving the first spike here, go ahead and do it. I don't. Those mountains over there look too ugly, and I see too much work ahead of us. We may fail, and if we do I want to have as few people know it as we can. Anybody can drive the first spike, but there are many months of labor and unrest between the first and the last spike."

COLLIS HUNTINGTON, SACRAMENTO, OCTOBER 1863

service from Sacramento to Roseville. In one week, it carried 298 passengers and collected $354.25 in fares. In June service to Newcastle began, and shortly thereafter the wagon road to Virginia City was completed. That road alone would soon be taking in one million dollars a year in tolls. As of yet, however, the revenues were a mere trickle compared with the torrent of expenses. The Big Four had stretched their resources to the limit and were still 10 hard miles short of the 40-mile requirement for federal assistance. As chief of construction, Charles Crocker was close to despair. "I could not get any money," he recalled. "They got all I had and all I could borrow."

In Washington, Congress was aware of the financial problems facing both the Central Pacific and the Union Pacific and was prepared to help them out by revising the two-year-old railroad act. The amended legislation doubled the railroads' borrowing power by authorizing the companies to issue bonds equal in value to the loans approved by the government and by giving the company bondholders priority over the government in case of default. And instead of withholding all government loans until 40 miles of track had been laid, the revised act offered two-thirds of the money due for a 20-mile section as soon as grading was completed. In addition, the amount of public land granted for each completed mile was increased.

Enthusiasm for this largess was not unanimous. Congressman Elihu Washburne of Illinois called it "the greatest legislative crime in history." Despite such opposition, Congress gave final approval to the new plan in July 1864, and President Lincoln signed the bill into law.

For all its generosity, the legislation did little in the short term to help the Big Four or their company. What cash they could muster was in paper currency, and in California, workers and suppliers insisted on being paid in gold. In the summer of 1864, the outcome of the Civil War was still in doubt, and lack of confidence in U.S. currency drove the price of gold to its historical high: $285 in currency bought only $100 worth of gold coin. Thus the Central Pacific was getting only 35¢ worth of labor or materials for every

paper dollar it expended. The company could afford to keep only 300 men at work through the winter of 1864, and the pace of construction slowed to a crawl.

The financial gridlock began to ease early in 1865, when the courts resolved a legal dispute that had prevented the California state legislature from backing the interest payments on Central Pacific bonds. The bonds were sold, and the cash was raised. The railroad advertised for 5,000 laborers, but nothing like that number showed up. There were too many other opportunities in the mines of Nevada and on the farms and ranches of California. Few were drawn to the backbreaking labor of railroad construction. For every 1,000 men who signed up, 900 moved on after a week. Many of those who remained agitated for higher pay, sometimes going on strike.

It was Charles Crocker who saw a way to solve the problem by tapping into a fresh source of cheap labor. He suggested offering construction jobs to Chinese immigrants. By 1860, about 42,000 Chinese were working as cooks, launderers, gardeners, and domestic servants in northern California. The Central Pacific's on-site construction boss, James Strobridge, whose harshness in dealing with the men made even the tough-minded Crocker blanch, objected strenuously, asserting that the Chinese were not "masons," or builders. Crocker pointed out that they had built the Great Wall of China and insisted that Strobridge hire 50 of them as an experiment.

In the first week, the crew of Chinese, few of whom weighed more than 120 pounds or stood taller than four feet 10 inches, graded farther and better than any other. Strobridge hired 50 more, and before the railroad was finished, the company would have 12,000 on the payroll. They were "the best in the world," said the astonished Strobridge. "They learn quickly, do not fight, have no strikes that amount to anything, and are very cleanly in their habits."

The 1,100-foot Secrettown Trestle, located several miles from Dutch Flat, was the largest structure of its kind on the Central Pacific. In this photo, Chinese crews haul fill in wheelbarrows and carts to cover the base of the trestle's timbers to lessen the chance of their igniting in the event of a forest fire.

The "celestials," as the new workers came to be called in contrast to whites, who were dubbed "terrestrials," followed a distinct regimen in camp that yielded benefits. Their diet, which included rice, bamboo shoots, salted cabbage, and dried fruit, was far more healthful than the beef, beans, and bread favored by white workers. The celestials also fared better for their insistence on bathing and donning clean clothes before the evening meal. Likewise, their taste for tea meant that they boiled their water, which often came from tainted sources.

By the summer of 1865, the Civil War was over at last, and the financial picture of the Central Pacific continued to improve, even as the grading crews approached the high Sierra. Between Illinoistown (present-day Colfax) and Dutch Flat, they came up against Cape Horn, a sheer cliff rising 1,900 feet from the bank of the American River. The plan called for a ledge wide enough to support the tracks to be blasted out of the rock high above the river and several hundred feet below the top of the cliff. While the construction bosses were considering how to accomplish this daunting task, a Chinese foreman deferentially asked Strobridge for a supply of wicker. Mystified, Strobridge complied, and the Chinese proceeded to weave large baskets in which men were then lowered by ropes from the clifftop to set explosives.

A visiting newspaper correspondent who followed the grading crews up into the high Sierra that August was awed by the sight of "a great army laying siege to Nature in her strongest citadel. The rugged mountains looked like stupendous ant-hills. They swarmed with Celestials, shoveling, wheeling, carting, drilling and blasting rocks and earth."

By 1866 the Central Pacific was actually making money on its existing line, clearing nearly $750,000 in the first nine months of the year, all of which went to pay for construction. Work proceeded swiftly. Charles Crocker told the *Sacramento Union* that the company was "working between 9,000 and 10,000 men and 1,000 horses." By July the tracklayers had reached Dutch Flat, and the grading crews were approaching Donner Pass. Near the crest, 12 tunnels had to be built, a monumental task that continued through the fall and winter. Some 8,000 men toiled around the clock, in three shifts of eight hours each, a pace that could be kept up all winter, since the workers were underground and out of the weather. The tunnels were 16 feet wide at the base, with 11-foot-high sidewalls. Eight had to be blasted through solid rock; the other four passed through softer material and had to be lined with timber supports to prevent cave-ins.

The work was grueling. After discharging each shot of black powder, the men had to haul away a few cubic feet of rubble and set the next charge. Although the crews were using 500 kegs of powder per day, the average daily advance of the tunnel diggers was a mere seven inches. To speed things up the crews started using nitroglycerin, an oily yellow liquid so unstable it had to be manufactured on site. It was eight times as powerful as black powder and led to more severe accidents. After two especially deadly mishaps, Charles Crocker ordered the crews to "bury that stuff" and resume the use of black powder. (Dynamite was invented in 1866 but never used by the Central Pacific.)

The completion of the route through Donner Pass would stand as a legacy to the tenacity of the Chinese road builders. The tunnels they worked in were shielded from the wind and snow, but their living quarters, mess halls, and supply lines were not. Early in the winter, the snowfalls were deceptively moderate. John Gilliss, a civil engineer on the project, thought the scene "strangely beautiful at night. The tall firs, though drooping under their heavy burdens, pointed to the mountains that overhung them, where the fires that lighted seven tunnels shone like stars on their snowy sides. The only sound

Stretching 1,659 feet through solid granite, Summit Tunnel, at the western end of Donner Pass, was the longest and deepest tunnel built on the Central Pacific. To speed the work, a shaft was sunk from the mountain's surface near the halfway point so excavation could proceed from the middle as well as from both ends.

that came down to break the stillness of the winter night was the sharp ring of hammer on steel, or the heavy reports of the blasts."

But the snow kept coming. There were 44 snow-storms in the Sierra that winter. One that began on February 18, 1867, dumped six feet of snow, followed after several days of drifting by another that left four more feet by March 2. Judah had seriously underesti-mated the problems of supplying the construction crews in deep snow and of keeping the trains running through the drifts once the railroad was built. The dense snowpack was impervious to "the largest and best snow plows then known," in the words of Arthur

A porter uses a yoke to transport tea to Chinese workers in this 1867 photo taken outside Black Point Tunnel, near the summit of Donner Peak. Chinese specialties shipped to the work sites from Chinatown in San Francisco helped alleviate the workers' homesickness. Chinese labor gangs, each of which had its own cook, practiced good hygiene and ate a well-balanced diet, and as a result they enjoyed better health than their less fastidious white counterparts.

Brown, the Central Pacific's supervisor of bridges and buildings. Brown realized that he would have to build snowsheds to keep the tracks open in the high Sierra. "Although the expense of building a shed nearly 40 miles in length was almost appalling and unprece-dented in railroad construction," he noted, "there seemed to be no alternative."

The summer of 1867 saw the grading crews at last making their way down from the moun-tains along the Truckee River. The chief problem now was not money, although keeping cash in the coffers would never be easy. Nor was it labor, although finding enough men required aggressive recruiting methods that bordered on coercion. What the Big Four needed now more than anything else was speed.

Congress had authorized the Central Pacific to "continue their road eastward until they shall meet and connect with the Union Pacific Railroad." This had set off a race with high stakes, considering the sizable loans and land grants the government offered for every mile of completed track. Moreover, the companies were allowed to grade up to 300 miles ahead of the tracklayers, collecting two-thirds of the government loans on the graded mileage before

track had been laid. By late in the year the Central Pacific grading crews were advancing briskly across the Nevada desert, while the tracklayers were coming down from the mountains.

Charles Crocker's New Year's resolution for 1868 was to lay "a mile of track for every working day." And he soon asked his men to do better than that. The Union Pacific had strung more than 500 miles of track across the plains and was halfway to Utah's Great Salt Lake from Omaha. The Central Pacific had built just 130 miles of track through more difficult terrain. Intent on picking up the pace, Crocker issued a chal-

With the 21st U.S. Infantry and its regimental band among the onlookers, the Central Pacific's *Jupiter* and the Union Pacific's *No. 119* prepare to touch cowcatchers after the golden spike was driven into place. One engineer called the event "a great deal of speechyfying and wine drinking," and a reporter noted that when the ceremony was over, the soldiers began "hammering away at the flanges of the rails, and had carried off all the pieces they could break, so that a new rail will soon be necessary."

lenge. He heard that Union Pacific crews under his counterpart, construction chief Jack Casement, were proud of having laid four and a half miles of track in a single day. "They bragged of it," Crocker exclaimed, and he prodded his men to outdo the competition.

By now, his tracklayers had their task down to a science. Each night a supply train groaned to a halt near the end of the stretch completed the day before with a load of track, ties, spikes, bolts, and joints. Each day began with a dawn blast from a locomotive whistle that brought hundreds of workers scrambling from their tents and bunkhouses. In organized pandemonium, they stripped the train of its freight.

The ties went forward on wagons drawn by horses and mules, to be flung in place and bedded, 2,500 to the mile. The rails, piled on low flatcars called iron-trucks, inched forward to the very end of the track, where a five-man squad on each side grasped a long rail weighing more than 400 pounds and lifted it from the car. They ran forward with their burden, forced the near end of the rail into its joint, placed the far end on the spot indicated by the gauger, then hustled out of the way. The spikers set the rails on the ties with 10 spikes each, and the bolters joined the rails end to end. While the bolters were still working, the iron-truck rolled forward one more rail length, and the process was repeated. At their best, the men could set a fresh pair of rails every 30 seconds.

Through such precise teamwork, Crocker's crews bested their Union Pacific counterparts and laid down six miles in a single day, only to have their rivals up the ante to eight miles by beginning the day at 3:00 a.m. and working until midnight. Crocker would respond, but not until the game was nearly over.

In early 1869 the grading crews of the two companies converged in the Promontory Mountains north of Utah's Great Salt Lake, then plunged on past each other without linking the grades. Since no junction had been designated, there was still money to be made by extending the two lines. On April 9, when the overlap was about 100 miles in length, Congress called a halt to the wasteful competition and decreed that the junction of the two lines would be at Promontory.

The engraving on this golden spike driven into a rail during the ceremony at Promontory, Utah, reads "May God continue the unity of our Country as this Railroad unites the two great Oceans of the world." The spike was later removed for safekeeping.

Only then did Crocker resolve to try once more for a one-day track-laying record. At 7:00 a.m. on April 28, with ties already distributed along the roadbed ahead and five 16-car trains loaded with supplies waiting in the rear, Crocker's seasoned army of loaders, rail handlers, spikers, and bolters started their march. From the leading pioneers who aligned the ties to the last tampers who made sure the rails were set firmly, the force was two miles in length. It advanced at a pace of nearly a mile an hour. By 7:00 p.m. the men had set 25,800 ties, placed down 3,520 rails, and tightened 14,000 bolts. They had laid 10 miles and 56 feet of new track—a record that the men of the Union Pacific could hardly top, for their line was now less than 10 miles from Promontory. Unwilling to concede defeat, Dan Casement of the Union Pacific pleaded in vain with his brother and boss Jack to be allowed to tear up a few miles of track so that his men could try for a new record. Enough was enough, Jack responded. It was time to drive the last spike.

Only a few hundred people watched on May 10, 1869, as Leland Stanford's silver sledgehammer tapped the last golden spike of the transcontinental railroad. But within minutes the event was being celebrated by President Ulysses S. Grant in Washington, by a crowded service of thanksgiving in Trinity Church in New York City, by a seven-mile-long parade in Chicago, by fireworks and the firing of guns in other cities across the United States. Even the Liberty Bell was tolled in Philadelphia. "In reality," one of the dignitaries at Promontory observed, "the millions of our country were present."

All except for Anna Judah. "I refused myself to everyone that day," she wrote, for it was the 22nd anniversary of her wedding to Theodore. Sequestered at her family home in Greenfield, Massachusetts, she remembered the man who had carried the dream and kept it alive, who had charted the way through the Sierra. While the country jubilated, she mused alone. "It seemed the spirit of my brave dead husband descended on me," she related, "and together we were there unseen, unheard." ◆

THE WESTWARD MARCH OF THE RAILS

On December 2, 1863, 11 months after the Central Pacific began building its line east from Sacramento, California, the Union Pacific broke ground for its westward route in Omaha, Nebraska. Braving bitter cold, townsfolk pressed toward the riverfront to listen to band music, speeches, and cannon salutes and watch their governor raise the first shovelful of soil. It was a remarkable show of optimism amid the rigors of winter and a grueling Civil War that made both labor and construction capital scarce. The man who would complete the line for the Union Pacific—Grenville M. Dodge *(near right)*—was even then serving as an officer for the Union army, supervising such feats as the building of a 710-foot-long bridge across the Chattahoochee River in three days. He left the army in 1866 to become chief engineer for the U.P., and the pace of construction picked up dramatically. Between the summers of 1866 and 1867 his men laid 500 miles of track, reaching the mountain passes of Wyoming. In May 1869 they linked up with the Central Pacific in Utah, and Dodge himself drove the last spike of the U.P.'s 1,086 miles. It was an epic achievement. "On the plains and in the mountains," marveled contemporary journalist Charles Nordhoff, "the railroad is the one great fact."

Grenville Dodge later described the great undertaking in a book, *How We Built the Union Pacific Railway,* excerpts from which appear here along with views of the work in progress by Andrew J. Russell, the official U.P. photographer.

A tireless campaigner, Major General Grenville Dodge became chief engineer for the Union Pacific after the Civil War and forged its Platte Valley route, which followed that river through Nebraska and continued through southern Wyoming and northern Utah. After linking up with the Central Pacific at Promontory, Utah, the U.P. provided passenger service from Omaha to San Francisco in less than four days, as shown in the advertisement at right.

"*This route was made by the buffalo, next used by the Indians, then by the fur traders, next by the Mormons, and then by the overland immigration to California and Oregon. It was known as the Great Platte Valley Route. On this trail, or close to it, was built the Union and Central Pacific railroads to California, and the Oregon Short Line branch of the Union Pacific to Oregon.*"

U.P. construction supervisor Samuel Reed inspects the roadbed in Nebraska before tracklayers come through. Farther west, crews grading the line had to blast and dig through steeper terrain.

The organization for work on the plains away from civilization was as follows: Each of our surveying parties consisted of a chief, who was an experienced engineer, two assistants, also civil engineers, rodmen, flagmen, and chainmen . . . besides axmen, teamsters, and herders. When the party was expected to live upon the game of the country a hunter was added. . . . Each party entering a country occupied by hostile Indians was generally furnished with a military escort. . . . All hands worked from daylight to dark, the country being reconnoitered ahead of them by the chief, who indicated the streams to follow. . . . The party of location that followed the preliminary surveys had the maps and profiles of the line selected for location and devoted its energies to obtaining a line of the lowest grades and the least curvature that the country would admit.

The location party . . . was followed by the construction corps, grading generally 100 miles at a time. That distance was graded in about thirty days on the plains . . . , but in the mountains we sometimes had to open our grading several hundred miles ahead of our track in order to complete the grading by the time the track should reach it. . . .

The track laying on the Union Pacific was a science. Mr. W. A. Bell, in an article on the Pacific Railroads, describes, after witnessing it, as follows: "A light car, drawn by a single horse, gallops up to the front with its load of rails. Two men seize the end of a rail and start forward, the rest of the gang taking hold by twos, until it is clear of the car. They come forward at a run. At the word of command the rail is dropped in its place, right side up with care, while the same process goes on at the other side of the car. Less than thirty seconds to a rail for each gang, and so four rails go down to the minute."

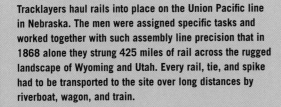

Tracklayers haul rails into place on the Union Pacific line in Nebraska. The men were assigned specific tasks and worked together with such assembly line precision that in 1868 alone they strung 425 miles of rail across the rugged landscape of Wyoming and Utah. Every rail, tie, and spike had to be transported to the site over long distances by riverboat, wagon, and train.

Vice president and general manager of the U.P. Thomas C. Durant *(seated second from right)* hosts a meeting of company officials in his luxurious rail car. Durant's financial wizardry kept the construction crews working, but his shady deals later embroiled the railroad in a national scandal.

Our Indian troubles commenced in 1864 and lasted until the tracks joined at Promontory. . . . The order to every surveying corps, grading, bridging, and tie outfit was never to run when attacked. All were required to be armed, and I do not know that the order was disobeyed in a single instance, nor did I ever hear that the Indians had driven a party permanently from its work. . . .

The entire track and a large part of the grading on the Union Pacific Railway was done by the Casement Brothers—Gen. Jack Casement and Dan Casement. General Casement had been a prominent brigade and division commander in the western army. Their force consisted of 100 teams and 1,000 men, living at the end of the track in boarding cars and tents, and moved forward with it every few days. It was the best organized, best equipped, and best disciplined track force I have ever seen. I think every chief of the different units of the force had been an officer of the army, and entered on this work the moment they were mustered out. They could lay from 1 to 3 miles of track per day, as they had material, and one day laid 8-½ miles. Their rapidity in track laying, as far as I know, has never been excelled. I used it several times as a fighting force, and it took no longer to put it into fighting line than it did to form it for its daily work. They not only had to lay and surface the track, but had to bring forward to the front from each base all the material and supplies for the track and for all workmen in advance of the track.

An irregular army of U.P. track workers, some of them Civil War veterans wearing their Union or Confederate uniforms, gather eagerly around the paymaster's car. Paid in cash, they earned on average three dollars a day, which was a good wage at the time. But their trade had its hazards, including skirmishes with Indians, who deeply resented the intrusion of whites into their land.

Wearing a Cossack cap and fur-trimmed coat and wielding a bullwhip, Jack Casement, U.P. construction boss and former Union general, pauses by one of his work trains. Although he stood just five feet four inches tall, he loomed large in the eyes of his men and kept them firmly in line. He once remarked wryly of his job, "It has been sufficient work to keep me out of a great deal of mischief."

Rough towns like Bear River City, Utah, aptly dubbed "hell on wheels," sprouted overnight—and often withered just as fast—as the Union Pacific crews advanced westward. Here, laborers spent their hard-earned money on greasy food, gut-burning whiskey, and prostitutes.

Bases were organized for the delivery of material generally from 100 to 200 miles apart, according to the facilities for operation. . . .

At these bases large towns were established, which moved forward with the bases, and many miles of sidings were put in for switching purposes, unloading tracks, etc. . . . I have seen these terminal towns starting first with a few hundred people until at Cheyenne, at the base of the mountains, where we wintered in 1867–68, there were 10,000 people. From that point they decreased until at Green River there were not over 1,000. After we crossed the first range of mountains we moved our bases so rapidly they could not afford to move with us. . . .

In the basin we found and rescued the [surveying] party headed by Thomas F. Bates. . . . They had been in the widest part of the basin for nearly a week without water, and were almost exhausted. When we discovered them they had abandoned the line and were taking a course due east by the compass, running for water. At first we thought them Indians, but on looking through my glasses I saw that they had teams with them. We went to their relief at once and saved them. They were in deplorable condition from thirst. . . . We had great difficulty in obtaining water for the operation of our road through the basin, being obliged to sink artesian wells to a great depth.

Laramie, Wyoming, where the U.P. installed this windmill-powered well and water tank for the steam engines and their crews, was one of the towns along the route that was built to last. General Dodge lamented that his men were so busy laying track that they spent little time boring wells: "We ought to have been at it long ago."

The bridge gangs always worked from 5 to 20 miles ahead of the track, and it was seldom that the track waited for a bridge. To supply 1 mile of track with material and supplies required about 40 cars, as on the plains everything, rails, ties, bridging, fastenings, all railway supplies, fuel for locomotives and trains, and supplies for men and animals on the entire work, had to be transported from the Missouri River. Therefore, as we moved westward, every hundred miles added vastly to our transportation. Yet the work was so systematically planned and executed that I do not remember an instance in all the construction of the line of the work being de-layed a single week for want of material. Each winter we planned the work for the next season. By the opening of spring, about April 1, every part of the machinery was in working order, and in no year did we fail to accomplish our work. After 1866 the reports will show what we started out to do each year, and what we accomplished.

A locomotive crosses the Green River in Wyoming over a temporary wooden bridge—one of many thrown up by the U.P. in its rush to lay track and thereby ensure a steady stream of government subsidies. Alongside the existing structure, masons are shown at left constructing piers for a permanent bridge, using stones moved into place with a railborne crane *(inset)*.

Surveyors clamber up a sheer rockface to reach a good vantage point, passing their instruments from hand to hand. The surveyors were the scouts of Grenville Dodge's advancing army, charting a path for the grading crews.

Laborers wield pickaxes to bring a steep slope down to grade near Ogden, in the Utah Territory. They first hewed out terraces, then blasted the rock and hauled the rubble away in mule carts or in rail cars, using temporary tracks.

Nearing their junction with the Central Pacific in northern Utah in early 1869, Union Pacific laborers transfer supplies from trains at the end of the existing tracks onto covered wagons, which will cart the material to crews preparing the last section of the line.

We made our plans to build to Salt Lake, 480 miles, in 1868, and to endeavor to meet the Central Pacific at Humboldt Wells, 219 miles west of Ogden, in the spring of 1869. . . . The necessary preparations were made to commence work as soon as frost was out of the ground, say about April 1. Material had been collected in sufficient quantities at the end of the track to prevent any delay. During the winter ties and bridge timber had been cut and prepared in the mountains to bring to the line at convenient points, and the engineering forces were started to their positions before cold weather was over, that they might be ready to begin their work as soon as the temperature would permit. I remember that the parties going to Salt Lake crossed the Wasatch Mountains on sledges, and that the snow covered the tops of the telegraph poles. We all knew and appreciated that the task we had laid out would require the greatest energy on the part of all hands. About April 1 [1868], therefore, I went onto the plains myself and started our construction forces, remaining the whole summer between Laramie and the Humboldt Mountains. I was surprised at the rapidity with which the work was carried forward. Winter caught us in the Wasatch Mountains, but we kept on grading our road and laying our track in the snow and ice at a tremendous cost. I estimated for the company that the extra cost of thus forcing the work during that summer and winter was over $10,000,000, but the instructions I received were to go on, no matter what the cost. Spring [1869] found us with the track at Ogden, and by May 1 we had reached Promontory, 534 miles west of our starting point twelve months before.

Minutes after driving the transcontinental railroad's last spike on May 10, 1869, Grenville Dodge *(facing the camera at center)* shakes hands with his Central Pacific counterpart, Samuel Montague. The ceremony sealed the peace between the rival crews, which had clashed sharply in the final weeks of construction. The two locomotive engineers entered into the spirit of the occasion by christening each other's cowcatchers with champagne *(background)*.

The Central Pacific had made wonderful progress coming east, and we abandoned the work from Promontory to Humboldt Wells, bending all our efforts to meet them at Promontory. Between Ogden and Promontory each company graded a line, running side by side, and in some places one line was right above the other. The laborers upon the Central Pacific were Chinamen, while ours were Irishmen, and there was much ill-feeling between them. Our Irishmen were in the habit of firing their blasts in the cuts without giving warning to the Chinamen on the Central Pacific working right above them. From this cause several Chinamen were severely hurt. Complaint was made to me by the Central Pacific people, and I endeavored to have the contractors bring all hostilities to a close, but, for some reason or other, they failed to do so. One day the Chinamen, appreciating the situation, put in what is called a "grave" on their work, and when the Irishmen right under them were all at work let go their blast and buried several of our men. This brought about a truce at once. From that time the Irish laborers showed due respect for the Chinamen, and there was no further trouble.

When the two roads approached in May, 1869, we agreed to connect at the summit of Promontory Point, and the day was fixed so that trains could reach us from New York and California. . . . The two trains pulled up facing each other, each crowded with workmen who sought advantageous positions to witness the ceremonies, and literally covered the cars. . . . The telegraph lines had been brought to that point, so that in the final spiking as each blow was struck the telegraph recorded it at each connected office from the Atlantic to the Pacific. Prayer was offered, a number of spikes were driven in the two adjoining rails, each one of the prominent persons present taking a hand, but very few hitting the spikes, to the great amusement of the crowd. When the last spike was placed, light taps were given upon it by several officials, and it was finally driven home by the chief engineer of the Union Pacific Railway. The engineers ran up their locomotives until they touched, the engineer upon each engine breaking a bottle of champagne upon the other one, and thus the two roads were wedded into one great trunk line from the Atlantic to the Pacific.

CHAPTER 4

AT WAR IN WYOMING

"The opening of spring may be more red than green for the horse thieves and cattle thieves of Johnson County."

THE *BILLINGS GAZETTE*, MARCH 10, 1892

Nate Champion stirred in his bunk as the rising sun threw thin bands of light between the logs of the dark cabin. For cattlemen along the Powder River in northern Wyoming, November was downtime, and neither Champion nor his partner, Ross Gilbertson, was in a hurry to get up. Champion petted his cat and drifted back to sleep. Suddenly the door burst open. "Who's there?" Champion barked.

"Tramps," came the reply, and then the voice became more menacing. "Give up—we've got you this time." Champion thought fast. The tiny cabin offered him nowhere to hide and no escape from the three pistol-wielding men who were silhouetted in the doorway. "What's up, boys?" Champion asked. Feigning a yawn, he stretched his hand toward the bedpost, where his six-shooter hung in its holster, turning his head in the same instant that a deafening blast singed his face and a bullet smacked against the wall behind him.

That instinctive movement saved his life. He thumbed a shot from his own revolver just as another bullet buried itself in the wad of blankets. Champion loosed two more shots at the intruders, who were now scrambling backward through the black-powder smoke and out of the cabin. He reached the

door to see the men running through the bushes, one holding his stomach as if he had been hit.

Glancing around, Champion spotted a Winchester rifle leaning against the house and another one next to the woodpile a few feet away. Shouting to Ross Gilbertson to cover him from the window, he stepped out to get them. As he did, another man jumped out from behind the corner of the house, his revolver leveled. Champion ducked back inside and fired through a gap in the logs, and the man fled.

Champion grabbed the rifles and, with the reluctant Gilbertson in tow, set off after the assailants. About 75 yards from the house they found four overcoats, and farther along the trail they came upon a campsite. Scattered bedding and cooking equipment signaled a hasty departure, and a tarpaulin gleamed with a slick of fresh blood.

To Champion, the camp's location was telling. Less than a mile away lay the NH Ranch, home of Mike Shonsey, who worked as a foreman for several well-heeled English-born cattlemen. No one camped on NH land without Shonsey's knowledge.

There was no love lost between Champion and Shonsey: They had quarreled a few months earlier when Shonsey's men had rounded up part of Champion's small herd on open rangeland. Given the bad

Honest, hardworking Nate Champion, the mustachioed cowboy on the horse nearest the chuck wagon at left, was widely regarded as one of the best horsemen and sharpshooters in Wyoming cattle country. His move from wage-earning cowhand to manager of his own herd thrust him to the center of the dispute between wealthy cattlemen and the cowpunchers they accused of cattle rustling.

At roundup time *(above)* man and horse were put to the test as droves of cattle were counted and beeves—fully grown fattened cattle—were cut out for shipping to market. Cowboys risked life and limb roping these heavyweights, and many horses' necks were broken in the rough-and-tumble of the roundup.

feeling between the two men, Champion had been surprised when Shonsey paid him an unexpected visit just the day before. The foreman's apparent purpose had been to talk about trading some horses, but Champion now wondered whether that had been only a ruse to disguise the real purpose of the visit— to make sure that Champion was at home and to have a look at the cabin's layout. If Shonsey was actually involved in the early-morning raid, Champion knew that he was up against some very powerful and determined enemies. They might have missed him this time, but they would be back for another try.

The attack on Champion, which took place on November 1, 1891, was an early round in what would prove to be a long and bloody feud in Johnson County in northern Wyoming. Trouble had been brewing there for some years between the large stock growers and the increasing number of settlers and cowboys who ran their own small spreads, in the shadow of the Bighorn Mountains.

According to the cowboys and settlers, the source of the problem was the big growers, who arrogantly claimed the right to run their huge herds on any and all land, trampling fences and gardens, and often making off with other folks' cattle in the process. It wasn't only the fences that the small ranchers built on formerly open rangeland that raised the hackles of the cattle barons; they accused the settlers and cowboys of harboring rustlers who branded the calves of the larger outfits and claimed them for their own.

The situation wasn't helped by encroaching civilization. Statehood had come to Wyoming in July 1890, and roads and telegraph wires already crisscrossed the open range. Buffalo, the county seat, was a thriving town of 1,000 people. But the large cattle growers refused to admit that Wyoming was changing—or that they would have to change along with it.

Tension between big ranchers and small was not limited to Johnson County, though it seemed to fester there the worst. Throughout the state of Wyoming the problem was exacerbated by a combination of greed and foolish business practices. The promise of easy profits had drawn East Coast and European-born speculators to the state's cattle business in the late 1870s and early 1880s. Along the several forks of the Powder River the knee-high grass was free for the grazing, and it seemed to the speculators that cattle obligingly fattened up and reproduced with little or no human interven-

tion. Returns on investment were touted to run as high as 40 percent.

But the green cattlemen often proved poor managers, overstocking the range and overestimating how many cattle they actually owned. Rather than count real, walking-around beef, they would look at the recorded number of branded calves (the only tally ever made) and multiply that number by four or five to arrive at a figure for their beef herds. According to one account, at least half the animals on which the cattle growers calculated their profits did not in fact exist. When the herds fell victim to nat-

Tied by the hind legs and dragged through the corral to the branding fire, a maverick—a motherless, unbranded calf—struggles to free itself as cowpunchers prepare to apply the hot iron. The T open A branding iron *(below, left)* comes from the TA Ranch, which figured prominently in the Johnson County war.

ural disasters such as prairie fires, bad weather, and plagues of grasshoppers that ruined grazing, many of the big ranchers fled to the more comfortable lifestyle and predictable business back east.

Those who stayed, anxious to explain lean dividends to their faraway investors, played down the risky nature of the cattle business and said nothing of their own mismanagement. Instead they pointed an accusing finger at a ready scapegoat: rustlers—those unscrupulous cowhands who would put their brand on any unclaimed cattle they found.

Nathan D. Champion had not always been a thorn in the side of the cattle barons. He had arrived in northern Wyoming in 1881, driving a herd up from Texas for a large outfit. He had been a trusted wagon boss during the great spring roundups, the huge gatherings when cowhands from several ranches would get together to drive in the cattle and newborn calves that had been on the open range over

The three-story, mansard-roofed, brick-and-wood Cheyenne Club (below), which was the headquarters of the Wyoming Stock Growers Association, boasted plush carpets, two grand staircases, wine cellars, and a library. In this opulent setting rich cattle ranchers—including titled Englishmen—dressed in white tie and tails to dine on caviar, pickled eels, and Roquefort cheese served by a liveried staff.

the winter. Over the course of several weeks, the men would sort out all the different herds and brand the unbranded calves. "A good man," one of Champion's admiring bosses had once said of him.

By 1891 the 34-year-old cowboy had become something of a legend among his fellow cowboys and settlers. Stocky, steely-eyed, and soft-spoken, he had earned a reputation for being unswervingly honest and for never using two words where one would do. He was a fine horseman, outstanding with a lariat, and one of the surest shots in Johnson County. Champion had also demonstrated his enterprise, accumulating 200 head of cattle of his own. That enterprise earned him respect in one quarter—and the label of rustler in another.

The cattlemen and the cowboys they employed were not cut from the same cloth. Men bred in the rigid social hierarchy of Europe or the somewhat more relaxed traditions of the East Coast did not understand how rough-and-ready hands like Champion and his fellows could possibly consider themselves equal to the owners of the

Attired in jockey's silks, the status-conscious cattle barons at left prepare for a harness racing meet sponsored by the swank Cheyenne Club. The moneyed members also enjoyed tennis and fox hunting, while in private they drew up a hit list of cowhands, small ranchers, and their sympathizers they wanted to see dead.

herds. The westerners, for their part, refused to recognize the superiority of their so-called betters. When one English visitor asked a cowboy, "Is your master at home?" the answer was blunt: "The son of a bitch hasn't been born yet."

To protect their own commercial interests, the cattle barons banded together. In 1879 they transformed what had been a little organization called the Laramie County Stock Association into the Wyoming Stock Growers Association. Headquartered at the luxurious Cheyenne Club in the territorial capital, the association's members enjoyed the patronage of Wyoming's governor, could count on newspapers that supported big-business interests to give them favorable coverage, and had clout with their representatives in Washington.

A few years after its formation, the cattlemen's association began stepping up its efforts to outmaneuver, if not eliminate, the small ranchers. In 1883 it drew up a blacklist, refusing to hire any cowboy who owned stock, on the assumption that he must have stolen it. When this happened to Nate Champion, he simply went independent and ran his 200 cattle himself, thereby earning the everlasting ill will of his former employers. The growers also began cutting wages and charging for the once free bunkhouse hospitality that had traditionally supported cowboys through the winter. With these mean-spirited acts the association succeeded in making a bad situation worse; denying men their livelihood only forced more cowboys to turn to ranching themselves.

Those who could afford it bought their own small herds, often a cow or a calf at a time. Others got started by falling back on an old law of the West about gathering unbranded calves: "The longest rope gets the maverick." An unwritten code stipulated when and where a man could and could not claim a maverick: A calf with its mother was to be left alone. However, as times got harder, not everyone abided strictly by this rule. Even competing big outfits often rustled calves from one another—a fact that rendered many juries sympathetic to small ranchers and cowboys accused of rustling. Convictions were so rare that frustrated members of the Cheyenne Club took to hiring stock detectives, who could earn $250 for each rustler they helped to convict. Joe Elliott was one, an unsavory character whom Champion had recognized as one of his attackers. So was Frank Canton, a gunman who had fled Texas after an apprenticeship in robbery, rustling, and murder.

At the behest of the growers association, in 1884 the Wyoming legislative assembly proclaimed all mavericks on the range to be the property of the association itself, which would then sell them at auction. Supporters argued that the ruling was aimed only at foiling rustlers. However, it also gave the association the right to seize the strays of any small rancher, who then found it impossible even to buy his own animals back. Auctions were rigged so that the small ranchers were always outbidden by representatives of the concerns belonging to the growers association, and when money actually changed hands, the association buyer always paid precisely $10 a head, no matter how high the bidding had risen.

The cowboys and settlers didn't take these injustices lying down. In 1886, a 25-year-old Virginian named Jack Flagg, who had a homestead on Red Fork, off the Powder River, was blacklisted after he led his fellow cowboys in a strike to protest a wage cut. Tall, intelligent, and a former schoolmaster, Flagg was by nature contentious and political. He was also seldom seen without a black hat. The following year he bought himself a small herd of cattle

and with four like-minded partners registered a legitimate brand with the county: the Hat. Like their friend Nate Champion, the Hat men hated the cattle growers who tried to deny them their living, and saw the conflict as a class war. The registration of the Hat brand, in turn, infuriated the cattlemen, who viewed Flagg and his partners as the rustler elite.

Then came the winter of 1886–1887. Even for Wyoming, it was a long, harsh season. Deep snow buried the grass for months at a time, and starving cattle wandered into towns or scavenged in ranch house garbage cans in a desperate search for food. Losses were enormous: According to some estimates, as many as half the cattle in Wyoming perished, though it was probably far less. The disaster only heightened the tension that was continuing to grow between the two sides.

Over the next couple of years, the members of the Cheyenne Club grew more desperate to regain the economic ground they had lost and prevent further erosion. In the spring of 1891 the growers' association took a step that was tantamount to a declaration of war. Under state law the association wielded control of the spring and fall roundups all over Wyoming, and they now drew up a new blacklist that banned all small ranchers from the state-sanctioned roundup. The association's aggressive move drew an equally aggressive response from the small operators of Johnson County. They armed themselves, formed their own stock association, and beat the Cheyenne crowd to the punch by holding their own roundup first, with Nate Champion as its captain. Where once they had branded mavericks because the law of the West said they could, it was now a gesture of defiance. Some of the settlers and cowboys went further, burning their own brands onto already branded cattle.

Out on the range, the conflict was getting personal. Feuds broke out between the cattlemen's employees and the cowboys who had once worked alongside them—and a feud could get you killed. Nate Champion was at loggerheads with

Mike Shonsey. Jack Flagg was sworn enemies with Fred Hesse, a foreman for a big outfit, and with Frank Canton. Frank Canton was a rancher with a nice spread south of Buffalo who in 1886 had gone to work for the growers association as its chief detective in northern Wyoming. Jack Flagg was one of the detective's chief targets. In a letter to his boss down in Cheyenne, Canton wrote of Flagg, "I am confident that the gentleman is crooked. . . . Jack Flagg is an old-timer here and is a hard man; he is cunning and it will take some good work to send him over the road." For his part, Flagg had no use for Canton. Before becoming a detective, Canton had twice been elected Johnson County sheriff, and in 1888 he decided to run again. Canton had a good record to run on, but it didn't count for much any-

there long when he saw Canton on the street in Buffalo and recognized him as the man who had tried to kill two of his friends back in Texas. Canton had escaped the enraged rancher by ducking into a store and running out the back door. Tisdale apparently was able to control his rage, for he did not go after the stock detective.

Besides being at odds with Frank Canton and a friend of Nate Champion's, Tisdale had a brother who was one of Flagg's partners in the Hat brand—all of which were good reasons for him to watch his back. As far as the big growers were concerned, there was more than enough proof of guilt—even if only by association.

On the snowy 30th of November, Tisdale drove his wagon into Buffalo to buy provisions and to do

> *"It was really wonderful to see him ride, he had such grip in his knees that he could fairly make a horse groan, and a horse could only pitch a short while until he would have to stop to get his breath. His strength was so great that he could handle the most vicious bronc as easily as an ordinary man could a Shetland pony."*
>
> JACK FLAGG ON RANGER JONES

more; he was widely regarded as a turncoat, a traitor who had gone over to the enemy camp. Jack Flagg campaigned for Canton's opponent, a bartender named W. G. "Red" Angus. Canton lost the election—and chalked up one more black mark against Jack Flagg.

Still, Canton's principal foe was not Jack Flagg but a man named John A. Tisdale who was a boyhood friend of Nate Champion's from Texas. Champion visited the small ranch on a fork of the Powder River where his friend lived with his wife and three young children. "There's going to be trouble," the worried cowboy confided to Tisdale, adding, "If it comes to fighting, I can fight, but I can't lead a fight."

Tisdale, who had gone to college in Texas and was better educated than the run of Johnson County residents, had become a leader among the settlers since arriving in Wyoming in 1889. He hadn't been

some Christmas shopping for his family. By all accounts, he was not himself. He drank heavily, though no one had ever seen him drunk before. And he told anyone who would listen—even a close friend of Frank Canton's—that he was terrified there would be an attempt on his life while he was on his way home.

Although he had his six-shooter, Tisdale bought a new shotgun. Another man agreed to accompany him on the 60-mile journey home, but Tisdale lingered too long and the man left without him.

It was afternoon when Tisdale left Buffalo, alone. Lumbering along at two or three miles an hour, the nervous rancher did not go far before stopping for the night, at the Cross H Ranch south of town. He told the foreman that he was expecting trouble and carefully pulled the window curtains shut for privacy, but he was too worried to sleep. Next morning he set off soon after 8:00.

DEATH ON THE SWEETWATER

The motive was simple: Cattleman Albert Bothwell wanted the spread on the Sweetwater River where Jim Averell ran a general store and saloon with buxom prostitute Ella Watson, the Queen of the Sweetwater to her cowboy clients. On July 20, 1889, Bothwell and five associates abducted the pair at gunpoint. Frank Buchanan, a cowboy who happened to be in the saloon, followed them to a dry gulch across the river, where he saw the men put ropes around the necks of Averell and Watson. Buchanan loosed a couple of shots from his six-shooter, but the lynching party returned fire with their Winchesters.

Buchanan rode 50 miles to Casper and brought back a sheriff's posse. They found the bodies of Averell and Watson hanging from a stunted pine tree, their toes barely off the ground.

An inquest identified all six men involved. But by the time a grand jury convened in October, all witnesses, including Buchanan, had vanished. No one was ever convicted of the crime, and Bothwell got the land he wanted.

JIM AVERELL

Ella Watson was wearing a new pair of beaded Indian moccasins when she was lynched. They fell off after she was hanged and were found lying on the ground below her body.

About two hours later, Charlie Basch, a rancher on his way to Buffalo, witnessed an unsettling incident at Haywood's Gulch, about eight miles from town. The horse trail he was riding on and the wagon road Tisdale had taken that morning dipped down into and across the gulch at about the same point. As Basch neared the gulch, he saw a man leading a horse across a hill that rose above it. Although Basch was still some distance away, he recognized his neighbor Frank Canton and Old Fred, Canton's horse.

Basch's first thought was that they could ride to town together, but Canton didn't seem to want company. Ignoring Basch he drew his gun and kept going. Basch lost sight of Canton for a couple of minutes in the hilly terrain, but when he had drawn closer and could see the bottom of the gulch, he caught another glimpse of Canton. He was leading a pair of horses hitched to an apparently empty wagon off the road. He disappeared from view, and a couple of minutes later Basch heard two shots coming from down in the gulch. Canton reappeared, galloping off at top speed in the direction of Buffalo.

Perhaps fearful of what he might find, Basch didn't stop to look for the wagon or to investigate the shots. Before he got to Buffalo he happened to meet the foreman from the ranch where Tisdale had spent the night and told him what he'd seen and heard at Haywood's Gulch.

In Buffalo the two men sought out Sheriff Angus, who after hearing Basch's story rode out to the gulch accompanied by a small posse. There they discovered John Tisdale lying dead in his wagon on top of the provisions and the Christmas presents he'd bought the day before. He had been shot once in the back, and both of his horses had been shot. Footprints in snow revealed the spot in the gulch where the murderer had lain in wait for Tisdale, about 20 feet from the road.

As news of the murder spread through the settler community, it caused particular alarm in one house out on Red Fork. Johnny Jones grew increasingly afraid for his brother, Orley, commonly known as

Ranger, because he had feuded with Fred Hesse. The 23-year-old Ranger had left for Buffalo around November 20, planning to be away for four or five days. He was soon to be married and had wanted to buy flooring for the cabin he was building for himself and his bride-to-be.

Johnny and his brother had come from Nebraska to Johnson County, where young Ranger had won some renown for his skill in breaking horses. As Jack Flagg would later note, "His strength was so great that he could handle the most vicious bronc as easily as an ordinary man could a Shetland pony." Ranger was a popular man, and he had had a good time in town—so good that he had stayed longer than he had intended, and went to a dance on Thanksgiving night. It wasn't until Saturday, November 28, that he had finally set out for home. He never got there.

On December 3 the search party raised by Ranger's brother set out to comb the gulches along his route home. About 15 miles outside Buffalo they found Ranger in his buckboard, his dead body frozen solid. He had been blasted three times in the back from no more than six feet away. When the men tried to lift Ranger Jones's body out of the buckboard, his blood-soaked, frozen hair stuck firmly to the wood.

The two murders struck terror into Buffalo's settlers. Everything about Tisdale's death pointed to Frank Canton, whose feud with the rancher was well known. Charlie Basch had witnessed Canton behaving oddly at the murder scene, and that same morning another man had seen Old Fred in Buffalo lathered and sweaty, sure signs that the horse had been ridden hard.

Sheriff Angus and the townspeople put their faith in the justice system. But the law was a manipulable commodity in Johnson County. At the inquest and hearing that followed, Charlie Basch changed his story, perhaps fearing retribution if he implicated Canton, whose friends provided him with an alibi. The judge, who was a friend of the cattlemen, allowed the prosecution no time to

The document below, citing Frank Canton's "integrity, ability and diligence," named him a deputy U.S. marshal of the district of Wyoming Territory on October 1, 1885. Less than a year later, Wyoming ranchers recruited him as their chief stock detective in northern Wyoming, with several assistants and the handsome salary of $2,500 a year.

Frank Canton *(left)* worked both sides of the law. At 26, after an early life of robbery and murder, he changed his name, moved from Texas to Wyoming, and served for four years as sheriff of Johnson County before becoming a stock detective. He later resumed his career as a lawman in the Oklahoma Territory and in Alaska during the gold rush.

examine Canton's story carefully. Canton was off the hook, and a week later he left town—to visit relatives in Illinois, he said. Justice was no better served in the matter of Ranger Jones's murder, which also went unsolved.

Within the comfortable confines of the Cheyenne Club, the leaders of the Wyoming Stock Growers Association had run out of patience with rustling. They singled out Johnson County as being a haven for cattle thieves and named Buffalo as the capital of Wyoming's rustlers. In the spring of 1891, John Clay, the new president of the W.S.G.A. and a member of the Cheyenne Club, gave an inaugural address bemoaning the sorry situation confronting his colleagues—"a question of life and death," he termed it. Clay, a Scot who had worked on Wall Street before moving west to advise stock growers in California and Wyoming, lamented the lack of state action against ranchers who fenced off prime grazing land and complained that stock growers paid their taxes but got nothing in return.

On Independence Day, Clay paid a visit to another disgruntled cattleman, Major Frank Wolcott. Wolcott was a thoroughgoing martinet, and Clay was one of a small minority who actually enjoyed the former Union officer's company. A Kentuckian who had earned his rank in the Civil War, Wolcott had served as a United States marshal in Wyoming Territory and now managed a ranch at Deer Creek, about halfway between Buffalo and Cheyenne. He was short and thickset, and his military bearing was marred only by the way he carried his head cocked to one side, the result of a neck injury he had received in a fight with a cowboy from Laramie. Most people hated Wolcott and many feared him—for good reason. He was known for a long career of driving stakeholders off their claims, and in 1886 he had gone to extremes, hiring a gunman to shoot down a man named Sumner Beach. Wolcott wasted his money: Beach proved quicker on the draw.

The Fourth was a bright, sunny day, and Clay and Wolcott went for a walk around the major's

place, where workers were harvesting alfalfa to feed the stock over winter. Naturally enough, the conversation turned to the sore subject of rustling. What northern Wyoming needed, Wolcott declared, was a lynching bee to rid it of rustling. His idea was bold, and it was violent: The big stock growers would bring to Johnson County a party of gunmen to settle the score with the cattle thieves once and for all. After hearing his friend, Clay said that he was "quite willing to draw a rope on a cattle thief if necessary," but he couldn't countenance the kind of wholesale

John Tisdale *(below, center)* was a friend of Nate Champion's and an enemy of Frank Canton's since their days in Texas. Before settling in Johnson County, he worked in North Dakota for future president Theodore Roosevelt, who gave the Tisdales a baby chair when their first son was born.

vigilante action Wolcott was proposing. He told the major to count him out and urged him to abandon the scheme. Shortly afterward, Clay departed on a long holiday in Europe. Nine months later, he was still abroad when he happened on an item in an Irish newspaper concerning a fight between cowboys and stock growers in Wyoming. The major, it seemed, had not followed his advice.

From his military experience Wolcott knew how valuable the element of surprise could be in an attack. He kept the plan for his lynching bee confidential, even going so far as to choose the Paxton Hotel in Omaha, Nebraska, as the site for an important meeting of cattlemen from northern Wyoming on March 10, 1892, to confer about the final details.

The scheme remained much as Wolcott had originally conceived it: A force made up of hired guns and cattlemen would invade Johnson County, march on Buffalo, kill the sheriff and his deputies, and seize the arms that the local militia had stored in the courthouse. They would then raise the general populace against the rustlers; Wolcott and his fellows were confident that the vast majority of Johnson County residents would back them. The war against the rustlers would then begin in earnest, as they were hunted down one by one.

An essential step had been to draw up a list of rustlers (or men falsely labeled as rustlers) that the big growers wanted to get rid of. Wolcott delegated this task to W.S.G.A. secretary Hiram B. Ijams, who, according to an acquaintance, talked about the lynching "in much the same manner that many people would talk about taking a picnic excursion." Ijams compiled a preliminary list from reports sent to him by ranchers around Johnson County, then passed the names to the association's executive committee to make the final decisions. The committee was ready to dispense justice to those they deemed guilty but was reluctant to unwittingly condemn innocent men to death. Exactly how long the list was remains uncertain because Ijams made only one copy, and it did not survive. Some people would say

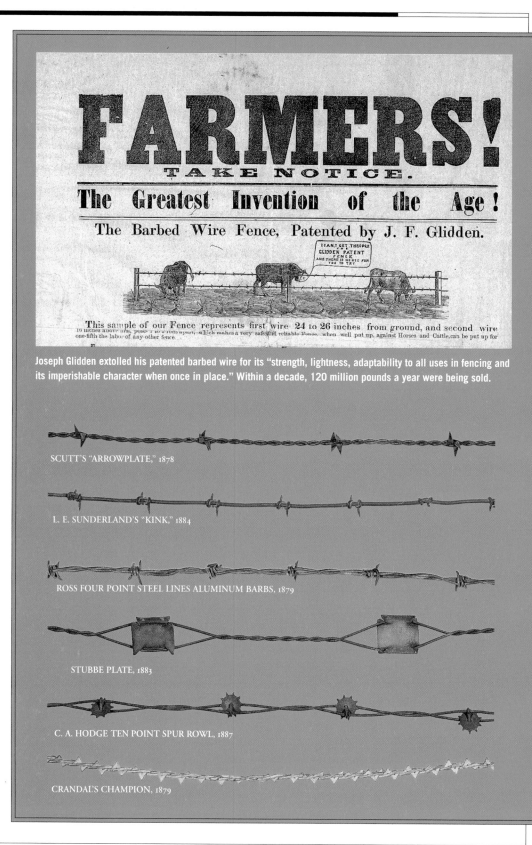

Joseph Glidden extolled his patented barbed wire for its "strength, lightness, adaptability to all uses in fencing and its imperishable character when once in place." Within a decade, 120 million pounds a year were being sold.

SCUTT'S "ARROWPLATE," 1878

L. E. SUNDERLAND'S "KINK," 1884

ROSS FOUR POINT STEEL LINES ALUMINUM BARBS, 1879

STUBBE PLATE, 1883

C. A. HODGE TEN POINT SPUR ROWL, 1887

CRANDAL'S CHAMPION, 1879

CLOSING THE OPEN RANGE

No single invention changed the landscape and the character of the American West as much as barbed wire. After the Civil War, the western territories began to fill up with homesteaders—small ranchers and farmers whose livelihood depended on keeping free-roaming herds of cattle off their property. Split-rail fences of the type that were used back east were impractical on the treeless plains, and experience demonstrated that simple wire fences could not discourage a determined cow.

In 1874 a clever Illinois farmer named Joseph F. Glidden devised an efficient method of attaching pointed barbs to interwoven strands of ordinary wire. Soon other inventors were developing variations on his idea *(opposite)*. Their combined efforts had a momentous effect: The wide open plains could now be fenced economically and subdivided into small parcels.

Cattle barons, who had long regarded the vast stretches of western rangeland as their private domain, did not take kindly to this development. Using hired guns to carry out their dirty work, they began a widespread campaign of vandalism, intimidation, and even murder against fence-building homesteaders. But they could not stem the tide of change: With the strength of numbers and the weight of the law on their side, the homesteaders prevailed.

In this staged photograph from the 1880s, four masked men demonstrate the common practice of fence cutting. Cattle growers bent on keeping the range open for their large herds would send out gangs, usually in the dead of night, to destroy the barbed wire enclosures of small landholders.

later that the list of the condemned ran to 19, or 38, or as many as 70 names.

Nate Champion was certainly on the list, along with Jack Flagg, whom the stock growers association considered the brains of the outlaws. Besides Sheriff Red Angus and his deputies, the county commissioners were to be killed. The editor of the *Buffalo Bulletin* went on the list because of his anticattleman stance, and the town's leading storekeeper, Robert Foote, was a likely target because he was said to sell rustled beef.

While Ijams worked up his list, others of his colleagues were busy garnering political support for the invasion of Johnson County. It had at least the tacit approval of Wyoming's senators, who were in Washington at the time.

Closer to home, the state's acting governor, Amos Barber, gave his blessing to the invasion, thereby relieving any worry the cattlemen might have had about breaking the state law stipulating that "no armed police force, or detective agency, or armed body, or unarmed body of men, shall ever be brought into this state for the suppression of domestic violence, except upon the application of the Legislature, or the Executive, when the Legislature cannot be convened." Barber saw to it that the militia of Johnson County would be hamstrung. In March he issued an order removing authority from sheriffs to call out the militia in case of trouble. According to the new regulation, local militia commanders would have to get permission from headquarters in Cheyenne before responding to calls for help from civilian authorities—in this case, from officials in Buffalo. Permission, the cattlemen were confident, would not be forthcoming, since the chief of the militia reported to Governor Barber.

The invasion was going to be an expensive business, and about 100 association members had contributed $1,000 each to pay for it. In January one man had gone to Colorado to buy the horses the cattlemen and their mercenaries would need; making such a large purchase in or around Johnson

The dapper Major Frank Wolcott rarely went without his 15-jewel, gold Waltham pocket watch *(above)*. An active member of the stock growers association, Wolcott was the resident manager of the VR Ranch, a large spread owned by overseas investors. It was said that the autocratic Wolcott could make an enemy of a man he had just met.

County would have been sure to attract unwanted attention and curiosity.

The job of hiring gunmen had been given to Tom Smith, a stock detective, who traveled to his hometown of Paris, Texas, in order to find recruits. Smith gave out the story that they would be serving warrants on a gang of dangerous outlaws. The pay would be five dollars a day, plus expenses, and each gunman would be insured by a $3,000 accident policy. (The Texans would find out only later that they were to shoot the so-called dangerous outlaws, rather than serve warrants on them. If a gunman had any scruples about murder, his reservations might be eased by the $50 bonus that would be paid for each man shot.) The generous terms raised 22 gunmen who, one witness remarked, looked "well able to take care of themselves."

On the afternoon of April 5, the train from Denver arrived in Cheyenne with a Pullman car with all of its blinds drawn. Inside the car were Tom Smith, the Texas gunmen, and Frank Wolcott, who had met them in Denver so he could get acquainted with the men who would be under his command during the long train ride. In Cheyenne the Pullman was switched to another train, along with three stock cars for the horses bought in Colorado, a flatcar carrying three new wagons, and a baggage car.

More people now came aboard, including a contingent of 19 W.S.G.A. cattlemen; Frank Canton and four other stock detectives; Dr. Charles Penrose, the expedition surgeon, who was riding with the invaders on the recommendation of Barber; three teamsters to drive the wagons; and two newsmen, Ed Towse of the *Cheyenne Sun* and Sam T. Clover of the *Chicago Herald*. Clover had traveled to Cheyenne on a tip and overcame the invaders' initial hostility by assuring them that his news reports would be sympathetic to their views.

The train pulled out of Cheyenne at around 5:30 p.m. and rumbled 150 miles northwest to Casper, which was the jumping-off point for Buffalo, another 125 miles away. The passengers detrained at about 4:20 the next morning and rode off into the sagebrush and snow. If Major Wolcott thought that the invaders had slipped away unnoticed under cover of night, he was wrong; curious railroad employees up and down the line had been watching the unusual group of travelers with interest. Practically speaking, however, the major's secret was safe. He had taken the precaution of having the telegraph lines at the station that relayed messages to Casper and on north to Buffalo cut, so there was no danger that word of a party of horsemen more than 50 strong was abroad. The Johnson County war was about to begin.

The invasion got off to a slow start. When Wolcott's men stopped for breakfast outside of Casper, some of the horses were tethered to sagebrush, which the animals uprooted with a strong tug. They ran off, and it took several hours to round them up. The members of the Cheyenne Club had brought everything they needed for comfort—a chuck wagon, tents, campstools. The heavily laden freight wagons moved at a slow pace and bogged down in ground made muddy by melting snow.

On the morning of April 7, the second day of the invasion, fresh snow began to fall, and by noon they had traveled only 30 miles from Casper. Leaving the wagons to plod along behind them, the horsemen went on ahead another 35 miles to their scheduled overnight stop at the ranch of a sympathizer. In the snowstorm, Wolcott got separated from the others, lost his way, and spent the night in a haystack.

Not wanting to strike out without their equipment and provisions, the invaders waited at the ranch for the wagons, which finally got there the next afternoon. Major Wolcott had also arrived, and the atmosphere was tense, because he had quarreled with Frank

The party of invaders commanded by Frank Wolcott traveled by train to Casper, where they saddled up and headed north to Buffalo in the foothills of the Bighorn Mountains. It took them three days to travel the 80 miles to the KC Ranch, shown on the map below. The next day they reached the TA Ranch, south of Buffalo.

Canton and Tom Smith. The Texans had sided with Smith, and the sulky major was threatening to relinquish command of the invasion.

Onto the scene rushed Nate Champion's enemy, Mike Shonsey, with the news that Champion and several other men were at the KC Ranch some 15 miles up the road. Fired by an afternoon of heavy drinking, the cattlemen argued fiercely about their next move. Frank Canton and most of the Johnson County cattlemen wanted to stick with the plan to get to Buffalo as fast as possible. But Wolcott and William Irvine, another architect of the invasion, were eager to begin executing justice: The invaders would head to the KC.

The horsemen set out around midnight and rode through what Sam Clover described as "one of the worst gales of snow and wind that ever swept over the country." After six hard hours they reached the KC, where a log house, stable, and small corral huddled together in a bend of the Middle Fork River. By daybreak on April 9, Wolcott had quietly deployed his men around the house, in the stable, and by the river.

After the attempt on his life back in November, Nate Champion had moved his winter quarters to the KC and was sharing the house with his friend Nick Ray. Both men had a reputation for generous hospitality, so when two acquaintances had shown up needing a place to stay, they found a ready welcome. Bill Walker was a cowboy turned trapper, and Ben Jones was an elderly out-of-work trail cook who had been trapping in the Bighorns with Walker. Champion and Ray were glad of company, particularly because Walker was a good fiddle player. The four men sat up late, taking turns singing old songs and making up dirty verses to a cowboy favorite, "The Old Chisholm Trail."

It was a quiet night, though Jones's dog howled in the yard a couple of times. Champion was up early next morning, fixing breakfast. Jones went out with a pail to get water from the river. As soon as he was out of sight of the house, he was quietly nabbed by the invaders. After a few questions they decided the old man was harmless and, following the policy not to harm any innocent people, simply kept him prisoner.

When an hour had passed and Jones had not come back, Walker went out to find his friend. He was passing the stable on his way toward the river when he heard whispers inside. Someone said in a low voice, "Hold on there—take it easy!" Walker turned toward the stable to find himself staring into the barrels of five Winchesters. The gunmen hustled Walker inside, where there were about 25 men, all with new guns and full cartridge belts. Walker, like Jones, was in no danger himself, but he feared for the men in the cabin.

The invaders sat tight and waited. About 20 minutes later Nick Ray came out looking for Walker and Jones. Major Wolcott was watching from inside the stable as Ray—one of the men who was on the W.S.G.A. list—took a dozen cautious steps from the door. One of the Texans in the stable was itching to use his new rifle and claim the first $50 bounty, and the major gave him the order to fire. The Texan's first shot felled Ray, who started crawling on his hands and knees back to the house. Gunfire erupted as half a dozen invaders fired at Ray while Champion shot back. As Ray reached the house, another shot hit him in the back and he fell forward. Champion leaped out the door and dragged his wounded friend inside.

The attackers now began aiming their fire at the windows of the house, but Champion was able to avoid the bullets as he did what he could for Nick Ray, who was in a bad way. Surrounded by an unknown number of killers and sure to be gunned down if he tried to flee, Champion thought that he was done for. He pulled out a pocket notebook and

A Customized Remington

Nate Champion modified the single-shot Remington-Hepburn .40-70 target rifle shown above to make it fit into his saddle scabbard. He shortened the octagon barrel by 10 inches, refitted the rifle with a more comfortable stock, notched the new stock with finger gouges to fit his hand, and removed the ring bolts that held a shoulder sling. These adjustments made it easier for him to shoot from horseback.

Remington sporting and target rifles were the firearms of choice for many of the cowboys and settlers of the American West. They were sturdy enough to withstand sustained firing and versatile enough to be used for hunting or military purposes. Chambered for a wide range of ammunition sizes, these all-purpose rifles sold for less than $25, a hefty sum in those days, but still within the reach of most workingmen.

a pencil and began keeping a terse chronicle of the violence, addressing it to his friends. If he didn't make it out of the cabin alive and the notebook found its way into their hands, at least they would know how he and Nick had died:

"Me and Nick was getting breakfast when the attack took place. Two men was with us—Bill Jones and another man. The old man went after water and did not come back. His friend went out to see what was the matter and he did not come back. Nick started out and I told him to look out, that I thought there was someone at the stable would not let them come back.

"Nick is shot but not dead yet. He is awful sick. I must go and wait on him.

"It is now about two hours since the first shot. Nick is still alive.

"They are still shooting and are all around the house. Boys, there is bullets coming in like hail.

"Them fellows is in such shape I can't get at them. They are shooting from the stable and river and back of the house.

"Nick is dead. He died about 9 o'clock. . . . I don't think they intend to let me get away this time.

"It is now about noon. There is someone at the stable yet. They are throwing a rope at the door and dragging it back. I guess it is to draw me out. . . . Boys, I feel pretty lonesome just now. I wish there was someone here with me so we could watch all sides of the house at once."

At about this time lunch was being served at the invaders' chuck wagon, which was drawn up on a bluff above the river. They were worn out after a sleepless night followed by the morning's action, and some of them lay down for a nap. The invasion leaders were also anxious to force Champion out of his house quickly, so they could chalk up their first dead rustlers and get back on the trail to Buffalo, about 45 miles away. Burning him out was the obvious solution, so several men were dispatched to a nearby ranch to look for hay to use as fuel; there was a little in Champion's stable, but not enough for a good blaze. The men returned from their errand empty-handed.

At about 3:00 p.m. Champion heard some excitement outside and looked out a window. "There was a man in a buckboard and one on horseback just passed," he wrote. "They fired on them as they went by. I don't know if they killed them or not. I seen lots of men come out on horses on the other side of the river and take after them. . . . I hope they did not catch them fellows."

The man on horseback was Jack Flagg, who was on his way to the town of Douglas as a delegate to the Wyoming Democratic Party convention. With him was his 17-year-old stepson, Alonzo Taylor, who was in front of Flagg driving two horses hitched to the chassis of a wagon carrying Flagg's suitcase and rifle. As they approached the KC, Flagg saw some 20 armed men jump out from behind the stable and order Taylor to stop. The young man was startled, but instead of stopping he urged on his horses and made a successful dash across a nearby bridge over the Middle Fork River as bullets flew around him. Someone ordered Flagg to stop and put up his hands, and Flagg shouted back, "Don't shoot me, boys—I'm all right."

Flagg was one of the men the invaders were out to get, and he'd practically fallen into their hands. One of the Johnson County cattlemen recognized him and shouted, "Jack Flagg! Jack Flagg!" identifying him as fair game—a rustler. A volley of shots rang out, and Flagg threw himself down on the flank of his horse and galloped for his life, with seven horsemen in pursuit. They had closed to within 350 yards when he overtook the wagon, yelling to his stepson to hand him his rifle. Flagg stopped to cover the boy while he cut loose one of the horses from the wagon. Facing a man with a rifle was altogether different from chasing an unarmed rider,

and the pursuers reined in their horses. They had no way of knowing that the gun had only three bullets in it. Flagg and Taylor galloped away to safety. Appropriating the abandoned wagon, the invaders retreated to the KC.

Jack Flagg's escape brought the invaders' simmering tension closer to the boiling point. There was little doubt that Flagg would raise an alarm about the band of gunmen at the KC Ranch. The Johnson County men wanted to quit the ranch immediately, but Frank Wolcott wouldn't hear of it and insisted that they finish the job at hand: "No, we will do one thing at a time," he declared. "We will get this fellow first while we are at it, and then we will go to Buffalo as fast as we can." The others reluctantly gave in.

Wolcott came up with a novel use for Flagg's wagon. He ordered several men to cut down and split some of the corral's posts and to pile the wood on the wagon. Champion heard the blows of the ax and realized what was in store for him: "I heard them splitting wood. I guess they are going to fire the house tonight. I think I will make a break when night comes, if alive."

Champion had even less time than he thought. While some of the gunmen fired steadily through the cabin windows to keep him from getting close enough to return the fire, others pushed the wood-filled wagon against the house, close to an open window on the breezy side of the house, and set the split posts on fire. Fanned by the breeze, the flames began to lick through the open window. Champion wrote the last lines of his courageous chronicle: "Its not night yet. The house is all fired. Goodbye, boys, if I never see you again."

The invaders surrounding the house watched as the roof and the log walls caught fire and smoke leaked out through the gaps in the logs. But there was no sign of Champion, and the waiting men grew edgy; perhaps, one said, he had shot himself. Then someone gave a shout as Champion ran out the back door through black smoke in his stocking feet. With his Winchester in his hands he ran some 50 yards to a ravine south of the house—straight at two sharpshooters. A shot hit his arm, and he dropped his rifle; three more caught him in the chest. Champion fell dead on his back. Sam Clover, who had abandoned the journalist's neutrality and had joined in the shooting, wrote a message of warning on a card—"Cattle Thieves, Beware," it read—and pinned it to the dead man's bloody vest. Frank Canton found Champion's bloodstained notebook on his body, and after it had been passed around for everyone to read, Major Wolcott handed it over to Clover. Nate Champion's last testament would be published within a few days in the *Chicago Herald*.

The shootout was still going on when Wolcott gave orders to the cooks to prepare dinner. Frank falo. Smith, who like Flagg was a delegate to the Democratic convention, was at home with several other convention-bound delegates. Shortly after 9:00, Flagg, his stepson, and three other men were on their way back to the KC.

The rescue party was about halfway there when it ran into a dozen armed settlers. Flagg, it seemed, had not been the first person to witness the shooting at the KC. A man named Terence Smith who had a spread nearby had heard the gunfire in the morning and went over to have a look from the safety of the far side of the river. From there he had ridden full tilt to Buffalo, spreading the alarm through the countryside as he went. The two groups were exchanging intelligence about the shootout at the KC when one of the men spotted a large party of horse-

"Boys, I feel pretty lonesome just now. I wish there was someone here with me so we could watch all sides of the house at once....I heard them splitting wood. I guess they are going to fire the house tonight. I think I will make a break when night comes, if alive.... Its not night yet. The house is all fired. Goodbye, boys, if I never see you again."

NATE CHAMPION'S NOTEBOOK, APRIL 9, 1892

Canton and Fred Hesse argued that they should skip eating and leave for Buffalo straightaway, but Wolcott prevailed, and shortly after 4:00 p.m. the cooks served up a hearty meal. Darkness was falling when the sinister procession got under way.

The snowy countryside was deserted, and Wolcott, at least, was satisfied that the plan was unfolding as he had envisioned, until two outriders who had been scouting ahead of the main column came back with disquieting news: They had spotted a body of horsemen on the road. Wolcott and William Irvine dismounted and walked cautiously forward, listening intently. They could hear nothing in the quiet night; the outriders, they agreed, must have been rattled by a bunch of range horses. Then a gunshot rent the darkness.

After escaping from the gunmen at the KC Ranch, Jack Flagg and his stepson had ridden to the ranch of John R. Smith, about 15 miles out from Buf- men in the distance, illuminated by the faint light of the setting moon. "There they are on the flat," he exclaimed, "a hundred strong." There were in fact only half that many, but the settlers could see they were significantly outnumbered. They decided to stay at a friendly ranch until daybreak and then ride into Buffalo to gather reinforcements.

Major Wolcott and William Irvine returned from their reconnoitering to find the invaders rattled by the gunshot they had just heard; in fact, one of the men in Terence Smith's party had accidentally fired his gun, but the invaders had no way of knowing that and were wondering if they were about to be attacked. Wolcott set about restoring discipline. Riding out in front of the men as if they were on a sunny parade ground, he snapped, "I can take ten good men and whip the whole damned bunch of you." He lined them up like raw army recruits and proceeded to put them through a military drill for more than an hour. When he was satisfied that he had his force back under control, he ordered them to cut a barbed wire fence and took them off the road and across the open fields to outflank whoever it was who had fired the shot in the dark.

The invaders had failed to strike quickly and without warning against Buffalo, but inexplicably Wolcott would not be hurried. After riding for a while, the invaders took a two-hour break at the ranch managed by Fred Hesse. They stopped again at the TA Ranch, approximately 14 miles outside Buffalo. The reason, according to Sam Clover, was that Charlie Ford, the ranch foreman and a member of the invasion force, wanted to see his wife.

Dawn was breaking on Sunday, April 10, and the vigilantes were once again on the move when a local cattleman and confederate galloped up on a lathered horse. "Turn back!" he yelled. "Turn back! Everybody in town is roused. The rustlers are massing from every direction. Get to cover if you value your lives." Things were not going according to Major Wolcott's plan, and he ordered a retreat to the TA. Disgusted by his caution, Frank Canton and Tom Smith insisted furiously that they ride on to Buffalo. As their leaders sat on their horses arguing, the Texas mercenaries waited for orders. The Cheyenne Club cattlemen were ready and willing to kill the rustlers of Johnson County, but the notion of a shootout with an army of citizens was appalling, and not at all what they had bargained for. They prevailed over Canton and Smith: The invaders would not march on Buffalo and take on the enraged populace, at least not this morning.

Sam Clover decided that he had seen enough action. Telling the invaders that he had to go and file his story, he left them to their fate and set out for Buffalo, hoping to contact a friend who was an officer at Fort McKinney, an army post that was located about a mile from the town.

Wolcott now set about planning for the defense of the TA, and his quick survey revealed several favorable features. Nestled in a bend of Crazy Woman Creek, the ranch looked out over rolling hills cut by ravines that would make an enemy attack in force extremely difficult. A log fence seven feet high surrounded the compound, which consisted of a house solidly constructed of 10-by-12-inch logs, a stable, an icehouse, and a dugout in which was stored a quantity of potatoes. A stack of heavy timbers recently purchased for a new building was commandeered to fortify a knoll 150 feet from the stable.

For the rest of the day and on into the night, the major drove his men to turn the ranch into a stronghold. With the timbers they built a fort that measured about 12 by 14 feet with openings in its walls through which the sharpshooters could cover anyone approaching the ranch. They also dug trenches within the fort's walls, threw up breastworks around the house, and blocked its doors and windows with logs, leaving only narrow cracks to fire through. The icehouse was similarly protected. Their work complete, the vigilantes retired behind their fortifications to wait.

While the TA Ranch was being readied for attack, Buffalo was in an uproar, as it had been since the evening before, when Terence Smith arrived with the news of trouble at the KC Ranch. The townspeople, along with the settlers out in the county, had been tense and jittery ever since the attempt on Nate Champion's life and the unsolved murders of John Tisdale and Ranger Jones back in the fall—all three men on the outs, in one way or another, with the county's cattle barons. Now Champion had been attacked again—nobody knew yet how he'd fared this time—and a large band of armed horsemen was riding around Johnson County. It was a terrifying prospect, and there was no telling who their next victim would be.

Sheriff Red Angus asked the commander of the Buffalo militia to call out his men, but the commander couldn't take action without getting permission from headquarters in Cheyenne first, because of the change in procedure that Governor Barber had announced in March. Around 11:00 a.m., the sheriff and a posse of half a dozen men set out for the KC to see what the situation was there. That afternoon, Jack Flagg and his companions rode into Buffalo, shortly before a cowboy galloped up Main Street with the news that the KC Ranch had been burned; worse, Nate Champion and Nick Ray were dead.

By now Buffalo's streets were filling with armed, grim-faced men, ready to finish what the cattlemen vigilantes had started. The men converging on the town were not rustlers; in fact, there probably weren't more than 30 rustlers in the whole of Johnson County. The vast majority of its citizens were honest ranchers, cowboys, storekeepers, and such—some of whom had challenged the hegemony of the cattle barons by fencing their own land or running their own small herds of cattle. They might have offended the old order, but they had been within their rights to do so. And they were now ready to defend those rights.

Rumors swept the town that the cattlemen had reinforcements coming down from the north.

Robert Foote, the merchant whose name probably figured on the W.S.G.A.'s death list as a receiver of stolen beef, threw open his store, offering free guns, blankets, clothing, and food to the ad hoc citizens army. Churches and schoolhouses opened their doors to the flood of arrivals, and townswomen prepared prodigious amounts of food for them.

Early on Sunday evening a force of men, including Jack Flagg, left town for the TA. They arrived around midnight, posted watchmen, and started digging rifle pits and throwing up breastworks of their own on the hills around the ranch. It was after midnight when Sheriff Angus returned to Buffalo from the KC Ranch, where he had seen for himself what the vigilantes had done. He quickly organized a party of 40 men, who reached the TA before daylight and took up positions on hills overlooking the ranch. Armed men, along with boys eager to be in on the action, continued to gather during the night, and by the time the chilly dawn broke, some

A row of holes drilled below the hayloft window of the log stable served as gunports for the vigilantes holed up inside during the siege of the TA Ranch (below). A small stream running through the corral to the left of the stable provided water for their horses, and the stable held plenty of hay and grain.

150 men and boys had surrounded the TA, and another 150 or more were on the way.

The TA Ranch was well known to many of these men. Only three winters before, it had been the venue for a large dance. The four-room ranch house had just been built, and the smooth floors were ideal for dancing. The host on that occasion had been the newly married Charlie Ford. Now the ranch foreman was about to shoot it out with his guests; one estimate had it that among the forces facing him were 9 out of every 10 men who had been at the dance that night.

The shooting began early on the morning of Monday, April 11, and the man in charge of the citizens was Arapahoe Brown, the manager of Buffalo's flour mill. He was filling the void left for the moment by Sheriff Angus, who was back in Buffalo organizing the reinforcements into small platoons to be escorted to the TA by deputy sheriffs. Brown was a huge bearded man who belonged to the town's rougher element, and it was rumored that his property was edged by unmarked graves.

Whatever his shortcomings, Brown began giving orders, and others followed them. As Major Wolcott had foreseen, it was going to be very hard to dislodge the vigilante band; the hilly, ravine-riddled terrain around the ranch and the formidable fortifications that the major had engineered were a daunting challenge to men whose only weapons were rifles and other small arms. The enterprising Robert Foote rode off to Fort McKinney and asked the commanding officer, Colonel Van Horn, for the use of a cannon, offering $500 for the loan, but was politely yet firmly refused. The fight going on at the TA was, in his opinion, the business of the state of Wyoming, and he wasn't going to get dragged into it.

This diagram, drawn shortly after the siege, shows the rectangular fort the invaders built west of the ranch house, along with the guidons, or flags, planted nearby. Positions occupied by the army of citizens appear as short squiggly lines. The U.S. Cavalry arrived from the northwest.

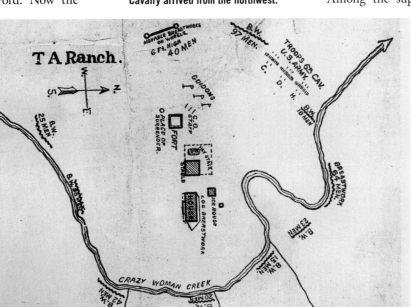

"Which do you prefer, being killed going up the hill or being killed right here? You white-livered son-of-a-bitch, you will either do as ordered or I'll kill you myself."

MAJOR FRANK WOLCOTT TO
A TEXAS GUNMAN

At around 9:00 a.m. on Monday, the citizens caught sight of the vigilantes' wagons, bringing up the rear as usual, on the brow of a nearby hill. They captured the wagons and were pleased to find several thousand rounds of ammunition, two cases of dynamite, fuses, and handcuffs. They also discovered a medical bag left behind by Dr. Penrose. Among the supplies in the bag was a bottle of bichloride of mercury, a well-known antiseptic used to prevent infection in wounds. Like any compound containing mercury, it was extremely toxic, and a rumor spread like wildfire that the cattle barons had been planning to poison the county's wells. The settlers treated the men who had been driving the wagons as neutrals and took them to Buffalo, where they installed themselves in a saloon.

Hunkered down within the walls of the ranch compound and listening to gunfire coming from all directions, the cattle barons were anxiously wondering when their friends in Cheyenne would get word of their embattled state and send help. The invaders had friends in Buffalo whom they could count on to send a telegram to Cheyenne—if it were possible. And, of course, sending a telegram from Buffalo was highly problematic since the vigilantes had arranged for the telegraph wires to be cut. Moreover, their confederates around Buffalo had orders to cut the wires again, if service was restored.

And in fact, linemen had been riding the snow-covered range for several days repairing the damage done by the cattle barons' allies. The connection between Buffalo and Cheyenne was restored on Monday, and Buffalo's acting mayor, Charles Hogerson, succeeded in getting word to Governor Barber that an armed force had invaded the county. Hogerson, a known rustler sympathizer whose name may even

have been on the death list, requested the aid of the militia. The governor responded by sending a message to Buffalo's militia commander, but it was simply a request for details of the situation and not an order to swing into action, as Hogerson had asked. Soon after this exchange, the wires were cut again—this time by Johnson County citizens eager to prevent the vigilantes' friends in the outside world from getting wind of their plight and coming to their rescue.

As Monday wore on, the mood inside the TA grew progressively grimmer. The invaders had only 100 rounds of ammunition each— not enough for heavy fighting—and nothing to eat except a cellarful of potatoes. Even now the mulish Wolcott refused to believe that he had misjudged the situation. He raged against the rustlers and against the Johnson County allies who had let him down. The only mistake in his plan, he insisted, was not coming with a bigger force.

Under the strain of siege, the rift between the Cheyenne Club gentlemen and the Texan gunmen, who had had little to do with each other from the beginning, was growing wider. The Texans muttered disapprovingly when one of the cattlemen, Frederic de Billier, a Harvard-educated New Yorker, retired to a back room of Charlie Ford's house for his midday nap. When Wolcott ordered some of the Texans up the hill behind the house to relieve the men in the fort, one of them refused, protesting that he would be killed going up. Wolcott exploded: "Which do you prefer, being killed going up the hill or being killed right here? You white-livered son-of-a-bitch, you will either do as ordered or I'll kill you myself." The Texan went.

"These people came in here with murder and destruction in their hearts and hands. They have murdered and burned and defied the law, and it was my duty to arrest them. They were mine. I had them in my grasp and they were taken from me."

SHERIFF W. G. "RED" ANGUS

Tension was also growing within the ranks of the cattle barons themselves. Wolcott let William Irvine in on his latest scheme: He would break out of the compound with 20 men and attack the forces ringing the TA; they had no stomach to fight, the major said, and would abandon the siege. When Irvine told Wolcott that the plan was foolish, the major flew into a rage, calling Irvine "a damn mutineer."

On Monday night a courier who brought a desperate message for Governor Barber from the vigilantes managed to slip through the army that was surrounding the ranch. Knowing that the telegraph lines south of Buffalo were probably out of commission, the courier headed east to the town of Gillette, some 70 miles away and outside the range of vigilante sabotage.

While the courier was speeding toward Gillette, Arapahoe Brown was also taking advantage of the cover of darkness. He directed some of his men to edge forward and dig a new ring of rifle pits closer to the ranch house. Another overnight project was to build a movable fort using the chassis of two of the captured wagons. They were lashed together, then piled with logs and bales of hay to a height of six feet. Big enough to shield 40 men, the go-devil, as the citizens called it, would be rolled forward inch by inch until it was close enough to the fort on the knoll near the stable for the men to lob sticks of the invaders' own dynamite into the compound.

Tuesday was another bad day for the invaders. No help materialized, and the citizens were, according to one of the stockmen, "constantly firing on the house, which was considerably shot up. They finally got the range of the doors and it was dangerous to go in or out." To prevent a breakout, sharpshooters fired at the invaders' horses in the compound's corral, killing five of them before the survivors were hustled into the stable. William Irvine was slightly injured when a bullet passed through a crack in the wall of the ranch house and grazed his foot. Others had nearly been hit. Apart from Irvine, however, the only other injury was self-inflicted. One of the Texans was crawling around with a cocked revolver strapped around his waist when the gun went off and hit him in the groin. He would die a few days later. Fortunately for the invaders, the citizens had not yet gotten their go-devil close enough to launch a dynamite attack.

Late on Tuesday night the major conceived another breakout plan: At 2:00 a.m. the Wyoming men would make a dash for it, abandoning the Texans. At the appointed hour the moon was shining so brightly on the snow-covered ground that the foolhardy major had to concede that attempting to escape would be suicidal.

Unbeknown to either side in the siege at the TA Ranch, word of the war in Johnson County was reaching the outside world. On Tuesday Governor Barber received a telegram describing his friends' predicament, probably the one carried by the courier to Gillette the night before. Barber sprang into action. Going straight to the top, he wired President Benjamin Harrison in Washington:

"An insurrection exists in Johnson County in the state of Wyoming, in the immediate vicinity of Fort McKinney, against the government of said state. . . . Open hostilities exist and large bodies of armed men are engaged in battle . . . United States troops are located at Fort McKinney, which is 13 miles from the scene of the action. . . . I appeal to you on behalf of the state of Wyoming to direct the United States troops at Fort McKinney to assist in suppressing this insurrection. Lives of a large number of persons are in imminent danger."

No reply came. The governor wired Colonel Van Horn at Fort McKinney to ready his troops pending orders from Washington. Barber also sent telegrams to the two Wyoming senators in Washington. They rushed to the White House and got the president out of bed. Within a matter of minutes, Harrison wired the governor: "I have, in compliance with your call for aid of the United States forces to protect the state of Wyoming against domestic violence, ordered the secretary of war to concentrate a sufficient force at the scene of the disturbance and to co-operate with your authorities."

The third day of the siege, Wednesday, April 13, promised resolution, and the citizens appeared to

Cavalrymen lead the captured invaders through the main street of Buffalo *(below)* on their way to imprisonment at nearby Fort McKinney. On the pretext that the locals might lynch the prisoners, their supporters arranged for federal troops to escort them to Fort Russell at Cheyenne. Because of their excellent connections there, the invaders had a much better chance of avoiding a trial.

NO. 1. TOM SMITH
" 2. A.B.CLARKE
" 3. J.N.LESLIE
" 4. E.W.WHITCOMB
" 5. D. BROOKE
" 6. W.B.WALLACE
" 7. CHAS FORD

NO. 8. A.R. POWERS
" 9. A.D. ADAMSON
" 10. C.A.CAMPBELL
" 11. FRANK LABERTEAUX
" 12. PHIL DUFRAN
" 13. MAJOR WOLCOTT
" 14. W.E. GUTHRIE.

NO. 15. W.C. IRVINE
" 16. BOB TISDALE
" 17. JOE ELLIOTT
" 18. JOHN TISDALE
" 19. SCOTT DAVIS
" 20. FRED DEBILLIER
" 21 BEN MORRISON

NO. 22. W.J.CL
" 23. L.H. PA
" 24. TESCHN
" 25. B.C.SC
" 26. W.H.T
" 27. J.A. GA
" 28. W.A.W

"THE INVADERS"
JOHNSON COUNTY CATTLE WAR. TAKE
(FRANCIS E. WARREN) MAY 4th 18

have the upper hand. Their go-devil had by now traveled 100 yards and was creeping ever closer to the invaders' stronghold.

Then, shortly before sunrise, a bugle sounded across the range. A cattleman with his eye to a crack in one of the barricaded windows yelled that he could see the flags of the cavalry. While the cattlemen gasped with relief, a Texan exclaimed in dismay, "What! United States troops! Have we got to fight United States troops too? Great God almighty, we sure are done up now."

Before the troops arrived, the citizens vented their anger in a last withering barrage of fire. But when Colonel Van Horn asked Sheriff Angus to order a cease-fire, the guns fell silent at once. The colonel conferred with the sheriff and Arapahoe Brown, who agreed that the prisoners could surrender to the military, as long as they were soon returned to the civil authorities for trial. The bugle blew again, and flanked by flagbearers, Van Horn, Angus, and two other officers led the column of troops toward the ranch house. With them marched newsman Sam Clover, in at the end as at the beginning.

From behind the breastworks of the TA Ranch's fortified outpost someone began waving a soiled white rag; another person appeared down the hill at the house. Major Wolcott stepped out of the door and strode briskly toward the column of men. He bowed to Colonel Van Horn, who told him that he had orders to quell the disturbance. "Are your people willing to surrender quietly?" the colonel asked. "I will surrender to you," Wolcott said, then pointed to Angus and added, "but to that man never. I know him well. Rather than give up to him we will all die right here."

It took two hours to place all the vigilantes under arrest and take their arms. Van Horn counted

JSSELL

NO. 29. J. BARLINGS
„ 30. M.A. MC NALLY
„ 31. MIKE SHONSEY
„ 32. DICK ALLEN
„ 33. FRED HESSE
„ 34. FRANK CANTON
„ 35. Wᵐ LITTLE

NO. 36 JEFF MYNETT
„ 37. BOB BARLINGS
„ 38. S. SUTHERLAND
„ 39. BUCK GARRETT
„ 40. G.R. TUCKER
„ 41. J.M. BENFORD
„ 42. WILL ARMSTRONG

No. 5174

Despite the weight of evidence against them, the stockmen and their hired guns appear self-assured in this group portrait taken at Fort Russell in Cheyenne. During their 10-week stay at Fort Russell they ate sirloin steak and mushrooms and passed the time playing high five, monte, hearts, and penny ante, and they were coached in baseball and football.

45 men, including the Texan shot in the groin; 46 horses, 45 rifles, 50 revolvers, and 5,000 rounds of ammunition. Around 8:45 a.m., as several hundred armed citizens of Johnson County looked on from the hills, the troops began marching the prisoners to Fort McKinney.

The cattlemen's friends now moved quickly to pull more strings on their behalf. Four days after their surrender, the invaders, cattlemen and Texans alike, were marched out of Fort McKinney in a freezing rain, on their way to Cheyenne and out of the legal clutches of unfriendly Johnson County. Furious settlers were in attendance to witness their departure. Sheriff Angus summed up their sense of injustice: "These people came in here with murder and destruction in their hearts and hands. They have murdered and burned and defied the law, and it was my duty to arrest them. They were mine. I had them in my grasp and they were taken from me."

After a six-day journey on horseback made miserable by a blizzard, they reached Fort Fetterman on the Bozeman Trail and there boarded a private Pullman car that whisked them in comfort to Cheyenne. For the next 10 weeks they endured the boredom and ignominy of being imprisoned at Fort Russell. They had been charged with the murders of Nate Champion and Nick Ray, but the case had greatly weakened when the chief witnesses against them, the trappers Ben Jones and Bill Walker, disappeared; it was said that they had been threatened at gunpoint to get out of town.

It was perhaps to be expected that the cattlemen would find a sympathetic judge in Cheyenne. He ruled that the trial should be held in that city—the only place, he declared, where they would receive an unprejudiced hearing. He then rubbed salt in the wound he had just inflicted on Johnson County by ordering it to pay for the prisoners' confinement, at a stiff $100 a day for each man. The county treasury went broke within a few weeks. The judge made yet another friendly ruling, releasing the prisoners without bond. The cattlemen and Texan gunfighters—the two halves of an army that barely spoke to each other—joined in a great celebration party. The Texans, unused to champagne, drank it like water and became so boisterous that they started fighting among themselves for hours. They were put on a train for Omaha, where they were handed postdated checks and dismissed. When they tried to cash the checks, they bounced.

In the end, the lack of funds forced Johnson County to drop all charges against the invaders. The cattle barons and their mercenaries had literally gotten away with murder. Vigilanteism had triumphed, thanks to the support of state and federal leaders, all the way up to President Harrison himself. The citizens of Johnson County had a great deal to be bitter about.

Buffalo buried the cattlemen's victims as heroes. On Saturday, April 16, three days after the siege lifted at the TA Ranch, the bodies of Nate Champion and Nick Ray were placed on display in town amid banks of flowers. Ray's body was little more than a charred trunk, without head or limbs. A funeral service was held for the two men in a vacant building on Main Street. The church organist, fearing trouble, refused to appear, and the organ was played for the occasion by a young girl. There were no untoward incidents during the funeral, which drew an enormous crowd for so small a town. The preacher urged the citizens to abide by the law, reminding them that punishment was not only theirs to dispense: " 'Vengeance is mine,' saith the Lord, 'I will repay.' "

As the funeral procession made its way up Main Street toward the cemetery, Jack Flagg walked directly behind the hearse, leading the dead men's horses with their empty saddles. Behind him came a procession of as many as 500 settlers, traveling in carriages and wagons, on foot and on horseback. One cowhand noted with satisfaction that the so-called outlaws Nate Champion and Nick Ray "were laid away with as much respect as any of the big cattlemen had ever been." ◆

ACROSS THE WIDE MISSOURI

"To say I wept bitterly would but faintly express the ocean of tears I shed on leaving my beloved home to take up residence in the 'wild and wooly West.' " MRS. W. B. CATON

Advertisements for prairie land trumpeted low prices and easy credit terms. Railroad companies tirelessly wooed potential buyers back east and in Europe for the millions of acres of land they were given by the federal government along their rights of way.

The vast, wide-open grasslands stretching westward from the Missouri River were, according to early-19th-century explorer Zebulon Pike, "incapable of cultivation." On maps the region was labeled "The Great American Desert," and goldminers and railroad builders considered it no more than an obstruction on their way west. But as arable land east of the Missouri became harder to come by, the land hungry turned their gaze toward the prairies.

Migration began slowly at midcentury and was aided by the passage of the Kansas-Nebraska Act, a law creating two new territories out of land previously reserved for American Indians. The pace picked up after the passage in 1862 of the Homestead Act, which offered 160 acres to settlers who built a house and lived on the land for five years.

Following the end of the Civil War, both railroad companies and the territories themselves advertised for settlers by promising, with a great many superlatives, "Land for the Landless! Homes for the Homeless!" People responded in ever greater numbers, traveling by wagon, steamboat, and rail to start new lives on the land that would become the states of North Dakota, South Dakota, Nebraska, and Kansas. "One year ago this was a vast houseless, uninhabited prairie, with no trace of approaching civilization to frighten the timid antelope, or turn the buffalo from his course," wrote a Nebraska settler in 1872. "Today I can see more than thirty dwellings from my door yard."

The hopeful arrivals found the prairies far less idyllic than the paradise promised in the advertisements. Some decided they couldn't live in a country where, as a woman commented after surveying a landscape with only sparse patches of trees, "there is nothing to make a shadow." The disappointed pushed on west to California or Oregon or gave up on pioneering altogether and went back home. As for those who stayed on, Mrs. W. B. Caton voiced an attitude shared by thousands of her fellow pioneers: "We had found God's own country, and were quite content to accept it as our future home."

A homesteading family arrives in Custer County, Nebraska, in 1886. Newcomers often lived in their wagons until they could build a dugout or a house on their new land.

Nebraskan settlers load blocks of sod onto a wagon *(right)*. To produce uniform blocks of "prairie marble," homesteaders cut the sod into rows of even width and depth with a breaking plow *(below)*, then used a spade to divide the strips into three-foot lengths.

A PLOW USED FOR BREAKING SOD

"Father made a dugout...when it rained, the water came through the roof and ran in the door. After the storms, we carried the water out with buckets." A KANSAS SETTLER

The settlers' first home was often a dugout that was made, a pioneer remarked, "without mortar, square, plumb, or greenbacks." Quick and cheap to build, the dwelling consisted of a room carved into the side of a hill, a front wall, and a roof of sod. One Nebraskan tallied the cost of his 14-foot-square dugout at $2.78; the total included one window and the materials for a door.

When time allowed, pioneers utilized sod, the prairie's only plentiful building material, to construct a freestanding house. Called a soddy, it took much longer to build than a dugout, but since it was aboveground it could be a larger and more comfortable home.

Although warm in the winter and cool in the summer, dugouts and soddies leaked when it rained hard. Insects and snakes also plagued these earthy homes. "Sometimes the bull snakes would get in the roof," recalled a Kansas pioneer, "and now and then one would lose his hold and fall down on the bed, then off on the floor. Mother would grab the

A swing hung from a roof timber for the children adds a playful touch to a dugout located at the edge of a cornfield in Nebraska. On the hill above stands a wagon loaded with sod to repair the dugout's roof.

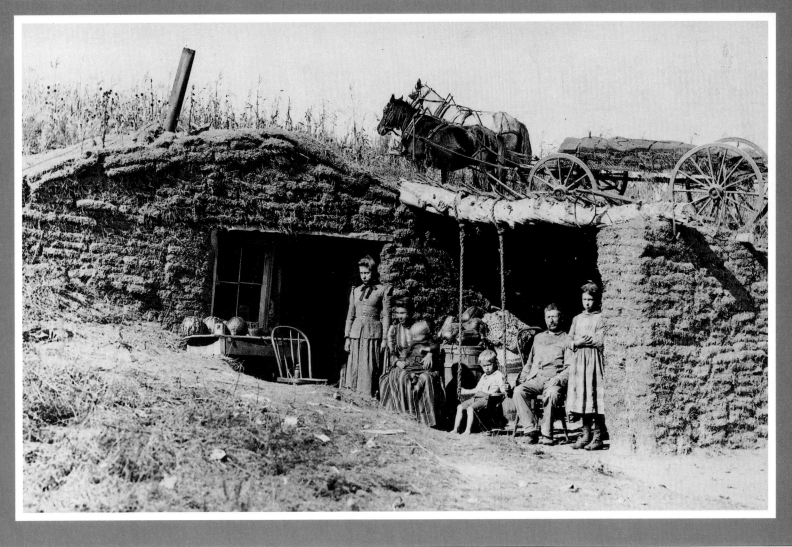

"Chips were plentiful, as the plains had for years been an open range, first for buffalo and then for cattle in great herds." EMMA SMITH, KANSAS

hoe and there was something doing and after the fight was over Mr. Bull Snake was dragged outside."

Once homesteaders had built a home, they turned to the task of breaking the ground and planting crops. Farmers needed a special sod-busting plow, several farm hands, and six or more yoke of oxen to cut through the tough, wiry roots of the prairie grass and turn it back in strips, roots up. Because most settlers had only one yoke of oxen, they often asked neighbors or hired established settlers to help prepare their fields. When this back-breaking chore was completed, the first crop planted was usually corn, and the women and children often helped with the sowing.

Although women did farm work when needed, they concentrated on feeding and cloth-

Settlers gathered buffalo and cattle dung for fuel *(inset)*. Leaving no ground idle, the Nebraskans below have planted corn close to their sod house.

172

This one-room dugout near Bloom, Kansas, was close quarters for a family, but one housewife discovered an advantage: "It don't take near the work to keep up one room that it does a big house."

BUTTER CHURN

ing their families with very limited re-sources. Ada Musgrave recalled how her in-genious friend Alzada Baxter cut up grain sacks stenciled with the family's name and "made trousers for her husband from the material. There was no danger of him being lost with his name brightly stamped across the seat of his trousers." Women traded milk and eggs for calico to make dresses for themselves; many made do with only two.

In the early days, even the cleverest house-wife had little choice but to serve very simple and often very repetitive meals. "Our living at first was very scanty, mostly corn coarsely ground or made into hominy," recalled one pioneer. "After we had raised a crop of wheat and had some ground, we would invite the neighbors, proudly telling them we would have 'flour doings.' Next it was 'chicken fix-ings.' And when we could have 'flour doings and chicken fixings' at the same meal we felt we were on the road to prosperity."

Nebraska settlers fight a prairie fire with gunnysacks and water in barrels *(above)*. "It came rushing down upon me, roaring, cracking, thundering," reported a witness to one such fire. "On it flew with lightning speed like a devouring demon." Tornadoes *(left)* were a yearly threat. A homesteader said of the prairie, "When it blows it storms, and when it rains it pours. When crops yield they are enormous, and when they fail the failure is complete."

"The grave was so little and pitiful and the prairie widened out from it so far;
I hadn't mistrusted before how big the prairie was." Kansas mother, 1879

The prairie's first settlers struggled against great odds for even a small measure of prosperity. Temperatures ranged from -30°F or less to more than 100°F. The winters brought deadly blizzards that would blow in without warning, and with the summers came dry, scorching winds. Tens of thousands of homesteaders fled the territory during a drought that lasted from June 1859 to November 1860, when there was not a single good rain.

Natural disasters—floods, fires, tornadoes, dust storms—regularly swept the prairies with devastating effects. Swarms of grasshoppers descended on the area from 1874 to 1877. "All, or many, of the elements of nature seemed to work together to discipline the early Kansas settlers," a pioneer commented. "They were not allowed to grow soft with ease and luxury, and as though hot winds, drought and Indians were not enough, the grasshoppers came along and did their part." With the exception of prairie grass, almost every kind of plant was attacked by the insects, and they left farmers with little more

Harvey Andrews and his family gather around the grave of one of his children for this photograph taken in 1887 in Custer County, Nebraska. Disease, injuries, and the privations of prairie life exacted a high toll on the pioneers, especially the young.

than "the barbed wire fence and the mortgage," in the words of one Dakota victim.

Nevertheless, many homesteaders were able to muster remarkable equanimity. "Life was wretchedly uncomfortable, we were poverty stricken, without the means to sustain life through the coming winter," wrote one woman. But, she continued, "we made the most of our circumstances and of one another. Life was worthwhile, even then."

Physical hardship was, for some, less burdensome than the effects of living on an isolated homestead. Settlers who had come from close families and communities were unprepared for the sometimes terrible loneliness of their new life. One pioneer woman later recalled of her early years, "The unbroken prairie stretched for miles outside, and the wistful-faced sheep were always near at hand. Often mother used to go out and lie down among them for company, when she was alone for the day."

Churchgoing was an antidote to loneliness. Until the area counted enough people

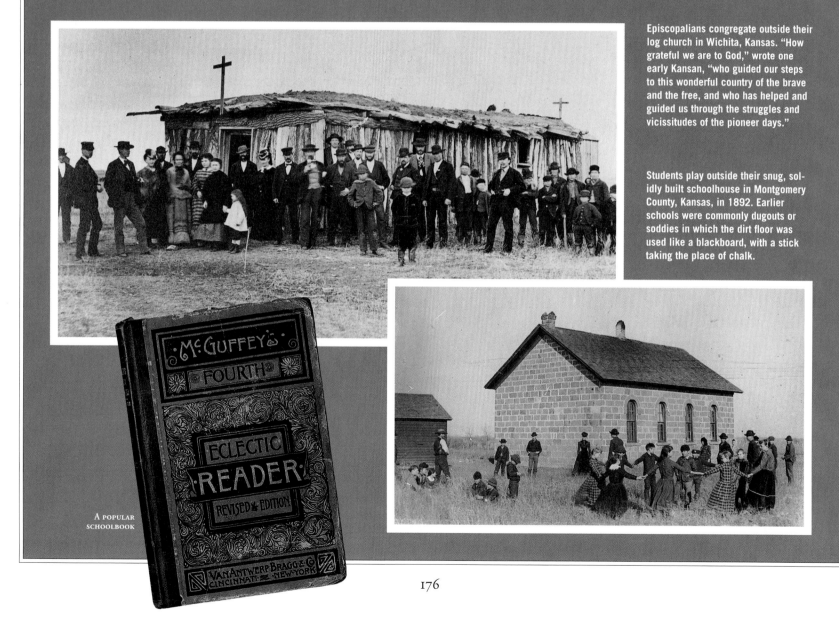

Episcopalians congregate outside their log church in Wichita, Kansas. "How grateful we are to God," wrote one early Kansan, "who guided our steps to this wonderful country of the brave and the free, and who has helped and guided us through the struggles and vicissitudes of the pioneer days."

Students play outside their snug, solidly built schoolhouse in Montgomery County, Kansas, in 1892. Earlier schools were commonly dugouts or soddies in which the dirt floor was used like a blackboard, with a stick taking the place of chalk.

A POPULAR SCHOOLBOOK

McGUFFEY'S
FOURTH
ECLECTIC
READER
REVISED EDITION
VAN ANTWERP BRAGG & CO
CINCINNATI NEW YORK

A MAP OF KANSAS
PATCHWORK QUILT
MADE IN 1887

Quilters apply the finishing touches to their communal handiwork at a gathering in the Pendroy, North Dakota, post office in the 1890s. Quilting bees provided a social break for the isolated women of the prairie.

Dressed in their best, Kansas women watch a friend's shooting skill during a picnic in 1878. Prairie women learned to handle guns for protection when their husbands were away.

of one denomination to build a church, the congregation held its services in houses, stores, or stables. A woman wrote of the services near her childhood home in Kansas in the 1860s, "These meetings were social as well as religious and were the only break from the hard toil of the empire-building, home-making pioneers, except an occasional quilting, sheep-shearing or sorghum-making gathering."

Intent on forging their own new communities, the settlers stuck together and helped one another out. The knowledge that "everybody else was facing the same hard times" bound people together, and in the process, many became "unbreakable friends."

The pioneers worked hard, but they also found ways to have fun. Many loved to dance. "During the five years we lived on the farm," a Kansas woman wrote, "I do not remember one religious service being held in town, but I do remember the dances that were frequently given to which I was sometimes allowed to go."

Single men greatly outnumbered single women on the frontier, and dances were one way that marriageable individuals could meet. Such encounters often resulted in brief courtships and simple weddings. "We went to Loup City, got the license, went over to the parsonage, and was married by Rev. Randolf, a Methodist minister, at two o'clock in the afternoon," a young man wrote his mother. He and his bride then drove back to her parents' home, "where a table well loaded was waiting for us. We ate our suppers and stayed there until about 11 oclock and then came on up home. They did not have but a few there on account of the house being small." A woman remembered her honeymoon as a "sixty mile ride in a lumber wagon loaded with things I was taking from home."

At its best, prairie life bred a sense of community, resilience, and trust in the future. As one pioneer recalled, "No matter what happened we always planned on next year being a good year and never quite gave up, for along with all the hard work and worry we had lots of fun and good times."

A PRAIRIE FAMILY'S PICNIC BASKET

U.S. STATISTICS

17,069,453 Population of the United States in 1840. Center of population: 16 miles south of Clarksburg, western Virginia.

23,191,876 Population of the United States in 1850. Center of population: 23 miles southeast of Parkersburg, western Virginia.

31,443,321 Population of the United States in 1860. Center of population: 20 miles southeast of Chillicothe, Ohio.

39,818,449 Population of the United States in 1870. Center of population: 48 miles northeast of Cincinnati, Ohio.

50,155,783 Population of the United States in 1880. Center of population: 8 miles southwest of Cincinnati, Ohio.

62,947,714 Population of the United States in 1890. Center of population: 20 miles east of Columbus, Indiana.

179,000 Population of western states and territories in 1850 (*including present-day Arizona, California, Colorado, Idaho, Montana, Nevada, New Mexico, Oregon, Washington, Wyoming, and Utah*)

3,134,000 Population of western states and territories in 1890

3,953,760 Number of black slaves in the United States, 1860

448,070 Number of free blacks in the United States, 1860

51,752 Number of Irish immigrants in 1846, the first year of the potato famine

1,186,928 Number of Irish immigrants between 1847 and 1854

2,808 Miles of railroad in 1840

30,626 Miles of railroad in 1860

163,597 Miles of railroad in 1890

400 Number of train rails to the mile

10 Number of railroad spikes to secure each rail

13,468 Number of communities served by U.S. Post Office in 1840

62,401 Number of communities served by U.S. Post Office in 1890

1,753,588 Land area of United States and its territories in square miles, 1840

2,973,965 Land area of United States and its territories in square miles, 1860

States admitted to the Union, 1840–1900:

Florida	1845	Nebraska	1867
Texas	1845	Colorado	1876
Iowa	1846	North Dakota	1889
Wisconsin	1848	South Dakota	1889
California	1850	Montana	1889
Minnesota	1858	Washington	1889
Oregon	1859	Idaho	1890
Kansas	1861	Wyoming	1890
West Virginia	1863	Utah	1896
Nevada	1864		

FRONTIER LINGO

Many colorful terms were coined by cowboys and others in the cattle trade or were freely adapted by them from Spanish words that had been used in Mexico for generations:

Bronco: an unbroken horse; from Spanish *bronco*, meaning rough or unruly.

Buckaroo: cowboy; from Spanish *vaquero*, cowman.

Cayuse: a horse; originally a range horse associated with the Cayuse Indians of Oregon.

Chaps: the leather leg coverings worn by cowboys; from Spanish *chaparajos*.

Chuck wagon: a wagon that carried bedding, water, and supplies on the cattle drive; the "chuck box" was the cook's worktable and pantry. The word *chuck* means food, but its origin is uncertain.

Dogie: a motherless calf; said to have originated from *dough-guts*, referring to a hungry calf's swollen stomach.

Hoosegow: jail; from Spanish *juzgado*, meaning tried or judged.

Lariat: a long, braided rope; from Spanish *la reata*.

Lasso: a sliding loop at the end of a lariat; from Spanish *lazo*, a snare.

Palaver: a discussion; from Spanish *palabra*, a word.

Passing the buck: giving someone else the blame or responsibility; originally a poker player's term for designating the dealer by placing an object such as a buckhorn-handled knife in front of that player. (Gambling also provided such colorful phrases as *poker face, raw deal, having an ace up your sleeve, loaded dice,* and *playing a wild card.*)

Pinto: a horse of mixed color; from Spanish *pinto*, painted.

Poncho: a blanket or cloak with a hole for the head; from Spanish *poncho*.

Son of a bitch stew: a one-pot meal that included brains, tongue, kidneys, hearts, tripe, or any other usable part of a freshly killed steer.

Stampede: from Spanish *estampeda*.

Waddy: originally a cowhand who filled in at busy times, later a rustler, then any cowboy; from *wad* or *wadding*, meaning something that fills an empty space.

Like the cattle business, the mining industry came up with terminology that soon found its way into popular usage:

Bonanza: a windfall. From Spanish *bonanza*, meaning prosperity, fair weather, success.

Bum: a shiftless person, applied to post-gold rush wanderers; from German *Bummler*, a loafer or wanderer.

Digs: short for diggings, the place where prospectors mine gold; it came to mean the place where a man slept, ate, and lived.

Hooch: a term derived from the name of a native Alaskan tribe called the Hutsnuwu, or "Hoochinoo," who distilled their own liquor; the term was shortened to "hooch" during the Klondike gold rush of 1896 and applied to any home-made or bootlegged liquor.

Pan out: from panning for gold. "Panning out" was the technique of separating valuable ore from worthless sand or gravel, and the term eventually meant to be successful.

Placer: a deposit of sand, gravel, or other loose material from which valuable ore could be panned out; from Spanish *placer*, a sand bank.

Slumgullion: a California gold rush term for a stew made with any available meat and vegetables.

Railroading inevitably produced yet another brand of slang, some of which caught the public's fancy and became entrenched in ordinary speech:

Hell on wheels: any of the rough-and-ready towns that served construction crews along the Union Pacific Railroad line. Such towns were far from peaceful, with gambling halls, saloons, and brothels attracting outlaws and consuming the railroaders' wages.

Jerkwater: a small town; originally a way station on a railroad line where crewmen obtained water for their steam engines by jerking on a cord that was connected to a railside water tower.

Make the grade: to achieve a goal, as when a train ascends a steep grade to the summit of a pass.

Railroad: to convict someone quickly and unquestioningly, as if with the speed of a locomotive.

Sidetrack: to deflect a person or object from a goal, as in the case of a train shunted from a main line to a siding.

CHRONOLOGY OF EVENTS, 1840S–1890S

1840-44	1845-49	1850-54	1855-59	1860-64	1865-69

POLITICS

1841 William Henry Harrison inaugurated ninth president but dies in office; vice president John Tyler becomes 10th president.

PRESIDENT WILLIAM
HENRY HARRISON

1845 James K. Polk inaugurated 11th president.

1847 Abraham Lincoln of Illinois elected to House of Representatives.

1849 Zachary Taylor inaugurated 12th president.

1850 President Taylor dies; Millard Fillmore becomes 13th president.

1853 Franklin Pierce inaugurated 14th president.

1854 Republican Party founded.

1857 Dred Scott Decision prohibits banning of slavery in U.S. territories.

1857 James Buchanan inaugurated 15th president.

1858 Lincoln-Douglas debates take place.

1860 South Carolina secedes from the Union.

1861 Abraham Lincoln inaugurated 16th president. Jefferson Davis inaugurated president of the Confederate States of America. Civil War begins.

1863 Lincoln's Emancipation Proclamation frees slaves in Confederate territory.

1865 President Lincoln assassinated. Andrew Johnson becomes 17th president.

1865–1866 13th and 14th Amendments grant full citizenship to former slaves.

1869 Ulysses S. Grant inaugurated 18th president.

1869 Elizabeth Cady Stanton and Susan B. Anthony form the National Woman Suffrage Association.

WESTWARD EXPANSION

1841 First covered wagon train reaches California in November, having left Kansas in May.

1844 Antipolygamy mob kills Mormon founder Joseph Smith in Carthage, Illinois. Brigham Young chosen new Mormon leader.

EMIGRANT'S TRUNK
CARRIED BY WAGON

1845 United States annexes republic of Texas.

1845 Editor John L. O'Sullivan justifies westward expansion as the nation's "manifest destiny."

1847 Mormons arrive in Utah.

1848 Oregon Territory created, encompassing today's Oregon, Washington, and Idaho.

1848 Gold discovered in California.

1850 California admitted as a state; Utah and New Mexico established as territories.

1850 Brigham Young becomes first governor of the territory of Utah.

1851 John B. L. Soule, in the *Terre Haute Express*, editorializes "Go West, young man, go West."

1853 Gadsden Purchase: United States buys 29,644 square miles from Mexico.

1856 Western Union Telegraph Company established.

1856 First railroad bridge across the Mississippi opens.

1858 Colorado gold rush popularizes slogan "Pikes Peak or bust."

1859 First major U.S. silver deposit, the Comstock Lode, discovered in Nevada.

1860 Pony Express carries mail from Saint Joseph, Missouri, to Sacramento, California, in 10 days.

1861 Transcontinental telegraph line completed.

1862 Homestead Act offers 160 acres of land to homesteaders who live on it for five years.

NOTICE FOR
PONY EXPRESS

1866 Charles Goodnight and Oliver Loving establish cattle trail from Texas to New Mexico.

1867 United States buys Alaska from Russia for roughly two cents per acre.

1869 Discovery of high-grade silver ore made near Denver, Colorado.

1869 Transcontinental railroad completed.

GOLDEN SPIKE USED TO LINK
UP TRANSCONTINENTAL
RAILROAD

SOCIETY

1841 James Fenimore Cooper publishes *The Deerslayer.*

1844 Charles Dickens's *A Christmas Carol* published in the United States.

1844 Samuel F. B. Morse sends first telegraph message, saying "What hath God wrought!" from Washington, D.C., to Baltimore, Maryland.

1846 Smithsonian Institution founded.

1846 Elias Howe patents the first sewing machine in the United States.

1847 Stephen Foster's "Oh, Susanna" first performed in concert.

1850 *Harper's New Monthly Magazine* begins publication.

1851 Isaac Singer patents his sewing machine.

1852 Harriet Beecher Stowe's *Uncle Tom's Cabin* published.

1854 Hoop skirts come into fashion.

SINGER SEWING MACHINE

1855 Walt Whitman publishes *Leaves of Grass,* and Henry Wadsworth Longfellow publishes *The Song of Hiawatha.*

1856 Gail Borden patents condensed milk.

1859 Minstrel and songwriter Dan Emmett composes "Dixie."

1859 First run of George Pullman's sleeping car.

1860 Charles Darwin's *On the Origin of Species by Means of Natural Selection* published in the United States.

1863 Ebenezer Butterick receives a patent for clothing patterns on paper.

1863 Thanksgiving becomes a national holiday.

1863 Congress standardizes railway gauge at four feet 8½ inches.

1867 National Grange, an organization of farmers, founded; by 1875 membership is 858,000.

1868 Bicycling becomes popular pastime.

1868 William Davis patents the refrigerated railroad car.

EARLY AMERICAN BICYCLE

POLITICS

1870 15th Amendment prohibits deprivation of voting rights to men on grounds of race, color, or previous condition of servitude.

1871 Indian Appropriation Act passes, making Indian tribes subject to federal law.

1872 Susan B. Anthony arrested for attempting to vote in presidential election.

1875 Civil Rights Act passes, ensuring blacks equal rights in public.

1877 Rutherford B. Hayes inaugurated 19th president.

1879 Women attorneys permitted to argue cases before the Supreme Court.

1881 James A. Garfield inaugurated 20th president, then assassinated; Chester A. Arthur becomes 21st president.

1882 Edmunds Act, aimed at the Mormon church, makes polygamy a felony.

1882 Chinese Exclusion Act bars Chinese immigration for 10 years.

1885 Grover Cleveland inaugurated 22nd president.

1886 Haymarket Riot; bomb thrown at police breaking up a Chicago labor rally.

1889 Benjamin Harrison inaugurated 23rd president.

PRESIDENT GROVER CLEVELAND

1890 Sherman Antitrust Act bars trusts and monopolies operating "in restraint of trade or commerce."

1892 Ellis Island opens to receive immigrants.

1893 Grover Cleveland inaugurated 24th president.

1894 Congress creates Bureau of Immigration and makes Labor Day national holiday.

1896 *Plessy* v. *Ferguson:* Supreme Court upholds doctrine of separate but equal treatment of black citizens.

1897 William McKinley inaugurated 25th president.

1898 Battleship *Maine* explodes in Havana harbor. United States declares war on Spain.

WESTWARD EXPANSION

1872 Yellowstone National Park established.

1872 Dodge City, Kansas, founded.

1873 Barbed wire introduced, giving homesteaders a cheap way to protect land from grazing by animals.

1874 Devastating grasshopper plague in western states.

1874 Colonel George Custer confirms reports of gold on land reserved for Indians in the Black Hills of Dakota Territory.

1876 Express train travels from New York to San Francisco in 83 hours 39 minutes.

1876 Custer and 263 troops killed by Indian warriors at the Battle of Little Bighorn.

1877 Desert Land Act provides 640 acres at $1.25 per acre to anyone willing to irrigate a portion of it.

1879 Exodus of 1879: 20,000 to 40,000 freed slaves immigrate to Kansas; most eventually return east.

1880 First major gold strike in Alaska.

1882 Rich copper strike near Butte, Montana.

1883 Telephone service links New York and Chicago.

1884 Dakota Territory land boom; claims for more than 11 million acres filed.

1885 Stanford University founded as Leland Stanford Junior University.

1886 Apache warrior Geronimo surrenders to General Nelson A. Miles.

1886 The first trainload of California oranges reaches the East Coast.

1887 Railroads establish four time zones to coordinate schedules.

1889 Oklahoma land rush begins.

1890 Sioux Indians massacred by U.S. Army at Wounded Knee.

1890 Oklahoma Territory created from Indian lands.

1892 Sierra Club founded by John Muir.

1893 Salt Lake City's Mormon Temple dedicated.

1895 Drought strikes the plains states; farmers forced to sell horses for as little as 25¢ each.

1896 Klondike gold strike attracts nearly 100,000 miners to Alaska.

1897 Oil strike at Bartlesville, Oklahoma.

1898 Hawaii annexed as a territory.

SOCIETY

1870 Standard Oil Company incorporated.

1870 Roller-skating is all the rage.

1873 Cable car makes its first run in San Francisco.

1873 Jesse James commits his first train robbery.

1876 The Centennial Exposition held in Philadelphia.

1876 Alexander Graham Bell patents the telephone.

1877 Charles Elmer Hires introduces bottled root beer.

1879 Incandescent electric lamp invented by Thomas Alva Edison.

1880 George Eastman patents photographic roll film.

1881 Thomas Edison directs construction of first central electric power plant.

1881 Clara Barton founds American Red Cross.

1883 Buffalo Bill Cody presents first Wild West show.

1884 Mark Twain publishes *Adventures of Huckleberry Finn.*

1884 Linotype typesetting machine patented.

1885 First-class postage drops to two cents an ounce.

1885 Sioux chief Sitting Bull and sharpshooter Annie Oakley join Buffalo Bill's Wild West show.

1886 Railroad workers strike for an eight-hour day.

1886 Statue of Liberty dedicated.

1891 Basketball invented by James Naismith.

1891 Thomas Edison patents the motion-picture camera and wireless telegraphy.

1893 Antonín Dvořák's symphony *From the New World* premieres.

1893 Whitcomb L. Judson patents the zipper.

1895 Westinghouse opens hydroelectric power generators at Niagara Falls, New York.

1895 Katharine Lee Bates publishes "America the Beautiful" as a poem.

1896 Henry Ford builds his first automobile.

1899 Ragtime pianist Scott Joplin's "Maple Leaf Rag" becomes a hit.

ALEXANDER GRAHAM BELL'S TELEPHONE

STATUE OF LIBERTY'S TORCH

ACKNOWLEDGMENTS

The editors wish to thank the following individuals and institutions for their valuable assistance in the preparation of this volume:

Gary Anderson, Jim Gatchell Memorial Museum, Buffalo, Wyo.; Diane Bruce, Institute of Texan Cultures, San Antonio; Kevin Bunker, California State Railroad Museum, Sacramento; Bob Clark, Montana Historical Society, Helena; Stephen Drew, California State Railroad Museum, Sacramento; Sarah Elder, Saint Joseph Museum, Saint Joseph, Mo.; Connie Estep, Museum of the Rockies, Montana State University, Bozeman; Ellen Halteman, California State Railroad Museum, Sacramento; Sandra Hilderbrand,

Gilcrease Museum, Tulsa; Don Hofsommer, Saint Cloud State University, Saint Cloud, Minn.; Nancy Jennings, Johnson County Library, Buffalo, Wyo.; Kirby Lambert, Montana Historical Society, Helena; Mary Lou Lentz, California State Department of Parks and Recreation, Sacramento; Jackie Lewin, Pony Express National Memorial, Saint Joseph, Mo.; John R. Lovett, University of Oklahoma, Norman; Hollie McHenry, Wyoming State Archives,

Cheyenne; Harriet C. Meloy, Helena, Mont.; Bonnie Morgan, Montana Historical Society, Helena; Patty Myers, Platte County Library, Wheatland, Wyo.; Craig Pindell, Wyoming State Archives, Cheyenne; Julie A. Pope, Kansas Research Services, Topeka; Jeff Sheets, Dickinson County Historical Society, Abilene, Kans.; Tom Shelton, Institute of Texan Cultures, San Antonio; Nancy Sherbert, Kansas State Historical Society, Topeka; Christie Stanley, Kansas State Historical Society, Topeka; Kathey Swan, Denver Public Library, Denver; Bruce Turner, Concord, Calif.; Sarah Wood-Clark, Kansas State Historical Society, Topeka.

PICTURE CREDITS

The sources for the illustrations that appear in this volume are listed below. Credits from left to right are separated by semicolons; credits from top to bottom are separated by dashes.

Cover: Denver Public Library, Western History Department/photograph by Henry Martinean. 8, 9: Map by Maryland CartoGraphics, Inc. 10: Courtesy Montana Historical Society, Helena. 12: Mansfield Library, University of Montana, Missoula. 14, 15: *Entering the Great Salt Lake Valley* by C. C. A. Christensen/courtesy Museum of Art, Brigham Young University, Provo, Utah; Church of Jesus Christ of Latter-day Saints, Salt Lake City (2). 16, 17: Courtesy Montana Historical Society, Helena. 18: M. & M. Karolik Collection/courtesy Museum of Fine Arts, Boston. 19, 21: Courtesy Montana Historical Society, Helena. 23: Smithsonian Institution, # 4703. 24: Denver Public Library, Western History Department—Library of Congress. 25: Map by Maryland CartoGraphics, Inc. 26: National Archives, neg. no. 069-N-19519. 27: Lane County Pioneer Museum, Eugene, Oreg./photograph by John G. Zimmerman. 28: Courtesy Montana Historical Society, Helena. 29, 30: © Museum of the Rockies, Bozeman, Mont./photograph by Bruce Selyem. 31-38: Courtesy Montana Historical Society, Helena. 40: Special Collections Department, University of Nevada, Reno Library. 41: Prints Collection, Miriam and Ira D. Wallach Division of Art, Prints and Photography, New York Public Library, Astor, Lenox and Tilden Foundation. 42, 43: Special Collections Department, University of Nevada, Reno Library; Nevada Historical Society, Reno; from *First Directory of Nevada Territory,* Talisman Press, Los Gatos, Calif., 1962 (reprint of 1862 edition). 44, 45: Nevada Historical Society, Reno; Bancroft Library, Berkeley, Calif. (2). 46: From *The Life and Remarkable Career of Adah Isaacs Menken, the Celebrated Actress* by G. Lippard Barclay, Barclay and Company,

Philadelphia, 1868—Nevada Historical Society, Reno. 47: Nevada Historical Society, Reno. 48, 49: Special Collections Department, University of Nevada, Reno Library; Nevada Historical Society, Reno (2). 50: From *We Pointed Them North: Recollections of a Cowpuncher* by E. C. Abbott and Helena Huntington Smith, University of Oklahoma Press, Norman, 1954. 53: *Charros at the Roundup* by James Walker, courtesy Elisabeth Waldo-Dentzel, Multi-Cultural Arts Studios, Northridge, Calif./photograph by Dean Austin. 54, 55: Library of Congress. 57-59: Kansas State Historical Society, Topeka. 60, 61: Western History Collections, University of Oklahoma Library; courtesy Garnet Brooks, El Reno, National Cowboy Hall of Fame, Oklahoma City, Okla./photograph by Ed Muno. 62-65: Dickinson County Historical Society, Abilene, Kans. 66: Institute of Texan Cultures, San Antonio, Tex. 67: Paul W. Stewart Collection—Denver Public Library, Western History Department. 69: Kansas State Historical Society, Topeka. 70: Library of Congress. 71: Kansas State Historical Society, Topeka. 72: © Gilcrease Museum, Tulsa. 73: Dickinson County Historical Society, Abilene, Kans. 75-77: Kansas State Historical Society, Topeka. 78, 79: Denver Public Library, Western History Department. 80: Frank and Marie-Thérèse Wood Print Collections, Alexandria, Va. 81: Kansas State Historical Society, Topeka. 82: Library of Congress; Dickinson County Historical Society, Abilene, Kans. 83: Kansas State Historical Society, Topeka. 84, 85: Dickinson County Historical Society, Abilene, Kans./photograph by Robert A. Paull; drawing by N. C. Wyeth, courtesy Adams Memorial Museum, Deadwood, S.Dak./photograph by Keith Shostrom; Kansas State Historical Society, Topeka. 86, 87: Kansas State Historical

Society, Topeka; Denver Public Library, Western History Department; Peter Newark's Western Americana, Bath, England. 88: Courtesy Adams Memorial Museum, Deadwood, S.Dak. 89: W. H. Over Museum, S.Dak.; Denver Public Library, Western History Department. 90: Western History Collections, University of Oklahoma Library, Norman. 91: Courtesy collection of Barney Hubbs. 92: E. A. Brininstool. 93: Copied by Charlie Brown, courtesy Irene R. Johnson. 94, 95: Western History Collections, University of Oklahoma Library, Norman. 96: De Grummond Children's Literature Research Collection, University of Southern Mississippi, Hattiesburg. 98, 99: New York Public Library, Astor, Lenox and Tilden Foundation; Huntington Library, San Marino, Calif. 100: De Grummond Children's Literature Research Collection, University of Southern Mississippi, Hattiesburg. 101: Courtesy California History Room, California State Library, Sacramento/photograph by Nikki Pahl. 102: Huntington Library, San Marino, Calif.; Pony Express National Memorial, Saint Joseph, Mo. 104: California State Department of Parks and Recreation/photograph by Nikki Pahl. 105: California State Department of Parks and Recreation/Sutter's Fort State Historic Park/photograph by Nikki Pahl—courtesy California History Room, California State Library, Sacramento/photograph by Nikki Pahl; California State Department of Parks and Recreation, Sutter's Fort State Historic Park/photograph by Nikki Pahl. 106: California State Railroad Museum, Sacramento. 107: Andrew J. Russell Collection, Oakland Museum of California, Oakland. 108: Bancroft Library, Berkeley, Calif. 110: Bancroft Library, Berkeley, Calif. 112: California State Railroad Museum, Sacramento. 114: Maps by Maryland CartoGraphics, Inc. 116: Southern Pacific Transportation Co. 117: Huntington Library, San Marino, Calif. 118, 119: Southern Pacific Transportation Company; art by Fred Holz.

120: California State Railroad Museum, Sacramento. 122, 123: Bancroft Library, Berkeley, Calif. 124, 125: Huntington Library, San Marino, Calif. 126: Andrew J. Russell Collection, Oakland Museum of California, Oakland. 127: Stanford University Museum of Art, gift of David Hewes. 128, 129: Union Pacific Museum Collection, Omaha, Nebr. (2); Library of Congress. 130, 131: Kansas State Historical Society, Topeka; Union Pacific Museum Collection, Omaha, Nebr. 132-141: Andrew J. Russell Collection, Oakland Museum of California, Oakland. 142: Wyoming Division of Cultural Resources, Cheyenne. 144, 145: Wyoming Division of Cultural Resources, Cheyenne—Jim Gatchell Memorial Museum, Buffalo, Wyo./photograph by Linn Costenbauer; Wyoming Division of Cultural Resources, Cheyenne. 146: Wyoming Division of Cultural Resources, Cheyenne. 147: Western History Research Center, University of Wyoming, Laramie. 150: Denver Public Library—Wyoming Division of Cultural Resources, Cheyenne (2). 152: Jim Gatchell Memorial Museum, Buffalo, Wyo./photograph by Linn Costenbauer; Western History Collections, University of Oklahoma Library, Norman. 153: Wyoming Division of Cultural Resources, Cheyenne. 154: Elisabeth Waldo-Dentzel, Multi-Cultural Arts Studios, Northridge, Calif.—Wyoming Division of Cultural Resources, Cheyenne (6). 155: Solomon D. Butcher Collection/Nebraska State Historical Society, Lincoln. 156: Jim Gatchell Memorial Museum, Buffalo, Wyo./photograph by Linn Costenbauer. 157: Map by Maryland CartoGraphics, Inc. 158: Jim Gatchell Memorial Museum, Buffalo, Wyo./photograph by Linn Costenbauer. 162: Wyoming Division of Cultural Resources, Cheyenne. 163: Western History Research Center, University of Wyoming, Laramie. 164, 165: Wyoming Division of Cultural Resources, Cheyenne. 166, 167: Western History Research Center, University of Wyoming, Laramie. 169: Baker Library/Harvard Business School. 170: Solomon D. Butcher Collection/Nebraska State Historical Society, Lincoln, neg. no. B983-2938A—Nebraska State Historical Society, Lincoln—Breton Littlehales/National Geographic Image Collection. 171: Solomon D. Butcher Collection/Nebraska State Historical Society, Lincoln, neg. no. B983-1653. 172: Kansas State Historical Society, Topeka—Solomon D. Butcher Collection/Nebraska State Historical Society, Lincoln, neg. no. B983-2023. 173: Kansas State Historical Society, Topeka—courtesy Oregon Historical Society/photograph by Harald Sund. 174: Nebraska State Historical Society, Lincoln—State Historical Society of North Dakota. 175: Kansas State Historical Society, Topeka—Solomon D. Butcher Collection/Nebraska State Historical Society, Lincoln. 176: Kansas State Historical Society, Topeka—courtesy Boot Hill Museum, Inc./photograph by Henry Groskinsky; Kansas State Historical Society, Topeka. 177: State Historical Society of North Dakota—Kansas State Historical Society, Topeka. 178, 179: Kansas Collection, University of Kansas Libraries; Kansas State Historical Society, Topeka. 182: Granger Collection, New York—Lane County Pioneer Museum, Eugene, Oreg./photograph by John G. Zimmerman; Huntington Library, San Marino, Calif.; Stanford University Museum of Art, gift of David Hewes—Culver Pictures, New York; UPI/Corbis-Bettmann, New York. 183: Granger Collection, New York—National Museum of American History, Smithsonian Institution, Washington, D.C./photograph by Dane A. Penland; Historical Society of Pennsylvania, Philadelphia.

BOOKS

Abbott, E. C., and Helena Huntington Smith. *We Pointed Them North: Recollections of a Cowpuncher.* Norman: University of Oklahoma Press, 1954.

Adams, Ramon F. *Western Words: A Dictionary of the American West.* Norman: University of Oklahoma Press, 1968.

The American Heritage Pictorial Atlas of United States History. By the Editors of American Heritage. New York: American Heritage Publishing, 1966.

Athearn, Robert G. *Union Pacific Country.* Chicago: Rand McNally, 1971.

Austin, William W. *"Susanna," "Jeanie," and "The Old Folks at Home": The Songs of Stephen C. Foster from His Time to Ours.* New York: Macmillan, 1975.

Baber, D. F. *The Longest Rope: The Truth About the Johnson County Cattle War.* Caldwell, Idaho: Caxton Printers, 1940.

Baker, Pearl. *The Wild Bunch: Robbers Roost* (rev. ed.). New York: Abelard-Schuman, 1971.

Bartlett, John. *Familiar Quotations* (16th ed.). Edited by John Justin Kaplan. Boston: Little, Brown, 1992.

Beebe, Lucius. *The Central Pacific and the Southern Pacific Railroads.* Berkeley, Calif.: Howell-North, 1963.

Blackburn, Forrest R., et al. (eds.). *Kansas and the West: Bicentennial Essays in Honor of Nyle H. Miller.* Topeka: Kansas State Historical Society, 1976.

BIBLIOGRAPHY

Boorstin, Daniel J. *The Americans: The National Experience.* New York: Vintage Books (Random House), 1965.

Bowman, John S. (ed.). *The American West Year by Year.* New York: Crescent Books (Random House), 1995.

Canton, Frank M. *Frontier Trails: The Autobiography of Frank M. Canton.* Edited by Edward Everett Dale. Boston: Houghton Mifflin, 1930.

Carruth, Gorton. *The Encyclopedia of American Facts and Dates* (8th ed.). New York: Harper & Row, 1987.

Chapman, Robert L. (ed.). *New Dictionary of American Slang.* New York: Harper & Row, 1986.

Claiborne, Robert. *Our Marvelous Native Tongue: The Life and Times of the English Language.* New York: Times Books, 1983.

Clampitt, John W. *Echoes from the Rocky Mountains.* Chicago: American Mutual Library Association, 1890.

Clark, Walter Van Tilburg (ed.). *The Journals of Alfred Doten 1849–1903* (Vols. 1 and 2). Reno: University of Nevada Press, 1973.

Clay, John. *My Life on the Range.* Norman: University of Oklahoma Press, 1962.

Collinson, Frank. *Life in the Saddle.* Edited by Mary Whatley Clarke. Norman: University of Oklahoma Press, 1963.

Combs, Barry B. *Westward to Promontory: Building the Union Pacific across the Plains and Mountains.* Palo Alto, Calif.: American West Publishing, 1969.

Cushman, Dan. *Montana: The Gold Frontier.* Great Falls, Mont.: Stay Away, Joe Publishers, 1973.

Custer, Elizabeth B. *Following the Guidon.* Norman: University of Oklahoma Press, 1966.

Davis, Jean (comp.). *Shallow Diggin's: Tales from Montana's Ghost Towns.* Caldwell, Idaho: Caxton Printers, 1962.

Dick, Everett. *The Sod-House Frontier 1854–1890.* Lincoln, Nebr.: Johnsen Publishing, 1954.

Dimsdale, Thomas J. *The Vigilantes of Montana, or Popular Justice in the Rocky Mountains.* Virginia City, Montana Territory: Montana Post Press, D. W. Tilton, 1866.

Discovering America's Past: Customs, Legends, History and Lore of Our Great Nation. Pleasantville, N.Y.: Reader's Digest Association, 1993.

Dobie, J. Frank:
The Longhorns. Boston: Little, Brown, 1941.
A Vaquero of the Brush Country (2d ed.). Boston: Little, Brown, 1957.

Dodge, Grenville M. *How We Built the Union Pacific Railway.* Ann Arbor, Mich.: University Microfilms, 1966.

Dykstra, Robert R. *The Cattle Towns.* Lincoln: University of

Nebraska Press, 1983 (reprint of 1968 edition).

The Encyclopedia Americana—International Edition (Vol. 28). Danbury, Conn.: Grolier, 1995.

Farr, William E., and K. Ross Toole. *Montana: Images of the Past.* Boulder, Colo.: Pruett Publishing, 1978.

Ferrell, Robert H., and Richard Natkiel. *Atlas of American History.* New York: Facts On File, 1987.

Fielder, Mildred. *Wild Bill and Deadwood.* New York: Bonanza Books, 1965.

Fitzsimons, Bernard. *150 Years of North American Railroads.* Secaucus, N.J.: Chartwell Books, 1982.

Fletcher, Baylis John. *Up the Trail in '79.* Norman: University of Oklahoma Press, 1968.

Flexner, Stuart Berg. *Listening to America: An Illustrated History of Words and Phrases from Our Lively and Splendid Past.* New York: Simon & Schuster, 1982.

Forbis, William H., and the Editors of Time-Life Books. *The Cowboys* (The Old West series). New York: Time-Life Books, 1973.

Frink, Maurice. *Cow Country Cavalcade.* Denver.: Old West Publishing, 1954.

Frink, Maurice, W. Turrentine Jackson, and Agnes Wright Spring. *When Grass Was King.* Boulder: University of Colorado Press, 1956.

Frost, Lawrence A. *The Custer Album: A Pictorial Biography of General George A. Custer.* Seattle: Superior Publishing, 1964.

Galloway, John Debo. *The First Transcontinental Railroad: Central Pacific, Union Pacific.* Westport, Conn.: Greenwood Press, 1983 (reprint of 1968 edition).

Gard, Wayne. *The Chisholm Trail.* Norman: University of Oklahoma Press, 1954.

Granfield, Linda. *Cowboy: An Album.* New York: Ticknor & Fields (Houghton Mifflin), 1994.

Griswold, Wesley S. *A Work of Giants: Building the First Transcontinental Railroad.* New York: McGraw-Hill, 1962.

Hamilton, James McClellan. *History of Montana: From Wilderness to Statehood* (2d ed.). Edited by Merrill G. Burlingame. Portland, Oreg.: Binfords & Mort, 1970.

Hinckley, Helen. *Rails from the West: A Biography of Theodore D. Judah.* San Marino, Calif.: Golden West Books, 1969.

Historical Statistics of the United States: Colonial Times to 1970 (Parts 1 and 2). Washington, D.C.: U.S. Department of Commerce, Bureau of the Census, 1975.

Hogg, Garry. *Union Pacific: The Building of the First Transcontinental Railroad.* New York: Walker, 1967.

Holbrook, Stewart H. *The Story of American Railroads.* New York: Bonanza Books (Crown Publishers), 1947.

Holmes, Kenneth. L. (comp. and ed.). *Covered Wagon Women:*

Diaries and Letters from the Western Trails 1840–1890 (Vol. 3). Glendale, Calif.: Arthur H. Clark, 1984.

Horn, Huston, and the Editors of Time-Life Books. *The Pioneers* (The Old West series). Alexandria, Va.: Time-Life Books, 1974.

Hunter, J. Marvin (comp. and ed.). *The Trail Drivers of Texas.* New York: Argosy-Antiquarian, 1963 (reprint of 1925 edition).

Jensen, Oliver. *The American Heritage History of Railroads in America.* New York: Bonanza Books (Crown Publishers), 1975.

Johnson, Dorothy M. *The Bloody Bozeman: The Perilous Trail to Montana's Gold.* New York: McGraw-Hill, 1971.

Johnson, Enid. *Rails across the Continent: The Story of the First Transcontinental Railroad.* New York: Julian Messner, 1965.

Kane, Joseph Nathan. *Famous First Facts: A Record of First Happenings, Discoveries, and Inventions in American History* (4th ed., rev.). New York: H. W. Wilson, 1981.

Kane, Joseph Nathan, Janet Podell, and Steven Anzovin. *Facts About the States* (2d ed.). New York: H. W. Wilson, 1993.

Klein, Maury. *Union Pacific: Birth of a Railroad, 1862-1893.* Garden City, N.Y.: Doubleday, 1987.

Kraus, George. *High Road to Promontory: Building the Central Pacific across the High Sierra.* Palo Alto, Calif.: American West Publishing, 1969.

Kurian, George Thomas. *Datapedia of the United States, 1790–2000: America Year by Year.* Lanham, Md.: Bernan Press, 1994.

Langford, Nathaniel Pitt. *Vigilante Days and Ways.* Boston: J. G. Cupples, 1890.

Lord, Eliot. *Comstock Mining and Miners.* Berkeley, Calif.: Howell-North, 1959 (reprint of 1883 edition).

Love, Robertus. *The Rise and Fall of Jesse James.* Lincoln: University of Nebraska Press, 1990 (reprint of 1926 edition).

Luchetti, Cathy. *Home on the Range: A Culinary History of the American West.* New York: Villard Books (Random House), 1993.

McCague, James. *Moguls and Iron Men: The Story of the First Transcontinental Railroad.* New York: Harper & Row, 1964.

McCoy, Joseph G. *Historic Sketches of the Cattle Trade of the West and Southwest.* Kansas City, Mo.: Ramsey, Millett & Hudson, 1874.

McCrum, Robert, William Cran, and Robert MacNeil. *The Story of English.* New York: Viking Penguin, 1986.

McLoughlin, Denis. *Wild and Woolly: An Encyclopedia of the Old West.* Garden City, N.Y.: Doubleday, 1975.

Marcy, Randolph B. *The Prairie Traveler: A Hand-Book for*

Overland Expeditions. Cambridge, Mass.: Applewood Books, 1988 (reprint of 1859 edition).

Mather, R. E., and F. E. Boswell. *Vigilante Victims: Montana's 1864 Hanging Spree.* San Jose, Calif.: History West Publishing, 1991.

Mercer, A. S. *The Banditti of the Plains, or The Cattlemen's Invasion of Wyoming in 1892.* Norman: University of Oklahoma Press, 1954.

Miller, Don C. *Ghost Towns of Montana.* Boulder, Colo.: Pruett Publishing, 1974.

Miller, James Knox Polk. *The Road to Virginia City: The Diary of James Knox Polk Miller.* Edited by Andrew Rolle. Norman: University of Oklahoma Press, 1960.

Milner, Clyde A., II, Carol A. O'Connor, and Martha A. Sandweiss (eds.). *The Oxford History of the American West.* New York: Oxford University Press, 1994.

Miner, Craig:
West of Wichita: Settling the High Plains of Kansas, 1865–1890. Lawrence: University Press of Kansas, 1986.
Wichita: The Early Years, 1865–1890. Lincoln: University of Nebraska Press, 1982.

Morgan, Dale (ed.). *Overland in 1846: Diaries and Letters of the California-Oregon Trail* (Vol. 1). Georgetown, Calif.: Talisman Press, 1963.

Morgan, Ted. *A Shovel of Stars: The Making of the American West, 1800 to the Present.* New York: Simon & Schuster, 1995.

Morris, William, and Mary Morris. *Dictionary of Word and Phrase Origins.* New York: Harper & Row, 1962.

Murphy, Virginia Reed. *Across the Plains in the Donner Party: A Personal Narrative of the Overland Trip to California 1846–47.* Silverthorne, Colo.: Vistabooks, 1995.

Nabokov, Peter (ed.). *Native American Testimony.* New York: Penguin Books, 1991.

Nash, Jay Robert. *Encyclopedia of Western Lawmen and Outlaws.* New York: CrimeBooks, 1992.

Nevin, David, and the Editors of Time-Life Books. *The Expressmen* (The Old West series). Alexandria, Va.: Time-Life Books, 1974.

Nunn, Joan. *Fashion in Costume, 1200–1980.* New York: Schocken Books, 1984.

O'Neal, Bill. *Encyclopedia of Western Gunfighters.* Norman: University of Oklahoma Press, 1979.

Otero, Miguel Antonio. *My Life on the Frontier, 1864–1882.* Albuquerque: University of New Mexico Press, 1987 (reprint of 1935 edition).

Phillips, Paul C. (ed.). *Forty Years on the Frontier as Seen in the Journals and Reminiscences of Granville Stuart.* Glendale,

Calif.: Arthur H. Clark, 1957.

Prentice Hall Literature: The American Experience (2d ed.). Englewood Cliffs, N.J.: Prentice-Hall, 1991.

Reiter, Joan Swallow, and the Editors of Time-Life Books. *The Women* (The Old West series). Alexandria, Va.: Time-Life Books, 1978.

Riley, Glenda. *The Female Frontier: A Comparative View of Women on the Prairie and the Plains.* Lawrence: University Press of Kansas, 1988.

Romero, Patricia W. (comp. and ed.). *I Too Am America: Documents from 1619 to the Present.* New York: Publishers Co., 1970.

Ronan, Mary. *Frontier Woman: The Story of Mary Ronan as Told to Margaret Ronan.* Edited by H. G. Merriam. Missoula: University of Montana, 1973.

Rosa, Joseph G.:
They Called Him Wild Bill: The Life and Adventures of James Butler Hickok. Norman: University of Oklahoma Press, 1974.
The West of Wild Bill Hickok. Norman: University of Oklahoma Press, 1982.

Rosenstock, Fred A. *The Montana Gold Rush Diary of Kate Dunlap.* Edited and annotated by Lyman Tyler. Denver.: Old West Publishing, 1969.

Rybczynski, Witold. *City Life: Urban Expectations in a New World.* New York: Scribner, 1995.

Sabin, Edwin L. *Building the Pacific Railway.* Philadelphia: J. B. Lippincott, 1919.

Sanders, Helen Fitzgerald (ed.). *X. Beidler: Vigilante.* Norman: University of Oklahoma Press, 1957.

Schlesinger, Arthur M. (ed.). *The Almanac of American History.* New York: G. P. Putnam's Sons, 1983.

Schoenberger, Dale T. *The Gunfighters.* Caldwell, Idaho: Caxton Printers, 1971.

Scott, John Anthony. *The Story of America* (rev. ed.). Washington, D.C.: National Geographic Society, 1992.

Siringo, Charles A. *A Texas Cow Boy or, Fifteen Years on the Hurricane Deck of a Spanish Pony.* Chicago: M. Umbdenstock, 1885.

Slatta, Richard W. *Cowboys of the Americas.* New Haven, Conn.: Yale University Press, 1990.

Smith, Helena Huntington. *The War on Powder River.* New York: McGraw-Hill, 1966.

Spring, Agnes Wright. *Colorado Charley, Wild Bill's Pard.* Boulder, Colo.: Pruett Press, 1968.

Story of the Great American West. Edited by Edward S. Barnard. Pleasantville, N.Y.: Reader's Digest Association, 1977.

Stratton, Joanna L. *Pioneer Women: Voices from the Kansas Frontier.* New York: Simon & Schuster, 1981.

Tanner, Ogden, and the Editors of Time-Life Books. *The Ranchers* (The Old West series). Alexandria, Va.: Time-Life Books, 1977.

Trachtman, Paul, and the Editors of Time-Life Books. *The Gunfighters* (The Old West series). Alexandria, Va.: Time-Life Books, 1974.

Utley, Robert M. *Billy the Kid: A Short and Violent Life.* Lincoln: University of Nebraska Press, 1989.

Vare, Ethlie Ann, and Greg Ptacek. *Mothers of Invention.* New York: William Morrow, 1988.

Wallace, Robert, and the Editors of Time-Life Books. *The Miners* (The Old West series). Alexandria, Va.: Time-Life Books, 1976.

Wentworth, Harold, and Stuart Berg Flexner (comps. and eds.). *Dictionary of American Slang* (2d supplemented ed.). New York: Thomas Y. Crowell, 1995.

Wexler, Alan. *Atlas of Westward Expansion.* New York: Facts On File, 1995.

Wheeler, Keith, and the Editors of Time-Life Books. *The Railroaders* (The Old West series). New York: Time-Life Books, 1973.

Williams, John Hoyt. *A Great and Shining Road: The Epic Story of the Transcontinental Railroad.* New York: Times Books, 1988.

Wilstach, Frank J. *Wild Bill Hickok: The Prince of Pistoleers.* Garden City, N.Y.: Garden City Publishing, 1926.

Withuhn, William L. (ed.). *Rails across America.* New York: Smithmark Publishers, 1993.

The Woman's Way (The American Indians series). The Editors of Time-Life Books. Alexandria, Va.: Time-Life Books, 1995.

The World Almanac and Book of Facts 1996. Mahwah, N.J.: World Almanac Books (Funk & Wagnalls), 1995.

Yarwood, Doreen. *Costume of the Western World.* New York: St. Martin's Press, 1980.

PERIODICALS

Breeden, James O. (ed.). "Medicine in the West." *Journal of the West,* July 1982.

"The Chisholm Trail." *Kansas Historical Quarterly,* Summer 1967.

Dykstra, Robert. "The Last Days of 'Texan' Abilene: A Study in Community Conflict on the Farmer's Frontier." *Agricultural History,* July 1960.

"Early Pacific Railroad History." *Themis: Saturday Evening,* December 14, 1889.

Galenson, David. "Origins of the Long Drive." *Journal of the West,* July 1965.

Galloway, John D. "Theodore Dehone Judah—Railroad Pioneer." *Civil Engineering,* January-December 1941.

Harlan, Gilbert Drake (ed.). "The Diary of Wilson Barber Harlan, Part I: A Walk with a Wagon Train." *Journal of the West,* April 1964.

Havins, T. R. "Texas Fever." *Southwestern Historical Quarterly,* July 1948.

Huffman, Wendell W. "Iron Horse along the Truckee: The Central Pacific Reaches Nevada." *Nevada Historical Society Quarterly,* Spring 1995.

"Is It War?" *Wyoming Derrick,* April 7, 1892.

"Journal of Henry Edgar—1863." *Contributions to the Historical Society of Montana* (Vol. 3), 1900.

Leonard, Carol, and Isidor Wallimann. "Prostitution and Changing Morality in the Frontier Cattle Towns of Kansas." *Kansas History: A Journal of the Central Plains,* Spring 1979.

Long, Vivian Aten. "Tim Hersey Built Abilene's First Home, and Wife Named Town." *Kansas City Star,* March 8, 1958.

Smith, Annick. "The Two Frontiers of Mary Ronan." *Montana: The Magazine of Western History,* Winter 1989.

Wheat, Carl I. "A Sketch of the Life of Theodore D. Judah." *California Historical Society Quarterly,* September 1925.

Wilkerson, Charles J. (ed.). "The Letters of Ed Donnell, Nebraska Pioneer." *Nebraska History Quarterly,* June 1960.

OTHER SOURCES

"Early Recollections and Personal Reminiscences of Abilene in 1800's." Booklet. Abilene, Kans.: Dickinson County Historical Society, 1995.

Edwards, J. B. "Early Days in Abilene." Pamphlet. Reprinted from *Abilene Daily Chronicle 1938* (reprinted from *Abilene Chronicle 1896*), n.d.

Flagg, O. H. "A Review of the Cattle Business in Johnson County, Wyoming Since 1882 and the Causes That Led to the Recent Invasion." Unpublished manuscript based on accounts published in the *Buffalo Bulletin* from May 5, 1892, to July 14, 1892.

Judah, Anna Pierce. "Theodore Dehone Judah Letters, 1861, 1863." Photographic reproductions of letters from the Amos Catlin Collection of the California State Railroad Museum Library, Sacramento.

Penrose, Charles Bingham. "The Johnson County War: The Narrative of Dr. Charles Bingham Penrose." Manuscript, n.d.

"Transactions of the Kansas State Historical Society, 1905–1906" (Vol. 9). Edited by George W. Martin. Topeka, Kans.: State Printing Office, 1906

TIME LIFE® Time-Life Books is a
BOOKS division of Time Life Inc.

TIME LIFE INC.

PRESIDENT and CEO: George Artandi

TIME-LIFE BOOKS

PRESIDENT: John D. Hall
PUBLISHER/MANAGING EDITOR: Neil Kagan

THE AMERICAN STORY

SETTLING THE WEST

EDITOR: Sarah Brash
DIRECTOR, NEW PRODUCT DEVELOPMENT:
Curtis Kopf
MARKETING DIRECTOR: Pamela R. Farrell

Design Director: Dale Pollekoff
Deputy Editor: Kristin Baker Hanneman
Picture Editor: Jane Coughran
Text Editors: Glen B. Ruh (principal), Denise Dersin,
Charles H. Hagner Jr., Stephen G. Hyslop, James Lynch
Art Director: Alan Pitts
Associate Editors/Research and Writing: Annette Scarpitta,
Robert Speziale, Karen Sweet
Copyeditor: Judith Klein
Picture Coordinator: Catherine Parrott
Editorial Assistant: Patricia D. Whiteford

Special Contributors: Ronald H. Bailey, Timothy Cooke,
Thomas A. Lewis, Ellen B. Phillips (text); Roberta
Conlan, Eliot Marshall (editing); Susan Borden,
Christopher Hoelzl, Mary H. McCarthy, Elizabeth
Schleichert, Katya Sharpe, Mary Davis Suro, Marilyn
Murphy Terrell, Elizabeth Thompson, Jennifer Veech,
Barry N. Wolverton (research and writing); Magdalena
Anders, Catherine Chase Tyson (pictures); Barbara L.
Klein (index).

Correspondents: Christine Hinze (London), Christina
Lieberman (New York), Maria Vincenza Aloisi (Paris).

Vice President, Director of Finance: Christopher Hearing
Vice President, Book Production: Marjann Caldwell
Director of Operations: Eileen Bradley
Director of Photography and Research: John Conrad Weiser
Director of Editorial Administration: Judith W. Shanks
Production Manager: Marlene Zack
Quality Assurance Manager: James King
Library: Louise D. Forstall

The Consultants
Wendell W. Huffman of the Carson City Library in
Nevada is a specialist on 19th-century railroad transportation in the American West. He has contributed articles to
the *Nevada Historical Society Quarterly* and *S.P. Trainline,*
the magazine of the Southern Pacific Technical and
Historical Society.

Craig Miner is the Willard Garvey Distinguished Professor
of History at Wichita State University. His numerous books
about Kansas and the Indian territories include *West of
Wichita: Settling the High Plains of Kansas, 1865–1890.* He is
the former president of the Kansas State Historical Society.

Phil Roberts is assistant professor of history at the
University of Wyoming, where he teaches courses on the
American West, American law, and the environment. Dr.
Roberts has been a practicing attorney and newspaper
editor and is the author of *Wyoming Almanac* and the
editor of *Annals of Wyoming/Wyoming History Journal.*

Clark C. Spence has taught history for more than 35 years
and is professor emeritus of history at the University of
Illinois. He is the author of *Mining Engineers and the
American West: The Lace-Boot Brigade, 1849–1933* and other
books on the history of Montana and the development of
western mining. He is the former president of the Western
History Association.

Library of Congress Cataloging-in-Publication Data
Settling the west / by the editors of Time-Life Books.
    p.   cm.—(American story)
    Includes bibliographical references and index.
    ISBN 0-7835-6252-7
    1. West (U.S.)—History—1860–1890. 2. West (U.S.)—
History—1860–1890—Pictorial works.
I. Time-Life Books. II. Series.
F594.S49 1996
978'.02—dc20   96-33041
                                                          CIP

Other Publications

HISTORY
Voices of the Civil War
The American Indians
Lost Civilizations
Mysteries of the Unknown
Time Frame
The Civil War
Cultural Atlas

SCIENCE/NATURE
Voyage Through the Universe

COOKING
Weight Watchers® Smart Choice Recipe Collection
Great Taste-Low Fat
Williams-Sonoma Kitchen Library

DO IT YOURSELF
The Time-Life Complete Gardener
Home Repair and Improvement
The Art of Woodworking
Fix It Yourself

TIME-LIFE KIDS
Family Time Bible Stories
Library of First Questions and Answers
A Child's First Library of Learning
I Love Math
Nature Company Discoveries
Understanding Science & Nature

For information on and a full description of any
of the Time-Life Books series listed above, please
call 1-800-621-7026 or write:

Reader Information
Time-Life Customer Service
P.O. Box C-32068
Richmond, Virginia 23261-2068

On the cover: The rigors of their long journey are
apparent in the faces of this pioneer couple and
their barefoot children, resting at midday in the
foothills of the Rockies in northern Utah in 1870.
Settlers migrating westward often stopped for their
main meal during the hottest part of the day,
unhitched their covered wagons, and watered their
livestock before soldiering on until dusk.